DATE DUE

JAN 1 8 2004			

DEMCO 38-296

Handbook for Beach Volleyball

Acknowledgments

Developing and writing of this handbook would have been impossible without the support of my parents, Rudolf and Christa Hömberg - a big "Thank you"!
Another big one to my friend and co-author Athanasios as well as to his family - thanks for everything.

Thank you, Patricia, for all your love, help and support.

For their friendly support, we would like to thank the
**EUROPEAN VOLLEYBALL FEDERATION (CEV),
HEAD: MANFRED LOECKEN**

and the

**INSTITUTE FOR SPORTS GAMES AT THE GERMAN SPORTS
UNIVERSITY, HEAD: UNIV.-PROF. DR. KARL WEBER**

Thank you Brigitte and especially Thomas Haag, for your fast and perfect corrections.
Thank you, Ingo Ulrich, for always being there when the computer breaks down.
Thanks, Isabel Brammertz, for all the statistical work.
Another thanks goes to Bruk Vandeweghe for his professional advice.

Thanks also to the large array of players, scientists, students, teachers who helped to make this book possible. These include Uli Köhler, Jenny Ester, C.C. Sandorfi (VOLLEYBALL), LeValley Pattison (WPVA), Jon Hastings (VOLLEYBALL MONTHLY), Bryan Stewart (CE SPORTS), Ursula Tattermusch (CEV), Dr. Michael Gasse (FIVB), Peter Murphy (FIVB), Pierre Berjaud (FIVB), Jon Stevenson (AVP), Kent Steffes, Kathy Gregory, Mike and Patty Dodd, Linda Carillo, Pat Zartman, Steve Timmons.

We also want to thank all photographers who have helped us during the recent years with their material.

Stefan Hömberg
Athanasios Papageorgiou

Handbook for Beach Volleyball

Meyer & Meyer Verlag

Original title: „Handbuch für Beach-Volleyball“
© 1994 by Meyer & Meyer Verlag, Aachen
Translation: Stefan Hömberg

Die Deutsche Bibliothek – CIP Einheitsaufnahme

Hömberg, Stefan:
Handbook for beach volleyball / Stefan Hömberg ; Athanasios Papageorgiou. –
Aachen : Meyer und Meyer, 1995
Dt. Ausg. u.d.T.: Hömberg, Stefan: Handbuch für Beach-Volleyball
ISBN 3-89124-322-7
NE: Papageorgiou, Athanasios:

© 1995 by Meyer & Meyer Verlag, Aachen
cover: CEV, Luxemburg
cover design: Walter Neumann, N&N Design-Studio, Aachen
cover exposure: frw, Reiner Wahlen, Aachen
type exposure: Typeline, Dagmar Schmitz, Aachen
type: Times
Printing: Druckerei Queck, Jüchen
Printed in Germany
ISBN 3-89124-322-7

Table of contents

PART 1: BASICS

1   THESIS OF THE HANDBOOK AND OF THE TEACHING CONCEPT

The game of beach volleyball has made an significant impact on the whole world of volleyball in recent years. In the United States it has grown, during the last 70 years, from a recreational sport to a professional sport, which has already surpassed the indoor game. This is obvious, given the media coverage in the U.S. High numbers of spectators (40.000-50.000), have led to the interest of sponsors and the therefore high price money. These factors have been responsible for the great success of the sport:

> **The beach volleyball-game has been established as an Olympic medal sport for the 1996 Olympic summer games in Atlanta.**

In Europe, the game has not yet undergone the same level of development as in the U.S. The level of performance can be characterized as "mediocre".
With the integration of the game into the Olympic program, it can be assumed, that it will undergo a fast international development.

Unfortunately, few publications exist regarding beach volleyball. And given the limited amount of literature, none has any didactical or methodical approaches to training (see bibliography). This book shall contribute its share to the further development of the sport, particularly considering that no *instructional* handbook for this game has been published worldwide.

The handbook attempts to enable players, coaches and teachers to become familiar with the **introductional level** and the **basics** and with **higher levels of the training** of beach volleyball. It shall motivate everyone who is learning or teaching the sport, to pay increased attention to the game of beach volleyball. On one hand, it deals with the development and structure of beach volleyball, on the other it deals specifically with, detailed learning- and teaching-steps for the introduction and the training of techniques and individual tactics as well as of strategies concerning offense and defense.
Here, knowledge of the indoor volleyball game is implied, so that everyone who knows the techniques and tactics of the indoor-game will be able to work with this book.

▶ The structure of this handbook corresponds to the "Handbuch für Leistungsvolleyball - Ausbildung zum Spezialisten" by Papageorgiou/ Spitzley (1994). Action and motion sequences as well as training sequences, similar to the indoor-game, have been taken over from this handbook with the necessary modifications. The handbook "Volleyball - Grundlagenausbildung" by Papageorgiou /Spitzley (1992) serves as a prerequisite for the basic techniques and basic tactical considerations. The methodical sequences for the introduction and further training follow the principles of this handbook.

For a better understanding, the terms for areas on the court respectively the positions have been taken from the indoor game. Apart from the chapters on techniques and tactics, selected training sequences for beach techniques and strategies as well as recommendations for practice are offered. Moreover, the book primarily gives concrete hints with respect to the preparation of the European beach volleyball player, or for those players who have so far almost exclusively played indoor volleyball and who still regard beach volleyball as preparation for the indoor game. New developments, reflecting players and coaches who only want to concentrate on beach volleyball, will also be taken into consideration and dealt with.

The recommendations for the planning of training, the accompanying training measures and the principles are especially helpful for these people. Furthermore, all special forms of the game, for example, "3 versus 3", "4 vs. 4" and "6 vs. 6"- games, will be discussed. Readers interested from the recreational level should have general volleyball knowledge in order to be able to work with this book.

The education of a beach volleyball player should be arranged in small steps. In all areas of performance, the all-around education should receive extensive attention.

Due to the "2 vs. 2"- structure of the game, every beach volleyball player is a server, receiver, setter, attacker , blocker and backcourt defender simultaneously.

Knowledge of the indoor techniques, regarding setting and passing techniques, attacking techniques, blocking and defensive techniques as well as the service techniques are a prerequisite. Based on these preconditions, the technique and tactics of beach volleyball shall be derived and optimized. Due to the large number of motion and action sequences and their variations in beach volleyball, working on the beach-specific techniques will follow the structure of the game.

A detailed description of indoor techniques is intentionally neglected in the explanation and illustration of motion and action sequences, in order to especially be able to highlight beach techniques and tactics.

Since the mini or small-court games are a training tool for the learning and practicing of team tactics and strategies of the indoor game, the opposite didactical-methodical approach makes sense for the teaching of beach volleyball skills. This is why special forms of beach volleyball, such as '4 vs. 4' and '3 vs. 3' should be used for the introduction and the training of the '2 vs. 2' beach volleyball game

The teaching of techniques and of individual and team tactics will be offered according to the game situations of beach volleyball. Consequently, for example the improvement and the training of the attacker will be described along with the individual tactical training of the blocker and backcourt defender.

The differences in the women's and men's beach volleyball game will be discussed in the various chapters. If no distinction has been made, the explanations could be regarded as valid for both.

A detailed **analysis** with respect to the **game's structure** will be given, regarding the contents of every learning section. The preconditions and demands for certain learning goals, the motion and action sequences and their variations, the didactical and methodical considerations as well as general hints for training will be offered and discussed in this analysis. Selected forms of training, which include detailed execution and observation hints, will be presented for each learning goal. Here, small-court games are again of high importance. **Small-court games with each other** primarily serve the *learning* process while the **games against each other** are part of the *training* process. The explanations given in each analysis are based on scientific studies, primarily on Master's thesis's (HÖMBERG 1993 and BRAMMERTZ 1993) as well as on the author's observations and experience. Additionally, about 50 professional tournaments in the USA have been observed and analyzed since 1982. This has been done unsystematically ("casual" or "unbound" observation) as well as systematically, the latter using video footage. All statistical information, the results of systematical game observations are basing on the author's own studies (German national top-level of men: BRAMMERTZ 1993; US-professional level: HÖMBERG 1993).

From didactical and methodical points of view, the analysis tries to determine and to give reasons for certain sequences of the technical and tactical contents of training.

Here it must once again be emphasized, that the introduction and the learning of beach volleyball techniques, as well as their situation and game-like use, is the main focus of this handbook.

The presentation and the sequence of contents follow the structure of the beach volleyball game. However, *within* one game situation, the contents, their sequence and their method of teaching follow didactical points of views. With respect to the didactical and methodical aspects of training, the following advice should be taken for an optimum handling and application of this concept .

> Reception and defensive techniques, defense tactics and strategies shall be trained prior to or simultaneously along with the corresponding attacking techniques, tactics and strategies.

This demand is derived from the game structure, which clearly demonstrates a substantial dominance of the attack over the defense.

> All contents, all techniques, strategies etc. shall be trained purposefully, with all actions distinctly aimed at certain learning goals, and consequently under the most varying exterior conditions and during various times of the day.

Observations of US-professionals as well as at the German top-level are proving this fact. The results show, that an average of 3.5 rallies are played for scoring one point and that the overall playing time for one point is 98.6 seconds. For the teaching of individual tactics for the receiving players, the serving players should, for example, first take over only supporting functions. Subsequently, their individual tactical training should be integrated step by step.

This demand will not always be repeated in later chapters, since it is, after all obvious and absolutely necessary for an improvement of performance and for success.

From the beginning, the following factors are to be taken into consideration for the learning process and the teaching method:

- Promoting beach volleyball techniques in terms of a moving, running and jumping game,
- promoting the anticipation ability,
- promoting the communication ability.

The classification of the forms of training given in the book exclusively follow **pragmatic execution- and organization-aspects** instead of **didactical-methodical principles**:

a. Training of a single player with or without a coach,
b. training of two players with or without a coach,
c. training of three players with or without a coach,
d. training of four players with or without a coach,
e. training of five or more players with or without a coach.

This classification is on one hand trying to take the present state of the training of the beach players into consideration. It will probably remain this way for several years. On the other hand, it pays attention to the organization of the training that is similar to the indoor-game. This method will surely prevail in the future. In other words, always with four or more players and a coach.

The **training of one player** results in the attempt to involve other interested recreational beach volleyball players in order to economize the training (shorter running distances) by having them fulfill assisting functions. It shall be pointed out in advance that **single player training** is similar to technique training and that it usually takes place under simplified conditions. This means that the single player, as a server as well as an attacker, sets the ball to himself or tosses the ball in order to stabilize his technique skills.

Training with two players also focuses on the training of technique, but under specific beach volleyball conditions.

Training with three players represents the transition from the training of techniques to training of individual tactics.

The training of individual and team tactics first becomes possible when **four players** are practicing.

Additionally, **training with four or more players** contributes to a practice, where different teams play against their own team under consideration of various tournament formats.

The forms of training with three or more players, corresponding to the structure of the beach game, are therefore situation-like and game-like. The forms of training principally offered are, small-court games '1 vs. 1', '1 vs. 1 with a permanent setter (who is the setter for both players), '2 vs. 2' on a smaller court, '3 vs. 3' or '4 vs. 4' on the usual court and as the beach volleyball game '2 vs. 2'. Games with more than 2 players simplify the whole game of beach volleyball. In this case each player must execute only one or even no ball touch or action per rally. For example, the attacker can act without any preceding action and, for the time being, can solely prepare himself for the attack in order to be able to attack after his own passing or digging action. This is later required, in furthergoing stages and forms of play.

The above listed games should also be played *consciously* and *intentionally* as games **with** each other in order to practice on the one hand the ball-handling accuracy and the motion precision and on the other, aspects of team tactics and strategies under simplified conditions. In practice, each player should intentionally play with different partners and opponents since this creates new situations of play, resp. new learning situations for every player.

> Each partner has different abilities and skills, demands different interactions and gives different types of assistance.

While this point is important for the indoor-game, it is absolutely necessary for a beach volleyball player since even among the professionals, 2 players rarely play together for a whole season, let alone for several years. However, for the World-Series-Tournaments of the World Volleyball Federation **(FEDERATION INTERNATIONALE DE VOLLEYBALL, FIVB)** as well as other national tournaments, the prohibition or limitation of frequent partners changes is expected.

From the beginning, the beach volleyball player must be confronted with **'open action situations'**, meaning game situations with at least two solution possibilities and which therefore initiate decision-making processes. This is important because open action situations resemble the structure of beach volleyball.

> **The main goal for the education of a beach volleyball player is universalism.**

This self-evident demand for an in depth all-around education can be traced back to the fact that every beach volleyball player is a serving, receiving, setting, attacking, blocking, defending and covering player.

A **specialization** in beach volleyball is only applicable in the block and defensive situation. However, this does primarily apply to a pair of beach volleyball players with very different abilities in block and backcourt defense. This can often be substantiated given the different statures of the players. A further aspect, also likely to be characterized as a tendency towards specialization, is the fact that in every beach volleyball team each player, particularly in the reception and attack situation, takes his preferred side of the court. The reasons mentioned clearly show that the specialization should not be a learning goal and that consequently, no time should be provided for the education of any kind of specialization.

In general, training must be performed according to the specific sport:

The following parameters are results of the **structural analysis of the beach volleyball game** at the German men's national top-level:

Short or very short physical loads alternate with longer recovery phases. The **load-period** lasts about 8 sec on average.

The **period between the rallies** lasts about 20 sec. In one rally, a beach volleyball player executes about 0.6 jumps and 1.6 starts, and covers a distance of an average 5.4 meters.

From an energetic point of view, these short term muscular stresses lead exclusively to an anaerobic-non-lactic acid physical load. However, it has not yet been assessed, how far the recovery has been affected by "walking" in the sand.

The running distances are about 3.3 m per start. The density of starts averages one per 15.4 sec. Running actions in an hour of net playing time add up to an average of 234 starts. Jumping actions are executed about every 42 sec. There is an average 85 jumps per player in one hour of net playing time. The winner of a beach volleyball weekend tournament plays a minimum of 7 and a maximum of 10 matches. The duration of one match or one set is on average 40 min.

When considering all the above mentioned parameters, one must also pay attention to the fact, that each match takes place under difficult exterior conditions (sun, temperature, sand, wind, etc.)

As a result, it can be said of ball-training, that with the exception of endurance training and the training of mental abilities with a ball, the repetition method must be used. Therefore, the training should consist of short maximum-load phases as well as active and sufficient recovery breaks.

2 HISTORY

2.1 DEVELOPMENT OF THE GAME UNTIL 1976

If not marked differently, the book "Kings of the Beach: The story of beach volleyball" by SMITH /FEINEMAN (1981) was used as source for this chapter.

Beach volleyball was first played in the 1920's in Santa Monica, Southern California. People started playing "6 vs. 6" according to the rules of the indoor-game. This shows, that the beach volleyball game originated from the indoor-game.

In the early 1930's the game was played with teams of four, mostly due to the lack of players. Shortly afterwards it was played for the first time in its today's form of "2 vs. 2". This way of playing beach volleyball proved to be so popular that it was copied by all players - even in the early stages of the game. In the late 1930's the beach volleyball scene moved to the "State Beach", north of the Santa Monica Pier. Even today, a large beach volleyball community concentrates on this part of the beach.

Before the end of the 1940's neither the spike nor the block was used; the net was lower than today. For the reception of the service, the underhand pass with the forearms, the bump, was still unknown. Here, similarities to the indoor-game become obvious.

Photo 1: "Miss beach volleyball"

After the beach volleyball game had almost come to a complete stop in California due to World War II, the first tournament was played in 1948 at "State Beach". This tournament then became an annual event. Already in 1951 people thought about possibilities to make the game and therefore the tournament more attractive for the spectators. Due to the missing spike, the games lasted several (1 to 7) hours. Therefore, players and tournament directors decided to hold beauty contests during the tournaments. By doing this, the tournament received more attention by the media and the spectators. Soon, more tournaments were established in southern California.

The player Gene Selznik became the first star of the sport in the 50's, especially because he was the first player to use the spike. The "star-mania" around Gene Selznik and the following 60's were the origin of the beach volleyball lifestyle which is typical for the sport even today:

The combination of beach, sun, sea, athletic players and female fans brought the game the reputation to be a sport for lazy young people who like the easy way of living instead of pursuing a "normal" career. As the players, especially during and after the late 1960's, spent every day at the beach, celebrated parties and were in a way pursued by the their female fans, a way of life typical for California and the beach volleyball game established itself. This beach volleyball players' philosophy is described by Dave Heiser, a former tournament organizer, in a striking way:

"One: Don´t work at a straight job a minute more than you have to. Two: Spend every daylight hour on the beach. Three: Figure out a way to make money playing volleyball. Four: Sleep with as many women as you can." (In: SMITH/ FEINEMAN 1988, 64)

Photo 2:
Beach volleyball, early "80's".

In 1960, this development was still in its early stages, but the sport grew and 5 tournaments were organized. In the middle of the 60's, Ron von Hagen made the bump set popular for the reception of the service. He is one of the most successful players of all times, won his first tournament in 1964 and reached the final of the Manhattan Beach Open (near Los Angeles) in 1965, the at that time and even today most important tournament. The longest match in beach volleyball history was the final of the Manhattan Beach Open in 1968. After five sets and a total playing time of 7 ½ hs, Rundle/Bergmann won in the late evening in the light of parked cars.

By then, the number of players and the competition among them had become so large that it was difficult to find enough free nets for the teams even on normal training days. Apart from that, the number of tournament applications grew as well. In order to enable all players to train and to divide the tournaments into different classes of performance, the rating system was established. This system is valid even today. It distinguishes different classes of performance, for example beginner, professional etc. In between those two extremes many different levels can be found. In order to reach the next higher level, the respective player has to prove an exactly defined statement of success (STEVENSON/OBSTFELD 1989). On most training courts however, it is common to play "challenger games", which means that the winner stays on the court to expect the next challenger.

Until 1976, there was no considerable prize money in beach volleyball. The "beach-bum"-lifestyle characteristics by that time become obvious considering that the players managed to train several hours a day and to take part in the meanwhile 10 tournaments without any significant financial support.

Until then, beach volleyball in Europe and in the US outside of California had only recreational character, which means it was mostly played at the beach without a net.

2.2 BEACH VOLLEYBALL AS A PROFESSIONAL SPORT IN THE USA

The first World Championships in 1976 at the State Beach in Pacific Palisades were the starting signal for the professionalization of the sport. The winners Jim Menges and Greg Lee received 5000 $. More than 30.000 spectators attended this tournament (SMITH/FEINEMAN 1988, 94).

After this success the marketing agency "Event Concepts" began with the development of a professional tournament series. The number of tournaments grew to 12 until 1983, the total prize money rose to 137.000 $ during this period, made possible by "Jose Cuervo" and "Miller-Beer", the main

Photo 3: San Diego Open 1982

sponsors. The number of spectators (10-15.000) grew and the tournament series expanded into other US-states (BEACH VOLLEYBALL MAGAZINE 1/1982).

The promoter changed the rules of the game several times. For example, a new ball was introduced in 1982, without any regard to the resistance of the players. Apart from that, the promoter took the main share of the television- and sponsor-money. After they had already protested against the rule- and ball-changes, the players asked for an increase of prize money. When "Event Concepts" refused, the players demanded an open financial statement.

> The rejection of this demand led to the foundation of the ASSOCIATION VOLLEYBALL PROFESSIONALS (AVP) on July 21st 1983.

Through the foundation of the AVP, the players expected to gain more influence concerning the commercial development of the game. The climax of the conflict with "Event Concept" came at the World Championship tournament in Redondo Beach in 1984. The demand for more rights and for an open financial policy was rejected once again and led to a player's strike. The tournament was played with second class players. Because of that, the annoyed sponsors turned towards the AVP (Smith/ Feinemann 1988, 129-136).

The following year, the AVP was the only promoter and it succeeded to enlarge the tournament series to 17 places and a total price money of 275.000$ (Green/ Patterson/ Casey 1993, 42-62). Prize money, the number of tournaments, the number of spectators and the presence of the media have since then more rapidly increased than in any other sport. The increase rates of the prize money exceeded even those of tennis and golf. For the AVP, an end of the commercial development is not visible:

The center court is meanwhile surrounded by stands, 25 tournaments are played in 15-20 states of the USA (Photo 4). Moreover, 750.000 $ of bonus money is paid to the best ranked players at the end of the season. The tournaments are endowed with 65.000-250.000 $ (AVP Media Guide 1993, 18-22). Since 1992, entrance fees have to be paid for seats on the stands at the center court. The possibility to watch the match in the own beach-chair directly beside the court - which is very famous among the spectators - was, like in tennis, very much limited by the introduction of the so-called VIP areas.

Photo 4: "Cuervo Gold Crown"-tournament, Clearwater 1989

More than half a million spectators in 1993 show that the popularity of the sport has obviously not been harmed by the introduction of entrance fees (AVP Media Information 1993). Until 1996, further multi-million-dollar contracts with the title sponsors of the tournaments "Miller", "Jose Cuervo" (photo 5) and "Old Spice" as well as "Coca-Cola" have been signed. The national TV network NBC is telecasting 16 hours live. Moreover the AVP is already playing an indoor-event in New York in February. In 1995 the indoor-tour shall be expanded to a series of 4-events (AVP Newsletter 1/ 1993).

Photo 5: The winner's cheque for Mike Dodd and Tim Hovland (1989)

Figures 1 and 2 show the commercial development of the AVP during the past decade.

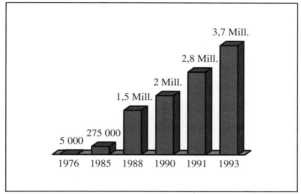

Fig. 1: Prize money 1976-1993 in $ (AVP)
(Sources: AVP MEDIA GUIDE 1990, AVP MEDIA
GUIDE 1993, AVP MEDIA INFORMATION 1993)

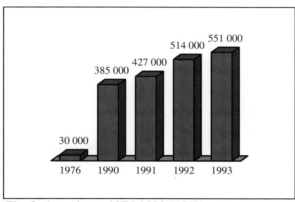

Fig. 2: Attendance 1976-1993 (AVP)
(Source: AVP MEDIA INFORMATION 1993)

At the end of the 1970's, players who are still dominating beach volleyball today, entered the scene for the first time. Sinjin Smith, Karch Kiraly, Mike Dodd, Tim Hovland and Randy Stoklos dominated the tournaments during the past 12 years. In the 80's the team Sinjin Smith/Randy Stoklos became the most successful team ever with far more than 100 tournament titles. Their finals vs. Hovland/Dodd characterized the past decade.

Among the male professionals, Karch Kiraly and Kent Steffes managed to break through the dominance with 51 titles won by them in the last three seasons. A similar dominance by them is expected for the following years (AVP Media Guide ,1993).

The fact that they never changed their partners is seen as a reason for the dominance of Smith /Stoklos and Hovland/Dodd. Even in the 60's, it was unusual to keep on playing with the same partner after a failure. Today, many players change their partners several times during a season. Smith /Stoklos in contrast to that, played together for more than ten years, due to that their "chemistry" worked well.

Most of the top-20-players of the AVP have passed over the peak of their career. The winners of tournaments during the last few years are 35 or even older. A new generation will consequently move up during the next few years.

The **professional beach volleyball game for women** (Photo 6) developed, although delayed, similar to men's beach volleyball.

The **WOMEN'S PROFESSIONAL VOLLEYBALL ASSOCIATION (WPVA)** has been founded in late 1986. The intention was to move out of the shadow of the men and to establish the women's beach volleyball game as a professional sport. Before 1987 no considerable prize money was paid, thus the players were amateurs.

Photo 6: Women's professional beach volleyball, Santa Barbara 1991

In 1988, several sponsors made a raise in total prize money from 50.000 to 105.000 $ possible. Like the men's game, women's professional beach volleyball experienced a rapid development: Until 1991, the total prize money was raised to 805.000 $, the number of tournaments to 17. Since 1988 the WPVA tournaments are aired on via television. The numbers of spectators do not reach AVP-dimensions (30.000 - 60.000 per tournament), but the growing attendance numbers (5.000 - 20.000) indicate without doubt an increase in popularity (WPVA TOUR GUIDE 1991). For 1992, 20 tournaments with an average prize money of 50.000 - 100.000 $ were planned. Due to a declining number of spectators, the loss of a TV-contract and an increase of organizing costs, prize money was cut by 20% and the number of tournaments reduced to 12 (FROST 1993, 50-56).

The year 1993 was therefore a year of financial consolidation for the WPVA. 12 tournaments were played, a single tournament being endowed with only 20 000 $. In 1994 the WPVA was able to increase the prize money (40.000$)and the number of tournaments (15) again.

▶ In addition to that the WPVA had to cope with the loss of 8 top players who left for the newly founded AVP women's tour in 1993. Parallel to men's tournaments the women play mini-tournaments. A safe yearly salary of 50.000$ is guaranteed by the AVP. At the end of the year the 8 players receive, a share of additional bonus pool money of 325.000 $ (AVP MEDIA GUIDE 1993) depending on their ranking. However, the latest development - with regard to the 1995 season - shows that the AVP was not able to put up a satisfying women's tour. Most of the female professionals playing for the AVP are expected to return to the WPVA-tour, since this organization has successfully completed its economic recovery.

Due to the fact that women's beach volleyball game has been overshadowed by the men's game for a long time, only few documents about players and tournaments before 1986 could be found. The most successful players before the foundation of the professional association were Nina Matthies and Kathy Gregory, who ruled the tournaments since the 1970's. The stars of the years 1987-1990 were the Brazilian Jackie Silva (41 titles), Patty Dodd (12) and Linda Chisholm-Carillo (28) (FROST 1993, 54).

Since 1990 the game has changed dramatically through a more athletic way of playing, which was first introduced by Karolyn Kirby and Angela Rock who managed to win 12 tournaments, and who are still dominating, however playing with different partners now. Since then a higher training volume and intensity has become common among the female pros', and connected with that, a more athletic way of playing, characterized by a high number of jump serves, blocking actions, and a more mobile backcourt defense can be observed.

The phenomenon of the "partner change" is even more common among female pros' than in the AVP. The magazine "Volleyball Monthly" (3/92) found that every player among the top 60 of the WPVA ranking has played with an average 5 different partners during one season. Here, those teams playing together for a whole season were also very successful. The average age of the 15 top players is about 30 years.

In the USA, several different organizations promote other tournaments for amateurs and professionals.

– In 1991, a tournament series with the name "**American Beach Volleyball League**" was created for "4-player teams" The tournaments are played in a group system. Each team consists of four players, the tournaments feature round-robin play with exclusively rally-scoring. (see part 3.5.2 for the rules).
Since the foundation of the league the Budweiser brewery has been the main sponsor. The team combinations are made by the "Draft" model known from other professional sports in the USA (Basketball, American Football etc.), the teams have sponsors, giving them their name. Since the 1992 season, a tournament series for women is played. Meanwhile the tournament series consists of 12 events (men and women) with a total prize money of almost one million dollars.

– The AMATEUR VOLLEYBALL ASSOCIATION (AVA) supervises the amateur events with the support of regional federations. It publishes the extensive annual tournament schedule of all open air tournaments. It is also responsible for the acknowledgment and the checking of the players' ratings (as well as local associations, like for example the California Beach Volleyball Association) and regulates therefore the admission of players to professional tournaments.

2.3   CEV BEACH VOLLEYBALL

(compiled by Ursula Tattermusch, Beach Volleyball Coordinator CEV)

The first CEV European Beach Volleyball Championships were held in 1993. One exclusive tournament was organized in Almeria, Spain, where 24 men's national teams entered the competition. In 1994, beach volleyball in Europe expanded, the European Championships then were played in a circuit format with five stops. Host cities included, among others, Palermo, Italy and Almeria, Spain. 26 national teams from 18 different countries took part in each tournament, playing in front of a capacity crowd of 2000 spectators, seated on stands.

The tournaments were played in a group format until 10 teams were eliminated from the field, then, the remaining 16 teams kept on playing in the double-elimination format. The ranking system of the European Beach

Volleyball Circuit takes only countries into consideration, and not the single player. In each tournament a 30.000 $ prize money was distributed, a bonus pool of 25.000 $ was paid at the season's end.

In 1994, the city of Espinho, Portugal hosted the first Women's European Beach Volleyball Championships. 18 teams originating from 12 different countries competed for the title and a prize money of 15.000 $.

The 1995 season, marks the final year before beach volleyball enters the Olympic arena in Atlanta. The European Beach Volleyball Circuit can be regarded as an good opportunity for European players to qualify for the Olympic games.

The CEV-tournament series in 1994 achieved reasonable success, consequently, the CEV has set up a calendar of six Beach Volleyball events for 1995. For the first time, all tournaments will feature entirely the double elimination format. There will be one qualification tournament and five final tournaments for men national teams, as well as two qualification tournaments and one final tournament for women national teams.

In 1995, the CEV plans to increase the standards regarding the local organization in order to provide an excellent atmosphere for the players, spectators, sponsors and officials. Therefore, all organization, communication and catering facilities will be provided in a special village area. Furthermore, TV-footage of each event will be produced and distributed to all interested TV stations all over the world.

The interest of the media, sponsors as well as the affiliated European Federations is remarkably increasing. More federations will send their teams into the circuit for participation and will host tournaments. The CEV recognizes with great pleasure the extension of beach volleyball in Europe and will strongly support this development in providing all organizational assistance that is needed.

2.4   FIVB WORLD-SERIES AND FURTHER INTERNATIONAL DEVELOPMENT

The ten-year development of the game as a professional sport by the AVP and the already existing resp. the still to be expected commercial profits were first noticed adequately by the FIVB in 1991.

The FIVB perceived the growing popularity of the beach volleyball game among players and spectators as well as the enormous chances of commercial development given through marketing. Consequently, the FIVB invented the "Beach Volleyball World Series" with, during its first years of existence, 3 - 6 annual tournaments. National champions from all over the world compete in this series. For the 1995 series, the number of tournaments is increased to

18 men's and 11 women's events. Meanwhile, prize money reaches dimensions of 100.000 $ - 200.000 $ for the men, resp. 50.000 $ - 100.000 $ for women's events.

Especially since beach volleyball has become an Olympic medal sport, the FIVB is striving to secure its status as the exclusive instance for international beach volleyball. The fact that the FIVB Beach Council determined the qualification regulations for the Olympic tournament, might serve as an example for that.

Photo 7: Beach Volleyball World Series, Rio de Janeiro 1993

Due to the growth of the beach volleyball game as a professional sport, a development similar to that of tennis is expected. The momentary number of tournaments (25 AVP, 18 FIVB) will further increase. The professional players/ teams can already choose between different tournaments on every weekend all over the world. A similar, maybe slower, development is expected for the women. The status as an Olympic sports event was established in September 1993 and is confirming the above mentioned tendencies.

The struggle between the AVP and the FIVB has been slowing down the sport's development during the last years. The recently founded agreement recognizes the AVP as the dominant professional beach volleyball promoter in the United States. It gives the AVP pros' allowance to compete in World Series events without being ejected from the AVP. On the other hand, the

AVP acknowledges the FIVB as the only instance for Olympic qualification procedures and for the Olympic tournament. Since this agreement will be newly negotiated after the Atlanta Games, more struggles can be expected in the future. For the women problems were solved in early 1994. The American Volleyball Federation USVBA (as representative for the FIVB) was acknowledging the tournaments of the WPVA as a qualification events for the Olympic games.

2.5   BEACH VOLLEYBALL IN GERMANY

In Germany, an organized tournament series has been existing since 1988. It was initiated by the German national coach, and organized until the end of 1990 by marketing agencies. Mainly the dissatisfaction of the players about the lack of organization during the first three years of beach volleyball in Germany has led to the fact that, since 1991 the German Volleyball Federation (DVV) organizes the Beach tournaments, or at least supervises the local organizers. In 1991 the so-called Beach-Commission met for the first time. It is now the main DVV-instance for beach volleyball.

In 1991, four tournaments were organized; in 1992 the number was raised to 7. So-called Masters tournaments have a minimum prize money of 20.000 DM. In 7 tournaments in 1992, a total prize money of 50.000 DM was distributed. The local organizers are relatively free referring to the marketing of the tournaments, but the DVV has reserved exclusive rights, for example determining the title sponsor of the tour and of events.

Photo 8:
German beach volleyball-championships Timmendorf 1993

That strategy led to the fact that in 1993 a total prize money of 100.000 DM has been distributed. In 1994 this prize money was even doubled. Meanwhile 10 Masters tournaments and 25 Beach-Cup-tournaments are played in Germany. Between 5.000- 6.000 spectators are usually attending a weekend-tournament.

Internationally the German top teams just play a subordinate role. Although the men's and women's national teams belong to the top European teams, the gap to the world's top teams can still be regarded as huge.

The national teams must necessarily get a coach, assistant coach/ match-analyst and physical therapist who should accompany the teams throughout the whole year. Moreover, financial support has to be sufficient enough to give the players' a chance to concentrate only on the beach volleyball game. Only by training in foreign countries for a whole year (esp. USA) the German top players will be able to reach the goals of the DVV, for example the qualification for the Olympic games.

3 STRUCTURAL ANALYSIS OF THE GAME

3.1 RULE-DIFFERENCES IN CONTRAST TO THE INDOOR-GAME

First of all, a survey of and some remarks on beach volleyball rules are given for a clearer understanding of the structural analysis, as well as for the explanation of technique and strategy. Here, knowledge of the indoor-game's rules is required.

Recently, standardized international beach volleyball rules were worked out. They are derived from the indoor game's rules as well the American professional rules.

American professional rules were developed mainly in accordance to the rules of the indoor game - under consideration of traditional beach rules.

It must be emphasized that currently there are two different kinds of rules, namely the FIVB-rules, where a game is decided by points and therefore sets, and the AVP-rules, where a game can also be decided by the playing time. The following descriptions correspond to the rules of the FIVB, the differences to the AVP rules are especially highlighted.

The games are structured as follows: The playing situation is a "2 against 2"-game on a volleyball court. The season consists exclusively of tournaments. In all tournaments, 32 teams play on 5 to 7 courts in a double-elimination format. The basic intention of this system is, that a team can not drop out after one lost game, it has to lose twice in order to be eliminated. After a defeat in the winner's bracket, the team keeps on playing in the loser's bracket and will be eliminated from the tournament after losing another game there. A set is played to 15 points with a two point minimum difference, but up to 17 points at the most. In this case, a one point difference will conclude the set resp. the game. The winners of the winner's bracket and the winners of the loser's bracket play the final. Two sets are played to 12 points. Here, the possible decisive set is played in the rally scoring format (Tie-Break) with a minimum 2 point difference.

USA: Basically, the US-professionals play with a rally clock. If neither team has won the set after an effective playing time of 8 minutes, the team leading at that moment would be the winner. Thus, even a one point difference would be enough to win the set/game. If the score is tied after the playing time has expired, the so-called "sudden death" will decide, which means that the team that wins the next point will be the winner.

Additionally, US-professionals are consistent in following the principle that a team has to lose twice in order to be eliminated. If a team, that won the winner's bracket, wins the first set of the final match (played to 15 points) it will be the overall winner of the tournament. If the champion of the loser's bracket has won that set, however, a decision set to 7 points with a 3 min. effective playing time, will be played. This is the so called double final. The rally scoring format is not used in this case, so that only the team with the sideout can gain points.

The 3 "Gold Crown Tournaments" as well as the "Kings of the Beach"-tournament are excluded from this format of double elimination. At these invitation tournaments, consisting of the top ranked 14 (16) players, the "group" format is used. On "Gold Crown Tournaments", sets to 11 points are played in the **round-robin format** (see glossary). Ultimately, the final match is played to 15 points. In the "Kings of the Beach"-tournament, the usual method of scorekeeping, in the shot-gun format, is employed. (see glossary).

During sets to 11 points such as during the double final (to 7 points) the teams switch sides after every two played points.

In order to meet the demands of TV networks, concerned with the playing time fitting into specific time slots, the AVP has been experimenting with a different duration of the rally clock (between 8 and 9 minutes) recently. Moreover, tournaments were sometimes played with or without the 7 point double final.

Fig. 3 on page 31 illustrates the double-elimination format:
The winner's bracket is shown on the left side, the loser's bracket on the right side. The team match-ups are noted on the horizontal lines of each small bracket. The sequence of matches is fixed and dependent on the **bold** numeration.

Numbers **A 1**-**A 31** determine matches of the winner's bracket, numbers **B 1-B 38** signify matches of the loser's bracket.

First round matches, in the left column in the winners bracket, are set up in accordance to a seeding list. The plain text-printed numbers from A 1- A31 in the loser's bracket indicate from which match of the winner's bracket, a team (loser of the winner's bracket match) is coming from. In the first round of the loser's bracket, the 16 losers of the first round matches of the winner's bracket, match up against each other. In the second round, the losers of the matches A 17- A24 start their play in the loser's bracket etc.

Accordingly, a team which, for example, has lost in the first round of the winner's bracket, but has still managed to qualify for the finals, has had to play 10 matches. On the other hand, a team which has won every match in the winner's bracket, will have played only 6 matches during a tournament weekend.

Photo 9

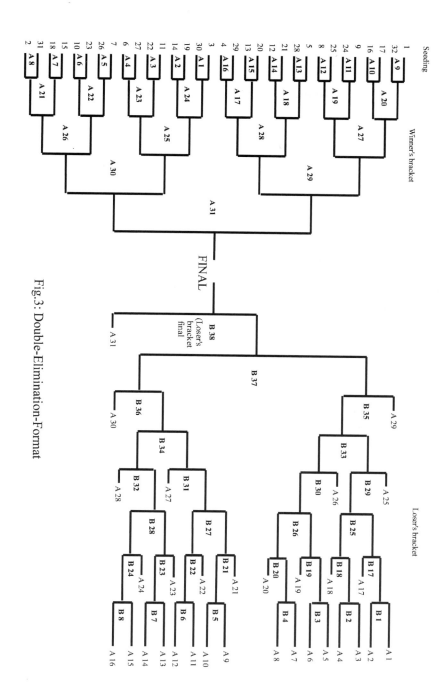

Fig.3: Double-Elimination-Format

The differences between beach- and indoor-rules are shown in keywords:

– In contrast to indoor volleyball, the beach volleyball game is profoundly influenced by exterior conditions, such as wind and sun. That is why teams change sides after every 5 points.
– The ball is hand-sewn and made of multi-colored leather (Mikasa Beach Champ). Due to its air pressure and surface, the beach volleyball is softer than a normal indoor ball. With a weight of 260-280 g, it is also heavier. The ball is inflated to 171- 221 mbar (0.175 - 0.225 kg /cm3), giving it a circumference of 65-67 cm.

USA: At the US-pro level, the ball is made of softer leather (Spalding Top Flite) and inflated to a pressure of 3,5 N/cm.

– The teams consist of two players who may not be replaced - neither during a game nor a tournament.
– There are no rules for rotation, so that each player can change his/ her position at any time before or after the service.
– With every sideout change, the serving player is alternated.
– An error in the service order of the serving players leads to a loss of the serving right.

USA: On the professional level, a wrong service order does not have any consequences. Neither is the match interrupted nor is anyone punished. Nevertheless, during the remainder of the game, the new service order has to be maintained in such a way that no player serves twice successively.

– During the serve, the non-serving player may not move. Moreover, he may not obstruct the receiving team's view in any way. At the request of the receiving team, or in the US, at the referee's request, the player must move in order to grant the opponent a clear view.
– The indoor rules were adapted concerning net contact. In addition to the rule barring contact with the net, such contact will not be called after the player has hit the ball, and if this action does not interfere with the subsequent development of the rally.

USA: Any net contact is prohibited.

– A player may cross under the plane of the net to the opponent's side in order to save the ball, as long as he/she does not interfere with the opponent's actions.

USA: Here, however, the opponent may be touched but his follow-up actions may not be influenced by this body contact. The opponent does not have to avoid the contact with the ball or player who is crossing into the court. However, the player or the ball may not be touched intentionally during the play. This last rule applies to both parties, so that no players can deliberately interfere with a possible play by the opponent. This rule is always interpreted in such a way that if a physical contact takes place, the interference by the player crossing under the net is called, although the rule does specifically permit the physical contact with the opponent.

- The ball contact must be played appropriately, meaning the ball may not be held, carried or thrown.
- In the defensive play of a hard-driven ball, the ball may be held momentarily. This can occur only in overhead actions with the fingers.

USA: The pro-rules do not restrict this rule to only overhead action.

- The ball may be touched with any part of the body. Simultaneous contact of different body parts with the ball is permitted.
- A team's first hit during the defense of a hard-driven ball, in the USA also a hard spike rebounding from the block, may be played by the same player with consecutive contacts during one playing action for example with open hands. As mentioned above, the FIVB even permits a momentarily held ball.

USA: On the pro-level, this rule only applies to the defense of hard-driven balls, and therefore not generally to the team's first defensive ball contact. Spin spikes, attacker and setter trick attacks as well as all other kinds of shots may not be defended open-handed.

The hand set must be played with two hands at the same time, the one-hand set is not permitted.

In the USA, the most recent rule change concerning the hand set took place in 1990. It now resembles the hand setting rules of the FIVB. Previously, the requirements for a precise set were not defined exactly. Only one ball rotation was allowed in order to call the set a clean hit. This led a situation where most players used the bump setting technique more often, in order to avoid mistakes. Observations and statistical analysis following the rule change show, that teams who are still mainly using the bump set, get worse results than teams who favor the hand set. Despite the rules being adjusted in favor of the indoor game, the rules, concerning clean ball contact, are interpreted more strictly in the USA than in FIVB or national tournaments.

- The lateral set to the partner is permitted, the lateral set across the net to the opponent is prohibited.
- The ball may be hand-set to the opponent, but only with the shoulders perpendicular to the ball's trajectory.
- The attacker's and setter's trick attack, such as a one-handed set is not permitted.
- The double-handed jump set, played as an attacking action will be called by the referee. This play across the net may only be performed from a standstill.
- Ball contact through the block will always be counted as the team's first hit, nevertheless, the blocker who touched the ball may carry out the second ball contact as well.
- In case of a simultaneous ball contact by the attacker and the blocker, the ball may be contacted with open hands by both players, it may therefore be held.
- 4 time-outs, each 30 sec., may be taken, also consecutively.

USA: Among the US-professionals, two time-outs, of 45 sec. each, and 4 so-called sand-time-outs, each 20 sec, may be taken. In a double final each team gets one full and two sand-time-outs. During sudden death, no additional time-outs can be taken. No more than two time-outs may follow another.

3.2   STRUCTURE OF THE GAME

In regards to the structural analysis of beach volleyball, its main characteristics and its differences to the indoor game will primarily be discussed.

While the indoor game is regarded as a team sport with some of the characteristics of racket sports (played back and forth over a net etc.), this can not be so generally applied to game of beach volleyball. It can best be described as a sport with a large resemblance to racket sports, and only with some of the characteristics of team sports. A large number of beach volleyball players increasingly see themselves more or less in an individual-sport. This opinion is especially supported by the players from the homeland of beach volleyball, the USA. Rankings appear for individual players and many play with different partners during the season. Here, the game is often regarded as a man vs. man competition. This trend is exemplified through the possible specialization of positions such as net blocking player and backcourt player defender.

However, the fact remains that those teams that practice and play together for longer periods of time are more successful. This supports the classification of the beach volleyball game as a team sport.

In any case, the FIVB as well as the German Volleyball Federation (DVV) are anxious to implement the prohibition of partner changes during one beach season. The intention is to increase the attraction of the game for spectators and the media through *team* identification and the subsequent marketing of the teams.

With respect to the game's athletic and mental characteristics, a partial similarity with the indoor game can be noticed. However, it can generally be said that, because of the size of the court and the number of players, certain physical demands have developed differently than in the indoor game. These are reflected in newly developed training techniques and their subsequent share of the overall training volume.

3.2.1 PHYSICAL DEMANDS

With regard to athletic abilities, a brief analysis of the demands on the beach volleyball player in terms of running and jumping, show results of trendsetting importance:

During one hour of net playing time, which refers to the total playing time excluding time-outs and unusual match interruptions, the following demands for a beach volleyball player on the German top level is displayed (see table 1). The player executes an average of 85 jumps, 234 starts, and covers 772 m of overall running distance. That means, that a player jumps every 42 sec and starts a running action every 15.4 sec. He jumps 20 times while serving, 39 times while attacking and 26 times during blocking actions. An average of 129 starts are executed, 54 while changing directions. Of these 54, 17 were backwards, 17 to the right and 17 to the left.

Jumps (overall: 85)			Starts (overall: 234)		
Serve	Attack	Block	forward	right left backward	changing direction
20	39	26	129	each 17	54
Density: 42 sec			Density: 15,4 sec		

Table 1: Jumps and (running) starts during one hour of net playing time

These figures are average results. Referring to one hour of net playing time, extremely high or low physical loads as shown in table 2, have also been noted.

With regards to the duration of one rally, the results of the German top level can be partly compared with those of the US-professionals:

1. Jumping actions:	
– in 117 sec 9 jumps = density 13 sec	
– in 472 sec 3 jumps = density 157 sec	
2. Running actions:	
– in 84 sec 13 starts = density 6,5 sec	
– in 102 sec 2 starts = density 51 sec	

Table 2: Extreme loads

On the German men's top level, one rally lasts about 8.5 sec, on the US-pro-level, men and women, about 7.5 sec. The interruptions between the rallies average app. 20 sec on the pro-level.

The average number of rallies per set is 84 in Germany, whereas it is 74 in the US men's professional game and 60 in women's pro-volleyball. These results, concerning the general game structure of US professional volleyball, are taking into consideration the introduction of the so-called "rally clock", used on AVP-tournaments. It is a clock which measures the effective playing time.

A German top player executes 0.6 jumps and 1.6 starts in the course of one rally. He covers an average running distance of 3.3 m per start. A male US-professional executes 0.65 jumps, a female pro 0.47. Analysis of the running action demands on the American top level has not yet been made.

In terms of the biological energetics, the short-term demands on the muscular system lead to an almost exclusive anaerob-alactacid load.

However, no studies have been undertaken so far about the influence of walking on the sand during recovery periods. In any case, the winner of a beach volleyball weekend tournament, of the double-elimination format, plays a minimum of 6 and a maximum of 10 matches.

> These points, as well as the analysis of extreme loads, justify the presumption that improvements in physical endurance, as well as the improvement of the mental abilities in terms of ball training are of a higher importance in beach volleyball than in the indoor-game.

Speed as a skill specifically in movement and reaction - as well as the speed strength with a high maximum strength, such as especially during serve and jump actions, are of paramount importance. This has been confirmed through interviews with American top players. They all regard strength training to be of a higher importance for beach volleyball, than for the indoor game (see chapter 10). Moreover, these facts can even be confirmed through free, informal observation. All the movements characteristic of indoor volleyball, e.g. jumping, running, stopping, starting, quick changes of directions, standing up quickly etc., can be observed in beach volleyball as well. When considering that all movements are executed on a sandy surface, it can be concluded that, compared to the indoor game, a higher level of maximum strength as well as other characteristics of strength must be developed (see chapter 11.5). Since all movements are executed on sand, reactive strength abilities are, in contrast to indoor volleyball, insignificant (see chapter 11.5). Coordinative abilities, specifically balance, have a substantially higher significance than indoors. The beach volleyball player needs also a highly developed ability of anticipation as well as excellent reaction skills in order to be able to defend balls hit at him from a distance of 4 - 10 m with a speed of 80 - 130 km/h. Corresponding observations show that, on German top level, the main action positions for backcourt defense are distributed as shown in figure 4:

7%	4,9%	6,6%
17,3%	30,5%	22%
2,9%	6,6%	2,2%

Fig. 4

The largest share of the backcourt defensive actions takes place on the middle third of the court. 30 % of all the defensive actions take place in the court's center, 22 % between pos. II and I and 17% between pos. IV and V.

About 19 % of the defensive actions take place in the front third of the court. The lowest share of defensive actions takes place on pos. I, V and VI with an overall 13 %.

Since the defender has to cover a much larger area, and as confirmed by many professionals, he must act closer rather than farther to the net, the elevated significance of anticipation and reaction abilities becomes obvious. It can therefore be stated that a beach volleyball player - especially as backcourt defender - can only be successful if he has many years of beach experience.

In addition to the already mentioned general data concerning the physical load in one hour of net playing time - 85 jump actions, 234 starts with an average running distance of 3.3 m; density of actions; one jump every 42 sec, one start every 15.4 sec - the following results can be added:

-   While the beach player has to execute one jump every 42 sec and one start every 15 sec, the indoor volleyball player on the German top level has to execute one jump every 51 sec and one start every 19 sec.
-   In one hour of net playing time, the beach volleyball player averages 20 jumps during the service, 39 while attacking and 36 while blocking. Consequently, the block has a share of 31 % of the overall total of

jumping actions, the service 23 % and the attack 46 %. In contrast to the indoor game, no jump set (whose share is there 12 %) has been observed.

- On the US-pro level (men), the share of jump serves, related to the overall total of jumping actions, is slightly higher (27%) than on the German top level. The share of the block is similar (about 31 %) and the attack's percentage a little smaller with 42 % (see table 3).
- The female US-professionals jump-serve with a percentage of about 17%, the attack's share is almost 60 % and the share of the block is relatively insignificant (23.7 %: see table 3).

	Block	Attack	Serve
US-Pro's - men	31%	42%	27%
US-Pro's - women	23%	60%	17%
German top men	31%	46%	23%
Jumps per set (nat. top level men)	15	23	14

Table 3: Percentages of techniques in jumping actions

- **Per hour of net playing time**, a beach volleyball player on the national top level executes 129 starts forwards, 54 with a change of direction and 17 (each) backwards, to the right or to the left (table 4).

	1-2 meter	3-4 meter	5-6 meter	7-8 meter	9-10 meter
forwards	41,0%	35,2%	21,8%	1,5%	0,5%
changing direction	17,8%	46,7%	26,1%	7,1%	2,4%
backwards	29,2%	49,2%	20,8%	0,8%	0,0%
sidewards	71,0%	25,9%	3,1%	0,0%	0,0%
overall	39,0%	37,5%	20,1%	2,5%	0,8%

Table 4: Running actions

- Especially in backwards starts (indoors 20 %, beach 7%), starts with a changing direction (indoor 2 %, beach 23 %) and sideward starts (indoor 24.5 %, beach 14 %), **differences** to indoor volleyball are evident.
- With respect to the total playing time, a German top beach volleyball player executes 76 jumps per hour, meaning he is jumping every 48 sec. In comparison, an indoor player jumps 66 times per hour with a density of 55 sec.
- The beach player jumps about 14 times while serving, 23 times while attacking and 15 times while blocking. Consequently, he executes 52 jumps during the course of one set.

- Substantial differences concerning the jumping demands can only be found occasionally, even among teams that are playing with a specialized blocker and backcourt defender. Due to the opponent's serve tactics and their own choice of serve tactics, the demand of jumping stress is usually distributed equally, although one player executes all blocks.

3.2.2   MENTAL STRESS

During a game of beach volleyball, various factors lead to a higher mental level of stress than during an indoor game.
Internal factors must be discussed, which are inherent to the match and its development.

- Every contact with the ball is very short and requires a very fast reaction,
- the technique requires high movement- and aiming-precision,
- the intensity of the game is high,
- the main characteristic, of the activity of a beach volleyball player, is the "play without ball", thus the readiness for a possible action which does not have to - but may appear.
- Every rally is short and always effects the result (sideout, win, or loss).
- The receiving, as well as attacking players are expected to react successfully. This is because the receivers play *like in the indoor game* in the 2-man reception formation, and the attacker because he is acting *against only two players* who have to cover 81 m², an area usually covered by 6 players. If the dominance of the attacker is high against 6 players in the indoor game, it is even higher in beach volleyball. This illustration shows that a very good performance is expected from the players. It therefore creates high levels of mental stress.
- The fear of failure is increased by the fact that only one other player can be made responsible for a team error,
- in the receiving situation, with only 2 players and a short time available for reaction, there is a requirement for the ability to maintain a high level of concentration. This is very demanding on mental stability.
- In most cases, the opponent's serving tactics aim to break a player's mental and physical resistance,
- the attack against one blocking player and one backcourt defender resembles the characteristics of the duel-like competition in an individual sport.

External factors may cause mental stress as well:

– The introduction of the 8 minute time limit in US-professional volleyball further increases the pressure on time and success. The players are forced to play more offensively and to take bigger risks while still attempting to be ultimately successful.
– **Sudden death** (only among the US professionals) happens in the case of a tied score, after the expired playing time. This leads to an excessively high mental level of stress, since a slight mistake may lead to the loss of the match and/or elimination from the tournament. The double-elimination format, as the common playing format internationally, is stress compounding as well.
– The high media-, sponsor- and spectator-attention levels lead to a high public expectations exerted on the players. This huge public interest, however, so far is mainly limited to the USA.
– A single fault or point-win is often the deciding factor for winning or losing high prize money.

The mentioned points allow the following conclusion to be drawn. The game requires high mental stability from all players.

Photo 10

3.2.3 NUMERICAL DISTRIBUTION OF THE TECHNIQUES COMMONLY USED

▶ Regarding the numerical distribution of the various techniques, the most relevant results will be presented in the following lines. Additionally, further descriptions, especially with respect to technique efficiency and the main action locations, will be analyzed in chapters 5.1, 5.3, 5.4, 6.3, 6.4, 7.4, and 7.5. All results come from observations of the German men's national top level and of the men's and women's pro-level in the United States.

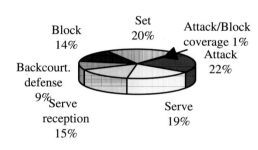

Fig. 5: Percentages of techniques

Figure 5 shows that the attack has the main share of all actions (22%). The serve makes up for 18.5%, the reception's percentage is 15.3% and the setting accounts for about 20 % of all actions. The share of the block is 13.8 %, that of the court defense 9.3 %. The attack coverage (0.9%) and the block coverage (0.2%) are of negligible importance.

– With a share of 56 %, the jump serve is of superior importance (see chapter 5.4, table 8). The results from the US men's pro-level show an even higher percentage (men 73.5 %, women 48%).

– While the spin serve in Germany still has a share of 13 %, it's percentage in US women's volleyball is only 6 % and among male pros it is an insignificant 0.5 %.

– The float serve plays an important role nationally (22%), as well as internationally (male professionals 22%, female professionals 50 %).

– While the skyball can only rarely be observed in Germany (0.7% of all serves) it is used more frequently among the US professionals (5 to. 4 % of all serves).

Almost all serve receptions (99 %) are played with the bump-technique (forearm pass).

Reception	Sidewards	Frontal	From a standstill	In a falling motion	In motion
	57%	43%	46%	17%	37%

Table 5: Reception techniques

- With a percentage of 57 %, the receiving actions on either side of the body are of decisive importance. The share of the frontal pass is 43 % (see table 5).
- While 46 % of all passes are played from a standing position, 17 % are played in a falling motion and 37 % in any other (running) motion (table 5).
- The German top players mostly use the overhead hand set (almost 72%).
- The bump set is played 26 % of the time, while the rest are emergency passes.
- In the USA, the share of the hand set is considerably lower, with 45 % for the male pro's and only 36 % for the female players. The bump set still has significant importance with a share of 55 % and 64% (see table 9 / chapter 6.3).
- Almost 92 % of all setting actions are executed frontally, with the player facing his setting target. For lateral (2%) or overhead sets (6%), the players use the bump-setting technique. These statements can not be transferred to the area of professional beach volleyball. American players use the lateral or overhead bump-set far more frequently, since they:
  a) use the bump set more often anyway (s.a.),
  b) move as non-receiving players with the perfect, attentive running timing (see chapter 6.2), which means they move to the setting location nearly parallel to the first pass.
- 62 % of the sets are played from a standstill, 26 % while moving and 12% while falling. Again, these statements can not be applied to the professional level of play, since hand sets in motion are likely to be called as a technical fault by referee.
- On the national top level, different variations of the hard-driven ball are primarily used by the attackers (52 %).
- Spin spikes, trick attacks, and any other such shots, make up for 41 %, the rest are saved balls and down-balls.
- The same distribution applies on the male pro-level, with 65 % of hard-driven balls and 34.5 % shots.
- The female pros' use hard-driven balls (51 %) and shots (49 %) almost equally.

In beach volleyball, the share of hard spikes with wrist rotations is especially high. Here the hard spikes are further divided into frontal hits, hits with a body rotation and hits with wrist rotations (table 6):

	Hard-driven balls			Tactical spikes (shots)		Others: Setter's trick,
	front.	body rot.	wrist rot.	spin spike	poke shot	bump etc.
US-Pro's Men	65,5%			34,5%		
US-Pro's Women	51%			49%		
National top level men	33,5%	11,2%	8,2%	23,6%	16,6%	7%

Table 6: Attack techniques

On 405 of 605 jump attacks, a block was up. Of these, 66 were fake blocks. One third of all attacks were defended without a block. Here, a big difference to the indoor game becomes obvious, since indoors nearly all attacks are defended with a block. Of the block and backcourt defense on the national top level, the following statements can be made (see table 11 in chapter 7.5):

- There are only single blocks,
- every 7th block attempt is played as a fake block,
- in backcourt defense, the forearm digging technique has a percentage of 63.2 % on the national top level,
- one-hand digs have a share of 27 %,
- the total share of specialized beach volleyball defense techniques, beach-dig and the tomahawk, is comparatively small (9 %),
- in most cases defensive actions are executed while moving (41%), about 34 % in a falling motion and 24 % while standing.
- The ball is mostly played sideways of the body (63 %), and less commonly frontally (37 %).

3.3 PROBLEMS OF SPECIALIZATION

For the sake of clarity and to avoid misunderstanding, it shall be emphasized here, that an all-around education is the most important goal for the beach volleyball player. Since he must perform all elements of play during the match, the player should develop them to total perfection. When "specialization" referred to here as a theme, the term can not be equated with specialization in indoor volleyball. Subsequently, the term "specialization" will only be used when referring to the following 2 aspects:

1. Every player usually has a weaker and a stronger side for the pass. First of all, this means that the player will try to hide his weak side during the competition. He will use a certain starting position prior to the serve. However, in training he tries to reduce this weakness. The same applies to the attack via the left or the right side of the net.

    As soon as two players get together to form a team, the strong and the weak points of each player must be analyzed in order to give each player their more suitable **passing** side. If both players have the same weak reception side, their strong attacking side will eventually be the deciding factor for the designation of that player's side of the court.

    Observations of beach volleyball show that the players choose their side of the court with regards to their favorite attacking side, and not, as would be more appropriate, with regards to their stronger reception side.

    If both players have different stronger sides of reception, the principle applies that each player must act on his stronger reception side, meaning on that particular half of the court.

    Here again the principle "reception prior to attack" is decisive.

2. A second aspect of specialization, which can also be observed among good teams, exists in the blocking and court-defending situation. If one of the two players is much more effective in blocking, then he, under consideration of the tournament's development, should take over the main blocking function as often as possible. Accordingly, the other player would take over the backcourt defense function. As a result, the blocker, who mostly takes over the defensive setting function, must have exceptionally good setting skills, particularly with the bump set.

    However, each player must develop his blocking and backcourt defensive skills rather quickly and must constantly pursue this goal because,

    a) in a tournament, where up to 10 matches may be played, physical overload and fatigue of the net player, who is constantly acting as blocker, may arise,

    b) each player often plays with different partners, with differing strengths and weaknesses.

These explanations show clearly, that the goal of specialization for a beach volleyball player can only be supported in the short term, but that it must be rejected as a long-term goal.

It is self-evident, that from the start, a beginning beach volleyball player has to train and to play **universally**.

3.4 PERFORMANCE-DETERMINING FACTORS

Here the main factors determining performance shall be assigned to the certain levels of play in male and female beach volleyball. Basically, these differences will be discussed in their respective chapters. However, here, the most important differences between beach volleyball and indoor volleyball shall be compared and explained:

Low performance level

The indoor medium level-player, as well as all **juvenile players** can be affiliated with this beach volleyball beginner's level:

- The match's decisive element, among women as well as men, is the serve, since it is executed without any influence of neither the partner nor the opponent.
- The exterior conditions, especially wind, confront the beginner, in the serving as well as in the receiving situation, with partially unsolvable predicaments. Due to its high effectivness, the serve is the preferred technique to be trained in single training. Therefore, reception training and attack build-up, resulting from the initial pass, must be intensified and considered more extensively in training.
- For the attack build-up following reception, the setting action undertaken as a deep-court set, in response to a pass of medium or bad quality, is also of decisive importance. This means that during the training process on the primary level, the precise half-height deep-court set must be trained thoroughly. The deep-court set, as a ball-saving action and/or as a setting action with a bump set, is also very important.
- Accordingly, after a set of minor or bad quality the ability to avoid subsequent errors, the execution of an exactly aimed spin spike or shot can be regarded as a factor determining performance.
- In block and backcourt defense, the defense without block, which resembles basically the receiving situation, can be regarded as an adequate defensive formation. Among women as well as men, an effective serve usually forces a down-ball situation for their own team.
- Especially in women's volleyball, defense without block is the only formation. This is because in addition to the above mentioned statements, women have reduced athletic capabilities (compared to men).
- The communication between players through calls regarding the direction of attack and through hand signals for the defensive strategy, should only be used if the players will spend many training sessions together.

> The most important training goal for both sexes is to avoid unforced errors.

The following measures can contribute to a reduction of the number of unforced errors:

- The serve should be executed from the center of the baseline and preferably be hit into the center of the opponent's court in order to avoid balls hit "out" due to the wind.
- The serve may, especially by the indoor player, be executed cross-court as well. The ball should be hit from right to left, in order to possibly force a counter-attack from the right side of the court, which is disadvantageous for a right-handed opponent.
- The first pass following the initial reception in defense situation should not be executed high but rather half-high and not too close to the net.
- The setter should use the hand set in response to a perfect first pass in calm wind conditions, and prefer the "safe set", using the bump technique as a response to passes of medium quality.
- The attackers should execute only tactical shots in response to a set of bad or medium quality. Additionally, tactical shots should also be preferred over hard-driven spikes after an optimum set.
- The court defenders, acting from the middle of the court, at a distance closer to 6 m rather than 5 m from the net, since trick attacks are rarely used successfully here. This is due to deficiencies in technical execution.
- If the court defenders have not mastered the beach defensive techniques above the chest and shoulder level, then they should act in a distance of about 7m from the net, shortly before the attacker's ball contact. Their position is also dependent on the set's quality.

Medium performance level

All players, who have played beach volleyball for more than 2 years and who belong to the upper performance level of indoor volleyball can be affiliated with this level. For female teams at this performance level, the lower performance level considerations are still valid. Performance-determining factors are:

- The serve, especially considering the tactical impact of weather conditions,
- the reception of medium quality, with the capability to set the ball using the hand or bump set,
- the set, and especially in the women's game, the deep-court set,

- the defense without blocking as the main defensive formation,
- the attacker's ability to drive a hard spike between his opponents' positions after an perfect set, without the block being up,
- the first steps concerning the communication between setting and the attacking player, as well as between the backcourt defending and the blocking player.

> Here, the reduction of unforced errors is still critical to the match's outcome.

The following measures make the transition to the upper level of performance easier and can be learned and used in a step by step method:

- Tactical serves from any given serving location, in order to put a certain player under pressure,
- execution of the first pass to the setting origin,
- the setting player executes the setting action with the hand set following a perfect first pass, while under normal wind conditions,
- the quality of the set may not be worse than the pass,
- the attacking player should be able to play tactical shots to all areas of the court,
- the build up of the attack out of a deep-court set from the defense is still a important training content.

Upper national performance level

For the women's upper national performance level, the explanations of the medium performance level apply. On the men's level, pertaining to the top 30 beach volleyball pairs, the following observations apply:

- The jump serves play a more important role in men's than in women's volleyball, where tactical serves dominate.
- Compared to the international level, it is noticeable, that only few service variations are used in a tactically intelligent way. This is especially valid for the skyball.
- The quality of the set is usually better than the pass quality, but worse than the set quality of the US professionals.
- The communication between setter and attacker is satisfactory and shall be further improved by systematic training.
- The communication between blocking player and court defender is already at a high level.

- Beach volleyball players usually master two to three attacking techniques, in contrast to the professional players.
- The block is regularly used, although its efficiency in comparison with the international level, could still be improved. Specifically, the zone block's efficiency could be increased.
- The fake block is too often used inappropriately and therefore relatively unsuccessful.
- Compared to the professional player, the court defender shows the largest deficiency concerning his overall actions. An improvement can be achieved through reaction and anticipation training, of defensive techniques. Especially, speed of motion towards ball and during the attack, could be honed during training. Likewise, the training of communication with the blocker could be improved.

> The main goal at this level is to play every action in the action sequence more effectively than the previous action..

In women's international beach volleyball (picture 11 + 12, the tendency to adapt the men's game may be observed among the 6 best teams in the world - concerning the technical-tactical side as well as the mental-physical side.

- Jump serves can be observed very frequently, hard-driven spikes often and block-defense formations relatively often.
- For all other teams at this level of play, the performance determining factors resemble those of the men's upper national level.

Photo 11: Women's professional beach volleyball (Gabrielle Reece)

Photo 12: Women's pro-beach volleyball

At the international performance level, there are about 40 players in the USA and several in Brazil, which display the following performance determining factors:

- perfect and natural athletic precondition,
- excellent execution of individual tactical actions in all game situations,
- intimate co-operation with the partner in all game situations,
- very high mental stability in all stressful situations,
- professional attitude in all aspects of life,
- systematic and purposeful training with coaching specific for competition,
- the presence of at least one excellent jump server on every team, who can execute the jump service successfully under all wind conditions.

3.5   BEACH VOLLEYBALL-VARIATIONS

3.5.1   BEACH VOLLEYBALL '3 VS. 3'

In some European countries, especially in France, the game '3 vs. 3' receives special attention, as a top-level sport (Photo 13) as well as a recreational sport. A tournament series is played at the top level, where it is divided into an international and a national category. The rules will be described in the following:

Photo 13: Professional beach volleyball '3 vs. 3'

– Each team consists of a maximum of four players and one coach, so that each team has one substitution player.
– A match is played as one game up to 15 points requiring a 2 point minimum advantage for the win. The final match of a tournament will be played in a "two out of three" match format. The decisive set will be played in the rally scoring format (Tie-Break).
– There is no rule for rotation, so that each player may attack and/ or block during the whole match. The rotation principle applies only to the service order.
– Open-handed dinks/ shots are not permitted.
– The ball my only be set over the net with a hand set, if the player's shoulders are "squared up", in other words, perpendicular to the ball's trajectory.
– In contrast to the '2 vs. 2' beach volleyball game, ball contact resulting from the initial block is not counted as the first hit of the defending team.
– Two player substitutions may be made. The replaced player may only come back into the game if he replaces "his" substitution player again.
– The court size in France is 7,5 x 7,5 m, in Switzerland and Italy 9 x 9 m.
– In recreational volleyball, the indoor rules may be used. It has to be observed here that the court size should be kept small (7,5 x 7,5 m).

The ideal three-person team

An ideal 3-man beach volleyball team is composed of two as far as possible tall all-around players, which are superior receivers as well as attackers and blockers. Additionally, one setter is needed who should have backcourt defensive capabilities which should be far above average.

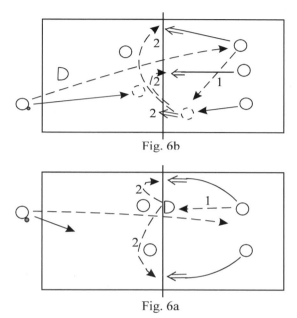

Fig. 6b

Fig. 6a

Reception formations

1. Two receiving resp. attacking players and one setter at the net (Fig. 6a).

2. If the opponent has a proficient jump serve, all three players form the reception formation. In this case, the attack build-up will depend on which player is executing the pass or on the direction of the serve. A prerequisite for the use of the 3-man reception formation is that the two all-around players have good setting qualities (Fig. 6b).

3. In recreational volleyball and in case of a weak reception, the attack build-up should be executed in the following manner: The reception should be played diagonally or as a high pass to the center of the court. This as well as other simplifying measures may be taken.

The only difference in service/ reception strategies to the main competition '2 vs. 2' can be seen in the opponent's opportunity to make the transition to the 3-man reception. Similarly, a shorter court (7,5 m) implies a different serving strategy; one with less risk.

Blocking and defensive formations

1. One blocking player and two backcourt defenders. This formation is recommended if the team's own blocker is very fast or if the opponent builds up his attacks with medium-high sets (Fig. 7a).

2. One backcourt defender and two block players (Fig. 7b). Here, the block-free net player always covers the cross-court attacking direction. This formation can be recommended when the opponent frequently uses fast outside attacks and the team's own blocking player is barely able to form a single block. Under these conditions, two blocking players will always be able to defend, using a well positioned single block (Fig. 7b).

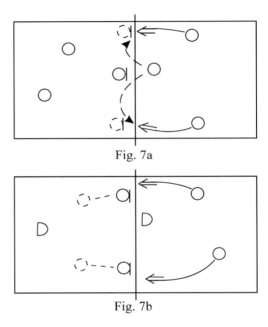

Fig. 7a

Fig. 7b

Attacking tactics

Again, the offensive tactics are determined by the technical and athletic skills and abilities of the opposing players, and by the team's own technical-tactical and athletic abilities as well.

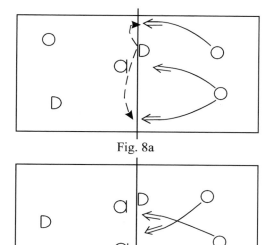

Fig. 8a

Fig. 8b

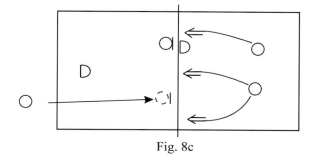

Fig. 8c

1. If the opponent uses one blocking player, the attack should be carried out using the entire width of the net (Fig. 8a). The execution of good quality blocks will be made impossible by use of medium-high sets to the outside. A tactic of equal value resp. efficiency, is the attack with one quick hitter to force the opposing block player to commit to a play.

2. If the opponent is playing with two blocking players, the setter must try, as much as possible, to have his best attacker hit at the opponent's weakest blocker. Combination attacks through the middle could be very effective, especially because neither of the two blocking players can back off early enough from the net to take over court defense. This of course, does not apply if the opponent uses a single blocker against the attack combination (Fig. 8b).

3. If the service is being executed by a blocking specialist, the attack tactic could be to attack with two simultaneous quick hitters or with one quick hitter and one outside hitter. In this case the ball is played at the part of the net that is the furthest away from the server (Fig. 8c).

3.5.2 BEACH VOLLEYBALL '4 VS. 4'

Photo 14: Professional four-man beach volleyball

At the **recreational level,** either the rules of the indoor volleyball game or the '3 vs. 3'-game apply. At the top- or professional-level, the following rules apply:

– A match is played as one game of up to 15 points with a 2-point minimum advantage required for a win.
– The teams switch court sides after every 5 points played.
– The ball may be served from any location behind the baseline.
– During the serve the teammates of the server may not obstruct the view of the receiving team. At the request of the receiving team, the server's teammates must move to allow a clear view of the server's actions.
– The service rotation must be observed, each time a team earns a sideout the teammates must alternate, following a fixed service order.
– There is no penalty for an error in service order. An incorrect server will be allowed to complete the duration of his service rotation, once he has initiated his service by contacting the ball. Immediately following the point, the offending team's serving rotation shall be changed in such a way that the offending player does not serve again until his three teammates have served in a previously established order. The opponent's service order does not change.
– There are no rules for rotation! Players may play at any position and hit from any location. Consequently all four players may act as front row players in any situation of play.
– The open-handed dink or shot is not permitted.
– There are no antennas! The ball must cross the net within the net poles.
– This rule has been established in response to the wishes of many professional players, since they have had experienced much difficulty to sideout while playing with antennas.

- With the exception of the poles, the ball may contact the extensions of the net (ropes, cables etc.) and may be played again afterwards. This does not apply to the serve.
- The ball may be played outside of the courtside banners if the player making the play remains fully inside the playing court area (inside the banners) with at least one foot on the ground at all times. Both feet must remain in the playing court area.
- For ball contact in regards to the attacker, defender and blocking player, the rules of the '2 vs. 2' - game apply.
- Regarding the hand set, the indoor volleyball rules apply, meaning the lateral set over the net is permitted.
- The ball contacting the blocker is not counted as first hit by a team.
- A player may cross under the vertical plane of the net if he does not interfere or threaten to interfere with an opponent's play. This is determined by the opinion of the referee.
- Two one-minute time-outs and one twenty sec sand-time-out may be taken.
- An injured player may be replaced.

The ideal four-person team
An ideal composition of a 4-man team consists of,

- Two good all around players with outstanding passing- and outside hitting qualities,
- one middle blocker with quick hitter qualities and
- one setter with very good defensive qualities.

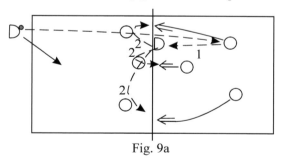

Fig. 9a

Reception formations:

1. 2-man-reception with 2 attackers and one quick attacker and the setter at the net (Fig. 9a).

2. For the reception of high quality jump serves, 3-man passing formations with the setter at the net (Fig. 9b).

3. At the recreational level it does make sense to use the 3-man formation at all times.

Block and defense formations:

1. Three block players and one backcourt defender (Fig. 10a). The front row players always try to form a double block. Behind the block, the free net player defends the cross-court area. The backcourt defender acts in the longline area or in the screened area.

2. Two players are constantly acting as blockers, while the other two are always defending the backcourt (Fig. 10b). This rarely observed formation, is used when the opposing team executes its attack using one dominant main hitter.

3. One blocking player with 3 backcourt defenders (Fig. 10c). Again, this is the best formation for the freetime-game, since the service reception is usually of poor quality.

Attacking tactics

Large similarities to indoor volleyball may be observed regarding offensive tactics. The teams constantly attempt to attack with all three attackers. The attack mounted against a single blocker is only made possible by the

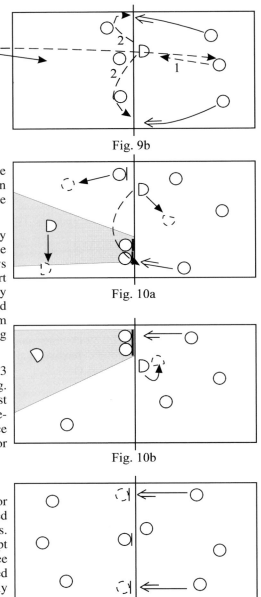

Fig. 9b

Fig. 10a

Fig. 10b

Fig. 10c

integration of the quick attacker, resulting in a committed middle blocker. A possible spike on the second contact by the setter makes a double-block formation even more difficult.

Explanations of offensive and defensive strategies are purposefully left out, since they are as numerous as in indoor volleyball and therefore too voluminous for this handbook.

4 BEACH VOLLEYBALL AS A RECREATIONAL SPORT

Photo 15: Recreational volleyball, here with Wilt Chamberlain, Bob Vogelsang and Bruk Vandeweghe

The **6 vs. 6** - game on sand can be found almost exclusively at the recreational level. Beach volleyball '6 vs. 6' or with more participants is recommended for all generations and for all calibers of play. It is ideal as a recreational sport or seniors' sport. It has been increasingly observed that all generations of both sexes with player constellations of '10 vs. 6' up to '9 vs. 9', '6 vs. 6' or even without a net or a court, will play with rules created on their own.

The character of the game as an open air sport existing in connection with sun, water, wind etc. makes for special experiences. Because of the informal composition of participants, the game imparts only positive experiences. Athletes, as well as people who are not in competition condition, experts as well as beginners can all join into the game without the danger of injury. The game may be adjusted to every level of play or any level of participant motivation by usually slight rule and/or organizational changes.

After these short general remarks on "volleyball on the beach", the following suggestions are given for the non-volleyball player who is playing on the sand recreationally (Photo 15, basketball-legend Wilt Chamberlain as a leisure time volleyball player together with former and current beach volleyball stars Bob Vogelsang and Bruk Vandeweghe):

- Any ball, from a soccer to a plastic ball, may be used.
- A net may even be built by connecting two sun umbrellas posts with some type of a cord or leash. A "road work line" or a "police line" may also replace this cord to gain better sight of the situation.
- The court boundaries may be crudly drawn in the sand using feet.
- The first ball contact could be a "catch" instead of a volleyball pass.
- In case of a very low net/leash, the game should be played without jumping.
- Beginners can use the indoor rules they already know.
- "Volleyball in the sand" can be played **with each other** or **against each other** with any number of team members. It does not matter if the sides are even or unmatched.

The following suggestions apply for indoor players who play "volleyball on the sand" in their freetime:
If there are differences in game performance or in the caliber of play between the participants,

- the teams/ groups should be formed of equal strength. Therefore there will be a balance of powerful and less powerful players,
- the better players should execute the key functions, such as the set, and/ or
- have their freedom of action limited through special rules, such as being allowed to "attack only with the weaker hand" and/ or
- have games with an uneven number of team members, such as '3 vs. 6', '1 vs. 3' or '4 vs. 10'!

If too many faults are being committed and therefore inducing long delays,

- a catch with a subsequent pass of the ball could be allowed with each ball contact and/ or
- the court size could be reduced and/ or
- the net/ leash could be taut higher and/ or
- the attack efficiency could be reduced through special rules, f.e. all attacks should be executed as spin spikes without jump.

If too many players are present and, as a result, a game, for example '10 vs. 10' can not efficiently be played,

- smaller teams should be formed and the games should be played with a time limit of at least 5 and no more than 7 minutes.
- If problems appear regarding the action playing height of play between women and men in the game of recreational beach volleyball,

- women should act as net players and men as backcourt players while playing at a net height corresponding to the women's height,
- men should be acting as front row players and women as backcourt players while playing at a "men's net" or
- men should only attack with their weak hand and block without jumping when they are front row players.

Drills, forms of play or game forms have purposefully not been described, or recommended in this chapter. First of all, the freetime sports fan just wants to *play* and secondly, the reader who is looking for such examples can easily find those in any volleyball book for the beginner's level.

Photo 16: Basketball legend Wilt Chamberlain as a recreational beach volleyball player

PART 2: TECHNIQUES, TACTICS, FORMS OF TRAINING

5 PASS AND SERVE SITUATION

5.1 ANALYSIS

The presentation and sequence of all subjects is organized by didactic and pragmatic points of view. Team tactics, in this case the 2-man reception, will be discussed prior to individual tactics. This is because the individual action is always executed within the context of the player's own team and against the opponent's team tactics. In order to serve effectively, taking into consideration outside conditions such as wind, sun etc., the server must know the strengths and weaknesses of the 2-man reception.

The training of the receiver's individual tactics must proceed the training of the server, since an optimum performance in receiving is a prerequisite for excellence in setting and attacking. The server, initially, serves only supportive functions. He trains, primarily, his aiming skills and doing so he consequently makes the first steps towards his individual tactical actions. The training of the individual tactics of the server is the last step, because it, as a precondition, depends on good receiving performances and, finally, on good receivers.

Referring to the frequency distribution of miscellaneous receiving techniques and receiving locations, the following observations show imposing results:

– Referring to the numerical distribution of techniques, the reception takes 4th place with 15,3% following attack, set and serve.

– Evaluations of the locations of reception at the German national level show that, looking through the depth of the court, 72,5% of all receptions are executed in the middle third, 25,5% on the back third of the court (see Fig. 11a). Looking across the width of the court, most of the receptions (45%) were played in the middle third of the court (see Fig. 11b).

– Almost all passes are being played using the standard two-arm technique. Other techniques, like the one-armed pass or the tomahawk (see chapter 7.5.1) can only be seen when the standard technique can no longer be used.

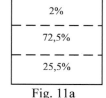

Fig. 11a

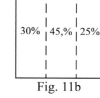

Fig. 11b

- With 57%, more lateral passes are played than receptions in frontal positions (43%; see table 5 in chapter 3.2.3). The overwhelming importance of the lateral pass could also be seen in observations of the US-professionals. Covering 46% of all passes, the reception in a standing position is of the highest significance. Because the size of the space that each receiving player has to cover, there are also a lot of passes being played **while moving** (37%) and **in a falling motion** (17%; compare table 5 in chapter 3.2.3).

5.2   RECEPTION FORMATIONS

The only reception formation in the beach volleyball game '2 vs. 2' is the 2-man reception. Theoretically, a one-man reception is possible against skyball-serves. However, this has yet not been observed. Since, in this case, the serve has a very high vertical trajectory, the speed of the receiver is not a critical factor. Instead, the decisive factor here is the ability of the player to receive skyballs significantly better than his partner.

The choice of starting position for the receiving players is generally equivalent to the positions displayed in Fig. 12a. A matching reception performance must be provided. Each player is therefore responsible for his assigned half of the court, as long as the server is standing in the middle of the baseline. If the player serves from the right hand side of the court, the responsibilities will shift according to Fig. 12b. For the server who stands on the left hand side the positions displayed in Fig 12c show the corresponding reception areas. These receiving area-changes, depending on the serving position, can be determined as follows:

The player opposite to the server has to cover a smaller area of the court because of the straight trajectory of the serve. In contrast, the player positioned diagonally to the server has to cover a larger area because of the longer trajectory of the serve and the therefore corresponding longer reaction time.

Basically, a beach volleyball team can only be successful when both players have matching reception skills. It is even better when they both have excellent receiving qualities. If one of the players is clearly the weaker passer, and the opponent recognizes the situation, the team will not be able to play successfully. Consequently, **the receiving skill is the determining factor** for the construction of a beach volleyball team.

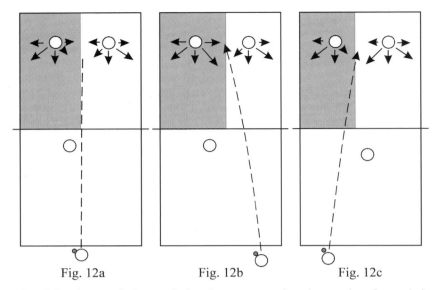

Fig. 12a   Fig. 12b   Fig. 12c

The following variations of the 2-man reception have, therefore, their justification in specific beach volleyball situations. The 2 receivers move depending on the wind direction. The receivers move about 1m forward when the wind is coming from behind (Fig. 13a+b). If the wind comes from the opponent's side, the receivers will move about 1-1,5m back (Fig. 13c+d), if there is a crosswind they will move to the off-wind side (Fig.13e+f). Wind blowing diagonally over the court, as well as crosswind, forces the receivers to adjust their position to a diagonally distorted formation in order to receive balls that are turning into or away from the wind (Fig. 14a+b). Serves with side spin which fly towards a player and then under the influence of wind, drift away, for example, serves going towards the middle of the court, have to be received by the player towards whom the ball is drifting to, never by the player the ball is drifting away from (see Fig. 42 in chapter 8.1). Independent from these considerations, the starting position of all described 2-man receiving formations may change according to the opponent's serving strategy or the current competition performance of the receivers and/or their current mental condition.

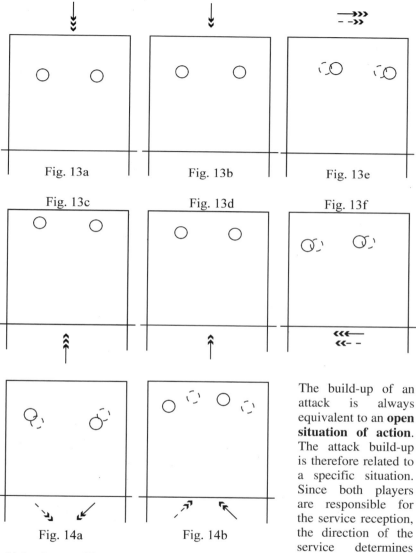

Fig. 13a

Fig. 13b

Fig. 13e

Fig. 13c

Fig. 13d

Fig. 13f

Fig. 14a

Fig. 14b

The build-up of an attack is always equivalent to an **open situation of action**. The attack build-up is therefore related to a specific situation. Since both players are responsible for the service reception, the direction of the service determines which player will pass and which one will set. Consequently both players must always be prepared to execute either the first and third or the second touch of the ball.

The action sequence of the attack build-up out of the service reception is executed as follows:

First and foremost, both players are responsible for the service reception. All following actions, such as set and attack, have to be clearly subordinated to the receiving action. The players have to concentrate their mental attention exclusively on service reception and they should not turn their attention to their setting function before they are absolutely sure that they will not be responsible for the reception.

The non-receiving player moves to the planned and probable setting spot. His time-space related behavior towards the setting spot depends on the service quality and the individual tactics-qualities of his partner. That is why the exact knowledge of the partner's abilities is a critical prerequisite for a successful co-operation.

> Observations clearly show, that all professional players move towards the net only after the receiving action of the partner in order to be able to run down bad sets, in other words, to save receptions of bad quality (Photo 17a).

The non-receiving player always runs to the setting spot *after* the reception - or at the earliest - *with* the reception. If he is expecting a reception of medium or bad quality, he must delay his movement to the net as long as possible and, if the occasion arises, orientate himself towards the middle of the court.

The late start of the non-receiving player to the setting spot, is possible if it is taken into consideration that beach volleyball players in contrast to indoor players do not need a perfect pass. In fact, the opposite applies:

The perfect first pass for indoor volleyball is comparable to a bad pass in the beach game, because it is very difficult to reach and to set passes that are played close to the net. Those passes are likely to cause even more mistakes thereafter. That is why a first pass of *medium (indoor) quality*, meaning 1 -

Photo 17a: Perfect timing of the setter while moving forward to the setting spot

2m away from the net with the option to set the ball with the hands overhead, can be considered the *perfect pass* for the game of beach volleyball. Because of the normally existing wind conditions, the **first pass must be played low** but still with the possibility to use an overhead hand set. The jump set is important in the indoor volleyball game but has no meaning in the beach game. Here, the overhead set in a standing position with an emphasis on the accuracy of the set is of exclusive importance.

The setting spot in the game of beach volleyball is dependent upon which player receives the ball and on which side of the court. The choice of the setting spot always pursues the goal where the attacking player can constantly and effortlessly see the ball and the opponent, no matter on which side of the court he has received the ball. That is why the location of the set may vary in different situations.

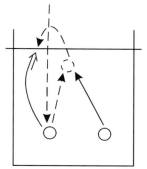

Fig. 15

If the player on the left side of the court receives the serve (Pos. IV/V), the setting spot will be on Pos. III, 1,5 - 2 m *off the net* and not, as in the indoor game, on Pos. II/III or II directly *at the net* (see Fig. 15).

The setting spot on Pos. III, although, often with a tendency towards Pos. IV, is on one hand shortening the ball's trajectory and on the other hand it involves, for beach volleyball, a decisive advantage. The danger of passing the ball over and beyond the setter is avoided. This would lead to inaccurate play and subsequent mistakes. Indoor players who start to play the beach game have not recognized this fact and still play a long first pass to the outside. This is either because they have not recognized the decisive advantage or because they believe to gain more time for their attack preparation through longer ball trajectories.

If the reception takes place on the right side of the court by the player in Pos. II/I, the

Photo 17b: Setting location II/III = 1. pass straight to the net

setting spot shifts from Pos. III more to Pos. II/III, and the first pass is played almost straight to the net (Photo 17b).

This gives big advantages for both situations of play:

1. In every service reception situation, the non-receiving player has a very exact idea or even better, exact knowledge, of the setting location.
2. The non-receiving and attacking player always has the ball and opponent in sight.
3. The approach of the right-handed receiver/ attacker may be straight to the net. The set may be played at medium height, as a "2-3meter-ball" over a short distance close to the setter in order to give the attacker the possibility to hit easily in all directions.
4. The straight pass to the net is easier to execute.
5. Likewise, the pass over the setter is avoided.

These advantages clearly prevail over the disadvantages, namely short ball trajectories and long running distances for the setter.

If a left-handed player is playing the left side of the court, the action sequence will correspond to the action sequence of the right-handed player on the right courtside - and vice versa. If a left-handed player is playing the right side of the court, the action sequence will match the sequence of the right-handed player on the left side of the court.

5.3   INDIVIDUAL TACTICS OF THE RECEIVING BEACH VOLLEYBALL PLAYER

The following results could be observed on the German national top-level with regard to effectiveness of the reception (table 7):

–   After almost 91% of all passes the ball was set in such a way, that the attacker could hit the ball while jumping (receptions of *good* and *very good* quality).
–   The percentage of direct reception *mistakes* is 6%.
–   56% of all receptions **in a standing position** are played with *very good* quality, 41% are of a *good* quality, and 2% *medium* quality. The share of direct *mistakes* while passing in a standing position totals only 1%.
–   The percentage of *very good* receptions, with a player **passing in motion** is 40%. Almost 51% of these "moving" passes have *good* quality, 3% have *medium* quality and 7% are direct *faults*.
–   Nearly one half of all passes that are played **in a falling motion** have *good* quality, only 26% of these passes are played *perfectly*. In contrast, the share of receptions of *medium* quality (6,5%) and in particular the percentage of direct *mistakes* (18%) is very high.

	Quality			
	very good	good	medium	mistake
All receptions	91%		3%	6%
standing position	56%	41%	2%	1%
falling motion	26%	49,5%	6,5%	18%
motion	40%	51%	3%	7%

Table 7: Reception quality

With a total percentage of 15,3% of all game actions, the reception has an even more important key function than it already has in the indoor game. This fact is important as well for the subsequent action as for the final outcome of the game.

Standing in the reception formation, the beach volleyball player always finds himself under high mental pressure because the spectators, in particular, expect the same level of performance as in the indoor game without taking into consideration, that external conditions such as wind, sun, high temperatures, different surface etc. make perfect passing more difficult and that these external conditions have an adverse effect on the beach volleyball player. Moreover, the passing player must receive a percentage of more than 60% of jump serves, even in windy conditions. This is why he has to perform under very demanding observation and reaction performance levels. This high

level of mental stress is maintained during one or even several games. Considering, that in indoor volleyball, jump serves are received using the 3-man reception formation, the even more difficult passing situation in beach volleyball becomes evident.

For many players, the game interruptions that preceed every passing action are the reason for the increase in their expectation of failure and fear and therefore increase mental stress. A direct passing mistake is a direct point for the opponent, confirming the special value of the reception. Since the target of the action, meaning the setting spot, is clear, bad or inaccurate first passes are recognized immediately by all and therefore they can also be considered as additionally mentally stressful.

Photo 18

USA: Moreover, the mental stress is increased in the game of the US-professionals by the use of the rally clock, especially in those situations where the effective playing time is about end.

The fact that the passing player always has the first action after a partner's mistake is also considered to be an exasperating factor in the level of mental stress. It is even more stressful when the receiver himself committed the last fault.

These explanations underline the extremely high mental demands for the receiving player and they require corresponding types of behavior:

– Positive strengthening of the receiving player by his partner or perhaps by the coach in practice and in competition.

– conscious avoidance of follow-up mistakes by the setting and also the attacking player after a bad first pass. Both should help each other, compensate each other's actions and exclude risky subsequent actions.

Because of these reasons, reception training must be planned and executed under game and competition-like conditions. Therefore, it is a definite **must** for the professional player, that he learns a mental relaxation technique.

5.3.1 IMPORTANCE OF BALANCE

In contrast to the indoor game, the coordinative ability of "balance" is of decisive importance for every action in the beach volleyball game (Photo 19).

The uneven surface causes balance difficulties in every game situation. In contrast to indoor volleyball, no action can be executed on a plane surface. Since sand is a soft surface, all balance-keeping motions are more difficult.

Accordingly, the elementary meaning of balance becomes obvious. The principle applies especially to all movements shortly before and during the ball contact, to all pass-, set- and defensive actions as well as to all jumps and all sprint starts.

A bad balance leads inevitably to **technical mistakes in all elements of play**.

These mistakes are either penalized directly by the referee or their consequences reduce the game success. Even actions which have obviously been executed correctly from a technical point of view, but during which the referee has seen balance difficulties or a wrong position of the player in

Photo 19: Perfect balance

relation to the ball, are, at least on the US-professional level, consequently called a fault by the referee.

Therefore it has to be emphasized, that a perfectly balanced posture is the absolute precondition to be able to start and react fast enough in each direction on sand surfaces and to play according to the rules.

The player constantly has to be in a low body position in order to keep his balance. He must try to reach the optimum position behind the ball, which will enable him to play accurately, in balance and according to the rules, by using intensive footwork and running steps. Wind-induced changes in ball trajectory, therefore, must be recognized at once and must be compensated for through short and fast-set steps.

A **perfect weight distribution** in form of a **well-balanced ready posture** is a **precondition for every action** in the game of beach volleyball.

The players always act starting in the above mentioned well-balanced posture. It allows a quick reaction in any situation of play. Especially the posture for the defending player enables him, for example, to dive fast for short hits or to get up in time to reach high shots overhead.

Description of the ready posture (Photo 20)

The legs of the player are bent. The feet are more than shoulder-wide apart with one foot slightly in front of the other. The upper body is bent forward. Most beach players prefer this step-like/squat feet position over the squat position. The body weight rests on the front part of the feet and is distributed *equally* to both legs.

The arms are bent at a 90° angle, with the hands open and at hip level. The arms point only slightly forward. They are positioned beside the upper body.

5.3.2 PASSING TECHNIQUES

The descriptions of the passing techniques imply a general knowledge of the techniques and motion sequences of the indoor volleyball game, so that only the differences will be discussed here:
The service reception is usually executed with the forearm passing technique (bump pass). Only in emergency situations, for

Photo 20: Ready posture

example after wrong anticipation of the ball trajectory, the ball is played overhead with the tomahawk digging technique (see chapter 7.5.1). Because of the 2-man reception over the whole court in addition to the high ball speeds of jump serves, the lateral passing techniques are of superior importance.

The increasing meaning of the overhead set has led to higher first pass-ball trajectories. That is why the pass is always executed from a very deep body position.

The frontal pass will only be used when the serve is aimed directly at the passers body or when the service target can be reached by a forward motion. The skyball in this case can be seen as an exception, because the passer always has enough time to reach a position that enables him to receive a skyball with a frontal pass. In all other game situations the ball is played exclusively with lateral passing techniques.

Motion sequence of the frontal pass

The motion sequence of the frontal pass in a standing position or in a falling motion is identical to the technique used in the indoor game.
Concerning the specific beach volleyball use of the pass, the following details have to be emphasized though:

The ready posture before playing the ball is perfectly balanced (see Photos 19+20). While playing the ball, the following principles apply:

- The body movement and the energy of the arm movement depend on the speed of the ball:

70

- The faster the ball is flying, the *less* movement of arms and body is necessary. In order to receive very hard and fast hit serves, the *digging* techniques should be used. Then, the arms should be guided *underneath and "through"* the ball in order to give it backspin.

- The height of the pass must be controlled with the deflection angle of the forearm-playing platform:

  - High passes require a *more horizontal* platform in relation to the ball.
  - Likewise, high trajectories of the serve require a *more horizontal* platform.

- Also depending on the trajectory of the incoming ball is the posture of the passing player:

  - Low serves need to be received in *low* postures.

- Posture and deflection angle of the platform are moreover dependent upon the net distance of the passing player:

  - Short serves require *low* postures and *more horizontal* platforms.

Again, here the skyball is the exception: The player needs to be in a *very low* posture, so that the ball is passed with the arms *parallel* to the ground.

- The deflection of the ball to the target (the setting spot) is controlled by the position of the platform and the shoulders. The shoulders are always facing the incoming ball at a 90° angle. Their position is not influenced by the direction of the target. Only the rotation of the platform - following the principle "angle of incidence=angle of the direction of the target", along with a light "follow-through" of the arms gives the ball its new direction. This principle especially applies to the use of lateral passes.

The following variations of passes **in a falling motion** are used in emergency situations:
- Diving pass (Photo 21a),
- Single or both knee drop pass (Photo 21b).

If the passer is unable to reach a short incoming serve fast enough to pass it in a standing position, he must **dive** (Photo 21a). In this case, an active impulse on the ball is not necessary. In contrast to the indoor game, acrobatic dives without any cushioning techniques while "landing" are possible.

The frontal pass with a **single or both knee drop** is used for top spin serves which descend rapidly. In some cases for example, where serves get shorter and shorter, the player must change his knee drop motion to a **forward sprawl**, gliding low over the sand with his upper body.

Photo 21a: Diving pass

Photo 21b: Knee drop pass

The ball is usually contacted with both arms at the beginning of the dive with one knee slightly bend outwards and one knee on the ground. After ball contact, the gliding motion continues and the arms follow through underneath the ball (Photo 21c).

A *back roll* while passing the serve as well as *passes in motion* should be avoided!

Instead, lateral passes in a balanced posture should be used.

Photo 21c: Forward sprawl

Motion sequence of the lateral pass

The following differences to the frontal pass have to be observed:

–   If the player receives a ball on his right, *below or on hip level*, he shall make a long step with his right foot to his *right* (Photo 22a); if the ball is *over hip level*, he shall take a long step to his *right/backwards*. The principle is:

–   The higher the ball, the further the right foot has to be set backwards.
–   The right shoulder rises forward/ upward, the left shoulder drops.

–   The motion's execution is 'mirrored' similarly on the left side of the body (Photo 22b).

Photo 22a: Lateral pass

–   The deflection direction is controlled by the position of the platform. The alignment of the shoulders is always at a 90° angle to the incoming ball. At the moment of ball contact, the platform is turned by a rotation of the shoulders into the target direction.

–   When receiving very high or very fast balls the body must be moved sideways out of the ball's trajectory and the ball will be received with a lateral pass (Photo 22b).

– When reaching the passing spot "late", the body must be dropped quickly, either by a long step (see Photo 22a), a very deep squat posture (see. Photo 19), a knee drop (Photo 23a) or a dive (Photo 23b).

Photo 22b: Passing "high balls"

Photos 23a+b: Lateral knee drop pass and dive pass

5.3.3 INDIVIDUAL TACTICAL TRAINING OF THE PASSING PLAYER

The training of the beach volleyball player as a reception specialist, aims to find the optimum use of the *following action alternatives* depending on his own abilities and skills and the concrete pass situation:

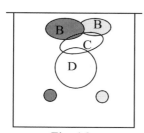

Fig. 16

1. To play the perfect pass to the **setting spot** - according to the tactical game concept (zone B in Fig. 16),

2. to play a good but not perfect pass **in the direction of the setting spot** in order to avoid unforced errors and/or following mistakes (zone C),

3. to give up the good pass in favor of a safe pass high to the middle of the court (zone D) in order to avoid a direct mistake and to be able to play a set from the deep court.

It has to be noted that the zones overlap, which means that the boundaries "flow" and that they are individually different for each beach volleyball player and depend on his reception performance and skills.

The improvement of the reception situation performance of the beach volleyball player is reflected in the changing percentages of his passing actions, from season to season, if possible from month to month in such a way that the percentage of direct mistakes in relation to ball rescue passes, the percentage of ball rescue passes in relation to good passes and the percentage of good passes in relation to perfect passes **decreases**.

The main training target for the beach volleyball player is to enable him to play the first pass, in a concrete game situation, deliberately into zone B, C, or D under consideration of all internal and external factors. The *internal* factors refer to the player himself and include his athletic and tactical but especially his technical and mental abilities. Also known as *external* factors are climatic and surface conditions, partner and opponent as well as the playing environment have an influence on the passing player. The most significant factors are:

– the consideration of the wind velocity (speed and direction) in order to take the correct starting position and anticipate the serve early, as well as to play the pass appropriately,

- the exact knowledge of the passing skills of the partner, particularly of his mental strengths and weaknesses,
- the exact knowledge of the partner's setting skills, especially his athletical and mental condition,
- the knowledge of the server's tendencies and the early anticipation of the type of service regarding the ball's trajectory and speed,
- the consideration of the partner's and the opponent's mental condition, especially with regard to successful or unsuccessful actions during the preceding rally,
- the observation of the competition's development, in particular, the development of the score and, for the US-professionals, the rally clock.

A requirement for the training of the beach volleyball player is that the mentioned exercises, drills and game forms must be adjusted appropriately to the player's and the team's caliber of play or their level of volleyball education. The key for good and effective training, is the correct choice of exercises, and a proper sequence of those exercises. Also important is an appropriate level of simplification or complication of those exercises. It has to be observed that these exercises still allow a competition and game-like practice without changing the structure of the game.

The first important step for the training of the individual tactics of the beach volleyball player is a detailed observation and analysis of his passing skills. This must be done under competition conditions, particularly under mental stress, in order to find out all his strengths and weaknesses. This is the only way to analyze the player's complete personality. The observer should pay attention to the following aspects:

- Does the player have more difficulties with the passing of jump serves?
- Does the player have more difficulties with the passing of float serves?
- Does the player show weaknesses when passing with the wind, against the wind or under crosswind conditions?
- Does the player show weaknesses when he is forced to move before or during his pass?
- Does the player have more difficulty with the passing of skyballs?
- Is the player able to act effectively after the reception of very short or very long serves?
- Does the player show passing weaknesses after unforced errors?
- Does the player show weaknesses when he is communicating with his partner?
- Does the player show weaknesses when he is receiving the serve below or above waist level?
- Does the player show weaknesses dependent on the serve's trajectory and length?

76

- Does the player show weaknesses in critical situations or is he able to show more responsibility in these passing/ attacking situations?
- Does the player show weaknesses after crucial mistakes by his partner or bad calls by the referee?
- Does the player have a weak passing side, for example his right side as a right-handed player?

Regarding this analysis of a player's skills, it must be emphasized, that the importance of scouting, of game and player observation has not yet been recognized in the world of beach volleyball, even at the professional level. Given the fact that the national team coaches do not only know the importance of player observation and scouting, but also have been using it successfully in the indoor game, it is clear that the player observation will have a great impact in the beach volleyball game within the next two years. Basically, it can be recommended to observe and analyze each single player in order to collect all information about that player's strengths and weaknesses. These files will be used for the most successful service strategy against this single player, regardless of his current partner. More detailed explanations about the prospects of player observation in the game of beach volleyball, as well as examples for observation methods, that have already been tested in competition, can be found in chapter 9.

Observations must be made at the highest women's and men's level of play, especially, during the preparation period prior to the season. Observations should also be made at lower levels of play. Only a few things that are important for a certain level of play should be observed on the middle and especially at the lowest level. Here, the principle "**less is more**" applies.

It is important to follow the specific beach volleyball-principles of training in all forms of exercises (see chapter 12). The training of the service reception is always connected to the training of the server. All the following forms of exercise should connect the pass with the attack as early as possible, since the passing player will always be the attacking player. Besides that, the training should take place under various wind and daylight conditions.

Fault analysis and corrections

The following selected training steps regard the observed weaknesses and faults of the passing player.

1. Example:

- *The service reception gets worse when the player must pass jump serves under windier conditions and under blinding sunlight conditions.*

1. Facing a strong headwind, the player will choose his ready posture to be 1 - 1.5 m (see Fig. 13c+d) in front of the baseline.

2. When passing with tailwind, the ready position should be approximately. 2 m in front of the baseline (see Fig. 13a+b).

3. Under crosswind conditions the player should leave more open space on the on-wind side (the side the wind is blowing from, see Fig. 13e+f).

4. When blinded by sunlight, the receiver tries to see and to visually fix the ball that is coming "out of the sun," according to his abilities. He fixes the ball no earlier than the jump server's ball toss and not later than his ball contact.

Principally, a beach player should get accustomed to wearing high quality sunglasses during practice and competition, in order to
–   eliminate unforced errors caused by blinding sunlight,
–   take precautions against eye injuries and diseases (see chapter 13).

FORMS OF TRAINING

a. The receiving player should deliberately be served several jump serves in a row, all of which should be hit according to his weaknesses and level of skill under the respective wind conditions and light conditions. He should always act on **his half of the court**.

b. Similar to 'a', but now the server constantly executes his jump serve from the same location behind the baseline. At first, for example, long serves to the backcourt, then short serves and finally serves to the right and the left side of the passer, should be performed.

c. Similar to 'b', but with varying service locations. For example changing from a position directly opposite to the receiver to a diagonally opposed position.

d. Similar to 'b', but with various types of jump serves.

e. Similar to 'c', but with a change of the service technique after each serve.

f. At first, all the above mentioned exercises may be played without an attack in order to concentrate on the service reception. Later, the normally subsequent actions should be included into the exercises.

2. Example:

–   *The reception performance gets worse when the receiving player must move in order to pass short or long serves.*

1. It must be tested to see if the player chose the appropriate ready position, according to the exterior conditions and the opponent's type of serve. In other words, to see, if the passer varies his position according to different situations.

2. It must be checked whether the perfect ready posture, according to the explanations in chapter 5.3.1, has been taken. This enables the player to start and move quickly in all directions.

3. One must pay attention to the early anticipation of the serve's trajectory and speed.

FORMS OF TRAINING

All forms of exercises for the improvement of the reception against jump serves, may be used here. It must be observed that all types of serves from varying service locations are used. Here, the passer should be forced to move back and forth. First the serve should be hit short, then later long.

3. Example:

– *The reception performance gets worse when the player has to pass low traveling serves.*

1. It must be checked to see, if the player uses the long forward step indoor technique to reach balls. This is a large mistake, since the long forward step has a negative effect on the player's balance. Moreover, the immediate transition to the subsequent attack will be more difficult.

2. It must be determined if the center of gravity is kept low and if the motion has ended early enough to reach a perfect balance before ball contact.

3. It must be checked to see if the arm positioning follows the principle "angle of incidence=angle of deflection".

4. It must be checked to see if the passing weaknesses can be explained with anticipation deficiencies.

FORMS OF TRAINING

a. A fault's cause may be avoided by practicing the motion, first without a ball and then later with a short distance-spin spike.

b. Similar to 'a', but with a spin spike from the other side of the net.

c. Similar to 'b', but with hard and low serves from different service locations.

d. Similar to 'c', but with different service techniques as well as different service locations.

4. Example:

− *The passing performance gets worse when the player must pass high and very high traveling serves.*

1. Check to see if the arms and the playing platform are positioned horizontally and if the player acts out of a well-balanced ready posture.

FORMS OF TRAINING

a. All exercises that urge the player to pass the ball several times in a row - out from a very low body position - are highly recommended. Moreover, the player should choose different positions with respect to the sun, he should especially practice his serve reception while facing direct sunlight.

b. Passing of balls that are thrown over the net with a high trajectory. Later, the ball should be served by the partner. At first the throws, in other words 'serves', should travel exactly to the passer. Later, they should be tossed/ 'served' more inaccurately.

c. At first the passer should receive serves with a high ball trajectory. Later he should pass real skyballs. As much as is possible, the skyballs should travel at the passer "out of the sun".

d. The server should mix skyballs with other types of serves, such as jump serves and float serves.

5.4 INDIVIDUAL TACTICS OF THE SERVER

In the beach volleyball game, the serve is of superior importance and effectiveness. This fact is easy to understand, taking into consideration that the serving and therefore defending team has no chance to defend against an attacker who is able to execute his spike after a very good service reception. Additionally, when one considers that one attacker almost dominates a 6-person team indoors, it becomes clearly visible that the 2-person team in beach volleyball faces an enormous domination of the attack. Consequently, a beach volleyball team can only be successful if it acts perfectly in the serving situation and if it makes perfect use of the service strategies in connection with its own defensive strategies. This should lead to many situations in which the opposing team must attack out from a pass of mediocre or bad quality.

Photo 24

Following the attack, and the set, with a percentage of app. 19%, the serve is the third most frequently used element in the beach volleyball game. The following tendencies may be observed with regard to the service strategies (see table 8):

–   At the German men's top level, the jump serve has the highest significance with a percentage of 57%. The percentage on the men's professional level in the USA almost reaches a superior 74%.
–   This development towards the use of the jump serve can also be seen in the women's game, where for example the female US-professionals serve a share of approximately 40% jump serves, with increasing tendency.
–   At the German national level, the float serve is used with a share of approximately 30% and the spin serve with a percentage of app. 13%. The skyball has no significance. The male US-professionals serve app. 22% float serves, just 0.4% spin serves and app. 5% skyballs.
–   The female professionals serve one half of their serves as floaters, 6% as spin serves and 4% as skyballs..
–   All beach volleyball players use the jump serve, some of them use it exclusively.

	Jump	Float	Spin	Skyball
AVP-Pro	74%	22%	0,4%	4,6%
WPVA-Pro	40%	50%	6%	4%
German top level/ men	57%	30%	13%	-

Table 8: Serve techniques

–   Studies at the national level have shown that 41,5% of all serves were hit from the serve zone behind pos. I, 16,5% behind pos. VI and 42% behind pos. V.

- Most of the spin serves were hit from the zone behind pos. V, whereas more jump serves were hit from pos. I.

The following observations have been made regarding the service quality:

- The will to hit risky serves can be clearly shown by the ratio of aces to service faults. At the professional level, there is an average of app. 3 aces and 6-7 service faults per game.
- At the German national level, app. 6% of all serves are aces. The share of service mistakes amounts to app. 15%, which again, is very high. This shows the will of the players to take risks in the service situation. Upon reception of app. 76% of all serves, the opponent was able to mount an attack at the net.
- At the German top-level, the various types of serves did **not show big differences concerning their effectiveness**.
- Float serves from a medium distance behind the baseline and even more from long distances, show a clearly decreasing effectiveness.
- Variable and precisely aimed tactical serves, even hit as jump serves, have an increasing importance. This is because they create big problems for the 2-man reception formation, made up of two attackers.

USA: In the US-professionals' game, which, according to the rules, is often decided by the rally clock, two serving strategies, that do not contradict each other, may be observed:

1. With risky serves, a team tries to gain a lead which can barely be made up in time by their opponents .
2. The losing team tries, as well, to shorten the opponent's lead by serving with a lot of risk.

The choice of the service location behind the baseline, the serve technique and the service direction and length are determined by:

1. the server's individual technical skills resp. abilities,
2. the external conditions, particularly the wind conditions,
3. the opposing players current level of performance (see also chapter 8.1).

The server may use only his two best competition serves shortly before and during the competition period in order to gain an increasing service stability and therefore security and an improvement of his individual tactical actions. Regarding the service spot behind the baseline, the player must be able to hit his competition serves with equal and constant effectiveness from each location. He must consciously practice his competition serves under the most variable external conditions. Only this method of practicing will result in the minimization of his service fault ratio and an improvement of his service accuracy. The beach volleyball player must know the serving strategies mentioned in chapter 8.1, and accordingly he must use the most effective variations of serves variable wind conditions. It can not be emphasized often enough that the serving strategy starts with the coin toss, meaning. the choice of court sides prior to the game (see chapter 8.1).

> It is an absolute must, that the side with headwind towards the server has to be chosen! This side must be preferred over the right to serve (ball) first!

Internationally, and nationally as well, the serve is and should be executed with risk, since the attack in beach volleyball is very effective after a good service reception. That is why the serves in beach volleyball are distinguished between *hard-driven* risky-serves and *precisely aimed* risky-serves. Both types my be hit with or without spin and utilize the external conditions always.

Hard-driven risky-serves with or without spin are aiming for a direct ace, minimally they are supposed to force a bad first pass.

Precise risky-serves are hit with the intention to make the attack build-up more difficult. They therefore lead to a weakening of the opponent's attack execution. Precisely aimed risky-serves cover all tactical serves, including the tactical jump serves. Since only two players are receiving the serves in beach volleyball, the accurate and well-aimed jump serve is of enormous importance. Teams in the indoor game will change from a 2-man formation to the 3-man reception formation if the opponent hits jump serves. This possibility of an improved court coverage is not applicable in the game of beach volleyball.

All players on top national levels and on the international level of play have to master at least one hard-driven risky-serve and one precise risk-serve from all locations behind the baseline. Since the skyball is a type of serve which can be very effective if hit under a high noon sun and or with a tailwind, it must also be learned and mastered by every beach volleyball player.

The conversion of individual tactical skills is very much dependent upon the mental state of the player. The serve situation creates highly stressful moments for the beach volleyball player. That is why the training of the beach volleyball player as the serving player must be performed under mental pressure and under high physical demands. Equally important is the training of concentration and focusing abilities while emphasizing endurance, particularly because the serving player must act after an interruption of play. The situation deserving special attention, is where a certain player, who has just forced the sideout by a spectacular attacking or blocking action, must now serve himself.

In order to pay special attention to the stress-release of the server during the training process, the principle of positive and negative support should be used for both players. Mental pressure situations, like that of sudden death in the US-professional game or like in the tie-break, should be included in the training as well.

5.4.1 SERVING TECHNIQUES

Motion sequence of the float serve

The technique of the float serve in beach volleyball is identical with the indoor technique. However, it must be observed that the server maintains a *well-balanced* ready posture before and during the motion.

The variations of the float serve can be identified by their different ball trajectories. With the exception of the following differences, the motion is similar to the usual float serve.

Deep and low floater:

The so-called **deep and low floater** travels low across the net and deep into the opponent's court and it will sink to the ground abruptly at the very end of the court, shortly before the baseline. This flight pattern can be created by a particularly short ball contact with no follow-through with arm or fingers. The arm swing should be a continuos whip-like motion without the input of too much power. The ball is struck at its center or slightly below the center.

Deep and high floater:

The so-called **lollipop serve** has a high-arched ball trajectory. It is exclusively hit as close as possible to the opponent's baseline. The power input is even more moderate than it is for the low floater. The ball is hit far below its center.

Short floater:

Directly after crossing the net, the so-called **short floater** sinks abruptly to the ground. This short serve may be hit with a low or a high ball trajectory. Both variations can be recognized by a very moderate power input. Their only difference is the contact spot. The short and high floater is struck below the ball's center, while the short and low floater is struck in the center.

Motion sequences of spin serves

The technique of the beach-spin serve is identical to the indoor technique. Again, a perfect execution will only be possible if the player maintains a well-balanced posture at all times.

The spin serves with a side spin can be regarded as special beach volleyball techniques. In the following, the differences to the usual top spin technique will be emphasized.

With the exception of the ready posture, the toss and the contact surface, the execution of side spin serves are similar to usual top spin serves.
If the ball should curve laterally to the right (right outside spin), it should be tossed in such a way that it would land on the server's left shoulder. The player stands in an open ready position, which means that the left foot and the left shoulder is slightly taken backwards, the shoulders are positioned at a 30°- angle to the baseline (Photo 25a).
The ball contact starts at the lower left section of the ball. The hand is wrapped over the left side *and* over the top of the ball with a forward snapping motion until it is completely roofing the ball. The outward turned palm of the hand with the thumb pointing downwards can be clearly observed during the follow-through motion (Photo 25b; the arm and body are following through, the left leg is making a forward step). Through the described wrist motion, the ball gets top spin and a right outside spin and will therefore,

Photo 25a: Ready position for the spin serve

Photo 25b: Spin serve with right outside spin

travel in a curve to the right, downwards into the opponent's court.

If the ball should be traveling in a curve to the left into the opponent's court (left outside spin), it should be tossed in such a way that it would land slightly behind the right side of the body. The ready position is also open, with the feet more than shoulder-width apart, the right foot and the right shoulder are positioned slightly backwards. The ball contact starts on the lower right section of the ball. The hand is wrapped with a snapping motion over the ball. It will be hit with a top spin and left outside spin, so that it will curve to the left into the opponent's court. The follow-through is characterized by an inwardly turned palm with the thumb pointing upwards.

Motion sequences of jump serves

Jump serves can be distinguished between the usual top spin and side spin variations and the relatively new floating jump serve. The floating jump serve was first introduced to the volleyball world in beach volleyball tournaments of the US-professionals.

The top spin variation of the jump serve reaches the highest ball speeds.

To a large extent, the jump serve technique is identical with the indoor technique. In beach volleyball, the jump server has to adjust to the external conditions, especially regarding his toss, approach, contact with ball and his balance.

The player takes a well-balanced ready position. Before the serve he has to make sure that his approach and takeoff will not be negatively influenced by "deep" holes in the sand. The toss and the approach are also dependent on the surrounding wind conditions:

– When serving into the wind or during calm wind conditions, the ball should be tossed so far forward, that it can not be blown behind the already jumping player;

– Accordingly, in case of a tailwind, the toss should be backwards;

– In relatively light wind conditions the toss may be higher than in strong wind conditions. The toss can be made with the player's hitting arm. It should be perfectly timed, so that the player has time for 1-3 approach steps and a maximum jump.

Photo 26: Jump Serve

- The toss should be considerably lower in strong winds. Thus the player should have time for at most 1 approaching step in addition with his maximum jump.

In order to convert the *run-up steps* into a high jump, the last conversion step (known as *the hop* in the indoor game) must be *shorter* than indoors. Takeoff and arm swing are identical to the indoor jump serve (Photo 26). An important attribute of the beach technique, is the perfect balance the player must maintain during the whole motion, in order to execute the technique successfully.

The takeoff location is close to the baseline in order to reach a hitting position that is as close to the net as possible. This will not only shorten the opponent's time to react, it will also help the server to reach his blocking or defending position as fast as possible.

The jump server in beach volleyball has to master the following techniques regarding the ball contact:

- For the **lollipop jump serve,** with its high and deep trajectory, that passes across the receivers to the baseline, the power input must be more moderate, compared to other jump serve variations. The ball is at first struck far below the center, then a snapping wrist motion follows with the hand finally roofing the ball.
- The **deep jump serve** with its low and deep trajectory is hit with strong to maximum power input, the wrist action is explosive. The ball is struck in its center or slightly below its center. The ball contact ends when the hand is roofing the ball.
- If the ball should sink to the ground **directly after the crossing of the net**, it should again be contacted far below the center. Moreover, the wrist action, the wrapping of the hand over and around the ball, should be far more intense.

The timing of the arm swing, in relation to the body and ball as well as the follow-through and the landing are like the indoor technique.

The motion sequence of the **side spin jump serve** is identical to the usual jump serve with top spin. In order to give the ball a left or right outside spin, the ball contact has to be changed. These contacting points and the types of spin and the trajectories are similar to the side spin serve variations hit in a standing position (see page 84).

Likewise, the motion sequence of the **floating jump serve**, is to a large extent identical to the usual jump serve. The ball trajectory is similar. In contrast to the float serve, however, the floating jump serve is hit with a slightly leaned-back body. The ball is struck in its center, will be contacted with an arm swing that resembles the shooting of an arrow with a bow. The player tries to avoid a long follow-through.

5.4.2   INTRODUCTION AND TRAINING OF THE SKYBALL

The perfect execution of the underhand serve, known from the indoor game, is a prerequisite for the introduction and training of the skyball.

Motion sequence of the skyball

For the more common **forehand-variation**, the player maintains a well-balanced ready position sideways to the baseline, the left foot slightly in front and the legs slightly bent. The shoulder of the *non-hitting arm* is pointing towards the baseline.

The ball is held with the tossing hand/arm (always the non-hitting arm), app. waist high (Photo 28a). The server's distance to the baseline depends on the current wind conditions:

– Facing headwind: close to the baseline;
– with tailwind: further away from the baseline, relative to the wind's strength.

The body's center of gravity is brought *down* by bending the knees to an angle of app. 45°, and by leaning the upper body forward (Photo 28b).

The non-hitting arm holds the ball close to the ground, the hitting arm swings backwards and upwards. The lowest body position is the turning point of the motion.

Right at this moment the whole body is extended explosively. At the beginning of this rising movement of the body, the ball is tossed very low or even dropped to the hitting hand. Because of the explosive rising body motion, the toss happens only a split second before ball contact. The hitting arm swings upwards and forwards, closely along the body. The ball is struck during the body's upward motion, app. between waist and chest level.

The ball is hit with either the inside of a half-closed hand (fist; Photo 27) or the upper edge

Photo 27: Skyball (Bruk Vandeweghe)

of the hand. It is hit slightly behind its center in order to give it the correct flight direction. The body extension continues; thus the whole body and the hitting arm follow through to a full extension which ends with the body weight on the toes, or with the player slightly leaving the ground (Photo 28c). However, during the whole motion, the body weight should be equally distributed to both feet.

This forehand-variation can also be performed as a floating variation. In this case, the ball is struck *at* its center. Then it will travel without spinning and with a very unstable motion which is difficult for the receiving player to anticipate.

With the exception of a different ready position and a different contact point, the **backhand-variation** of the technique is similar to the forehand technique of the skyball. The player also stands in a position sideways to the baseline, but now the shoulder of the hitting arm points towards the baseline (Photo 29a). The toss, arm swing and ball contact are all similar (Photo 29b). The ball is struck with the edge of the hand. The backhand-variation is executed solely as a *spin serve*.

Photo 28a-c: Skyball, forehand-variation

Photo 29a+b: Skyball, backhand-variation

Exercises:
1. Hit the ball from a medium to low ready position, like an underhand serve, very high in the direction of the net.

Hints
– Maintain a stable position sideways to the net, with the left foot slightly in front!
– Initiate the body extension motion shortly before the toss!
– Execute the whole arm swing with an first bent, later almost fully extended hitting arm!
– Toss the ball as low or short as possible just a split second before ball contact!
– Contact the ball with the inside of a half-open fist!
– Make the ball contact above waist level in front of your body!

Variations:
(1) Try to hit the ball high into the opposite side of the court.
(2) Try to hit the ball even higher into the opposite side of the court.

2. Similar to the basic exercise **1,** but now the motion, particularly the body extension, is initiated out of a low, and then later very low and well-balanced ready position.

90

Hints

– Pay attention to the fact that the body is constantly moving. From the start of the motion out of the ready posture, until the end of the follow-through, it never comes to rest!
– Initiate the explosive body extension when you have reached the lowest body position!
– The motion of the whole arm swing, backwards and upwards and then forwards and upwards, should be similar to that of a pendulum!

Variations:
(1) The variations of the basic exercise **1**.
(2) Similar to (1), but now the ball should be hit as high as possible.
(3) Similar (2), now the skyball should intentionally be practiced in all kinds of wind and sunlight conditions.

3. Game form: '1 vs. 1', only skyball-serves.
Player A serves a skyball from the baseline; Player B, in the opposite court must pass the ball and afterwards catch it himself. He serves the next skyball from the "catch position". He is sure not to pass skyballs that have been served "out".

Variations:
(1) '1 vs. 1', with 2 ball contacts following beach volleyball rules.
(2) '1 vs. 1', with 3 ball contacts.

4. '2 vs. 2' following beach volleyball rules, only skyball serves are allowed.

Variation:
(1) Special rule: If the skyball has been hit "out", a bonus point will be awarded to the opponent.

5. The games '1 vs. 1' and '2 vs. 2' under all wind and sun conditions.

Analysis and correction of technical faults

• Faults concerning the ready position
– Broad instead of step-like, narrow feet positioning.
– Incorrect feet positioning, for example, the right-handed player has his right foot in front.
– The player faces the net frontally instead of positioning himself sideways.
– The body weight is distributed to only one leg.

- **Solutions**
  - Discussion of the importance of the perfect ready position for the successful execution of the skyball.
  - Practicing the hitting motion without the ball. The body should be brought down and extended again several times consecutively, without changing the posture or a loss of balance.

- **Faults concerning coordination and momentum**
  - The ball is tossed too far to the side, too high or too far forward, instead of being dropped immediately before contact with the hitting hand.
  - The ball is dropped or tossed too early, for example during the backswing of the hitting arm.
  - The ball is struck too late during the follow-through, instead of being hit in the first phase of the body extension at slightly above waist level.
  - The body's weight is not equally distributed to both feet.
  - The hitting impulse is generated by the hitting arm only, instead of the entire body's momentum.

- **Solutions**
  - Practicing the toss and the ball drop without the actual execution of the serve. The ball should fall to the ground app. 40 cm in front of the back foot. Consequently, it falls down on the hitting arm side.
  - The ball drop should intentionally be executed very late, almost too late.
  - Acoustic aids for the right timing of the hitting impulse might be used.
  - Any service attempt out of an unstable posture must be stopped immediately, even during the motion.
  - Practicing the skyball with a slowed momentum. In this type of exercise, the ball will only be hit 3 - 4 m high. One should pay particular attention to the simultaneous body extension and the forward arm swing.
  - With regard to momentum, it should especially be noted that the whole motion should end with the server on his toes or even with a "jump/skip".

- **Errors concerning the contacting point**
  - The ball is struck too far behind its center.
  - The ball is struck in front of its center.
  - The ball is contacted with the palm of the hand.

- **Solutions**
  - Intentionally serving a *resting* ball from the non-hitting hand in order to control the exact contacting point.
  - Trying to hit very high skyballs.

- Slowing of the whole motion momentum in order to concentrate on the exact contacting point.
- Serving low skyballs, and subsequently balls of higher altitudes with the inside of the half-open fist, in order to find out the preferred hand positioning.

5.5 SELECTED FORMS OF TRAINING

All explanations of the handbook's thesis regarding practical application, chapter 1, should be observed in this chapter. All the following forms of training and drills will be presented as games/ small court games with more than 2 players per team. Depending on his goals, the player/ coach has the opportunity to make methodical changes regarding the organization of his training through the following steps:

1. Sideout-change after a certain duration of time (3 to 5 min.).
2. Sideout-change after a team reaches a certain number of points (3 to 5 points).
3. Sideout-change after certain series of services, for example one team has the right to serve 5-10 times before the other team gets the sideout.
4. Sideout-change after the execution of a certain number of successful actions by a team (5 or more).
5. Sideout-change after the execution of a certain number of successful actions **in a row** (3, 4 or more).

All forms of training, including the drills and the simplified games, have to be performed under competition-like conditions. The sideout-changes may be counted as so-called "big points":
The big point for winning the right to sideout will be awarded to the team that has reached this sideout change in a shorter time-span or by a smaller number of actions. Likewise, special points could be awarded for certain actions, for example for an ace-serve, (2 points), or conversely, 2 points for the opposing team in case of a service fault. With regard to the professional game of beach volleyball in the U.S., big points could be granted depending on a certain effective time of play for instance 30 sec or 60 sec. In order to intentionally increase the duration of rallies, 2 or 3 balls should be used. In that case, the first ball could be brought into play by a serve, while the other balls could be thrown in as so-called "down-balls". For the player/ coach, this form of game presents an outstanding opportunity to increase training intensity.

For the **introduction and further practice** of a single technique, it is of decisive importance that one side of the court with constant surrounding weather conditions will be kept for a longer period of time.

This does not apply to **training**. Here, practicing should be similar to competition situations, consequently the player/coach must pursue a frequent change of court sides. Likewise, relative to the weather conditions, different service directions from different spots behind the baselines should be chosen.

EXERCISES FOR ONE PLAYER

For the serve and pass situation, a single player can only practice serves, therefore, he should execute different types of serves from all spots behind the baselines to various targets. He must always consider the current external conditions (Photo 30). The following exercises for the single player may be executed in competition-like standards:

1. The player serves from one location to one target on the other side of the court. The number of serves is predetermined (5-10). According to the level of play, the number of successful and precisely aimed serves must be determinated prior to each series of serves.

Photo 30: Practicing serves (Bruk Vandeweghe)

Hints

- Always pay attention to the wind direction!
- Always serve out of a well-balanced posture!
- Your position behind the baseline, relative to wind conditions, should allow a precisely aimed serve!

2. Similar to the basic exercise **1**, but with a different service technique, for example jump serves. Because of energetic advantages, the jump serves should be practiced to a larger extent in single player training.

Hints

- Hit the first series of serves deliberately into the middle of the court in order to get a secure feeling!
- Choose service positions where your approach and takeoff will not be influenced by deep holes in the sand!
- Adjust the height of the toss to the wind conditions; do not toss the ball too high in strong winds!

3. Practicing the service reception in connection with a skyball serve by the lone player. Here, the player must hit the skyball intentionally into his own side of the court in order to play a game-like pass.

Hint

- This exercise should only be carried out when the player is perfectly skilled in skyball service!

All single player exercises should be combined with a competition-like following action. This can be done with or without a second ball, f. e.:

4. After his serve, the player runs as fast as possible (competition-like) to the net:

  - and makes an aggressive blocking jump or
  - fakes the block and backs off the net 3 - 5 m or
  - fakes the block, backs off, takes a ball from the ground and plays an attack after a self-tossed ball or
  - runs to his backcourt position after his serve and practices a defensive diving or falling technique or
  - imitates a defensive technique, takes a ball from the ground and plays a well-planned, precise attack after his own toss.

These additional tasks may be organized differently and practiced in various combinations. In any case, it must be made certain, that the physical load phase does not last longer than 10 s. The duration of the intermission phases must be at least 20 s.

EXERCISES- AND GAME FORMS WITH TWO PLAYERS

All the forms of exercises with one player may also be used with two players. The second player can take over helping functions, moreover he can correct the partner's technique.

According to the caliber of play, the below mentioned '1 vs. 1' - games can initially be played as games with each other, '1 **with** 1'. In case of deficiencies regarding the motion and action precision, this type of game, '1 with 1', should be played more frequently.

1. '1 vs. 1' with a jump serve over the whole court with the following special rules:

   – The server will get two points, if the passer does not touch the jump-served ball,
   – the server will win one point, if the passer "receives" the ball with one hand,
   – the server will not get a point, if the passer is able to receive the ball with both arms and catch it afterwards,
   – the server will get a "minus point", if he commits a service mistake,
   – the server will get a minus point, if the passer is able to build up a counter-attack within three ball contacts,
   – the server will get two minus points, if he is not able to touch the passer's counter-attacked ball.

Organization hints
   – Each server hits 10 serves in a row and counts his points or
   – the right to jump serve alternates until one of the players has reached 6, 10 or more points.

Hints
   – Use a jump serve hit with side spin into the wind, under crosswind conditions!
   – Vary the length of your serve when serving into the wind!
   – Vary the direction of your toss according to the wind conditions! For example, toss the ball a little more or little less back when serving with the wind!

Variations:
(1) The basic game form **1** with serves from a standing position.

Hints
   – Do not use jump serves if the wind is too strong!
   – Hit long float serves along the line when serving with tailwind!

- Serve spin serves with forward spin (top spin) and high power input into the wind and vary between long and short serves into the middle of the court!

(2) The basic game form **1** with skyballs.

Hints
- **Server**: Vary your distance from the baseline according to the wind conditions!
- Never change your "automated" motion sequence, no matter which exterior influences (wind) occur!
- **Receiver**: Pass skyballs out of a very low posture with an almost horizontal arm/ platform position!

(3) All types of serves are allowed.

Hints
- Put pressure, especially time pressure, on the passer by serving hard down the line!
- Receiver: Anticipate the service trajectory and your passing spot as soon as possible, no later than after one third of the balls flight path!

2. '1 vs. 1' with three ball contacts on the 3 x 9 m - court, later 4,5 x 9 m.

Hints
- **Server**: Vary short and long serves by utilizing the wind conditions!
- Hit hard-driven, risky serves longline "on" the sidelines!
- **Receiver**: Focus totally on the next pass and do not start to think about the attack unless you have executed this pass!

Variations:
(1) '1 vs. 1' with two ball contacts.

Hints
- **Server**: After your serve, move quickly to your backcourt position!
- **Receiver**: Play a pass that is high enough!
- Always act out of the basic ready posture in order to be able to move fast into any direction!

(2) Each player uses one type of serve.

Hints
- **Server:** Use your strongest/ best competition serve without regard to the wind conditions!

- **Receiver:** The first pass should be played low, so that the ball will not be influenced too much by the wind. However, it must be high enough to allow an overhand set!
- React to changes in the ball's trajectory, caused by wind, with short running steps!

(3) '1 vs. 1' on the diagonal court, at first with 3, later with 2 ball contacts (see Fig. 17).

Hint
- Serve spin serves with outside spin into the short cross-court!

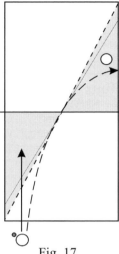

Fig. 17

GAME FORMS WITH THREE PLAYERS

All game forms and games with 2 players may be used here with a few adjustments, however, using the same sequence. Of course, the single player now has only one hit and is not allowed to contact the ball several times consecutively. Preceding the games *against each other*, all below mentioned games may be played in as games *with each other*, as well.

1. 1 vs. 1 with one player setting for both "teams" as,

The Beach Volleyball Player's Game
- Three players play '1 vs. 1' with one player serving as the permanent setter for each one of the opposing players. The game can be played on the usual court or on 4,5 x 9 m (Fig. 18a), 3 x 9 m (Fig. 18b) and on the diagonally arranged court halves (Fig. 18c). The winner will be determined over a certain period of time or by accruing a certain number of points. Points will only be awarded to the player who has the right to sideout. The setter can either be replaced after a predetermined period of time (for example 5 min.) or number of points (for example 7 points) or by following these rotation/ replacement rules:
- The passer who commits a mistake becomes setter and the setter moves to the free passer/ attacker spot, so that the remaining passer/ attacker has the right to serve. Each "team" must use all three hits in order to practice the reception according to real game-conditions.

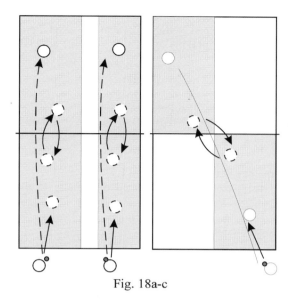

Fig. 18a-c

- Mistakes by the setter will be counted as a mistake committed by the passer.
- Depending on the level of play, the players can start their game with attacking only hard-driven balls, later they are free to introduce all different types of attacks.
- The court size has consequences for the goals of the individual tactical training of the server and the passer. Basically, the choice of a smaller court should always be paid attention to. This will on one hand increase the effectiveness of the reception and on the other hand it will limit the attacker's freedom of action. Consequently, by taking this measure, the attacker's actions can be trained. For example, a court size of 3 x 9 m makes the pass and the attack build-up very easy, on the other hand it requires more skill by the attacker.
- The game on the 4,5 x 9 m - court is more or less equal to the requirements of the beach volleyball game, concerning the demands in the serving and passing situation.
- With regard to the whole court-game, a reverse situation can be found. Here, the serving player acts under simplified conditions whereas the passing player faces much higher demands.
- Games on the diagonally arranged court-halfs must be emphasized.

Finally, in this **'Beach Volleyball Player's Game'**, the effectiveness of the serve is the determining factor for the choice of the court size.

Hint
- **Receiver**: Try to play the perfect beach volleyball pass at all times, while never too close to the net!

2. '1 vs. 2', one server against a beach volleyball team.
The '1 vs. 1' - games with conjoined setter can also be used here. Therefore, the server will always be playing against one passer/ attacker with his setter.

Organization hint
– After a certain period of time or number or points, the functions of the 2-man team may be changed, later the functions within the whole group should be changed.

Hints
– Serve with increasing frequency between the passers!
– **Receiver**: Communicate early, the player positioned diagonally to the server takes the middle!

3. '1 vs. 2' on the beach volleyball court.
The server fights against the two other players (the beach volleyball team). The following special rules apply:
– After the serve, the server must to move to either the left or the right half of his side of the court to defend this area. Accordingly, the receiving and attacking team must direct their attack to this court area, defended by the server. At first, only hard-driven balls may be hit to the close range of the defender. Later, all types of attacks may be used. In case of a successful defensive action by the server, he retains two more hits for the build-up of his counter-attack. The "win" will be awarded to either the server or the team, depending on who has reached the most points during a predetermined period of time or number of serves (Fig. 19).

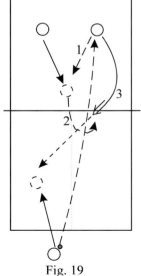

Variations:
(1) The server has to use the jump serve.
(2) If, because of daytime and weather conditions, the skyball is the preferred serve, the server must use it.
(3) The server should serve with the wind, against the wind and under crosswind conditions.

Hints
– **Server:** Serve with risk by using the wind conditions!

Fig. 19

- **Receiver**: Receivers: Relocate your passing position according to the wind conditions:
  - 1 m backwards when passing into the wind,
  - slightly forwards with tailwind,
  - slightly to the off-wind side when passing in crosswind conditions!

TRAINING WITH FOUR PLAYERS

Basically, all the above shown exercises, games and game formats may be used.

1. All the games that are played in the '1 vs. 1' format could also be played here, on all possible court sizes. With regard to this fact, the following type of organization offers a very good opportunity. The player who made the fault will be replaced by a player who is already waiting behind the baseline. This player will now execute the serve. Since the player who has earned the point or has not committed a fault stays in the game, the new player has the right to serve.

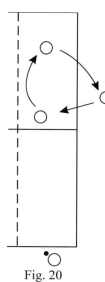

Fig. 20

2. The "**1 vs. 1 Beach Volleyball Player's Game**" with predetermined setter (Fig. 20).
    Here, this game is played with four players and waiting position. The rotations are executed as follows. The passer and attacker who makes a mistake moves to the waiting position. The player in the waiting position becomes the setter and the setter replaces the passer/ attacker.

Hints
- **Receiver**: Try to make the server feel insecure by "offering" one area to him!
- Try to avoid the use of a long step into the broad side squat (indoor technique)!

3. '2 vs. 2' on 4,5 x 9 m.
    Each player of each team has a predetermined function, so that one is only responsible for the set. The other has the task of passing and attacking. Now, according to the rules, the ball may be played to the opponent *on two*.

Hints
- **Receiver**: Play the perfect beach volleyball pass, low and not too close to the net!

Variations:

(1) Similar to the basic game **3** but with diagonally arranged 4,5 x 9m - courts.

(2) A combination of the basic game **3** and variation (1), which means that every time the ball has crossed the net, the counter-attack must be played into the other half of the court. If the ball has been received on the left half, the attacker must hit to the diagonally

Attack cross-court ——→ Attack longline

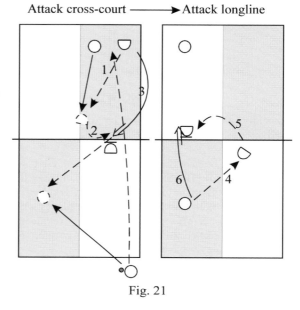

Fig. 21

opposing right half. The counter-attack again would have to be played to the frontally facing half. As a result, one team is attacking diagonally all the time, the other team is always attacking longline (Fig. 21).

4. '2 vs. 2' over the whole court according to the beach volleyball rules.
Special rule: A direct passing mistake or a service mistake will be punished by awarding two points to the opponent. At first, each team attacks diagonally, then later longline and finally towards any direction.

Hints
– **Server**: Choose a competition-like risk!
– **Receiver**: Play the first pass according to your abilities!

Variations:
(1) Only jump serves.
(2) Only serves from a standing position.
(3) Only skyballs.
(4) The players should choose the same serving technique from the same service location as well as the same serving target at all times (Fig. 22).

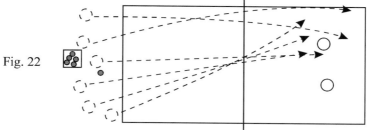

Fig. 22

Hints

- **Server**: Serve precisely, independent of the wind conditions and your service location. Use spin serves and the wind to achieve this goal!
- Never serve directly to an opposing player! Instead, serve in a way that forces the receiving player to move before or during his passing action!
- **Receiver**: Always try to avoid a passing action "in motion"!
- Only a perfect position relative to the ball will make a perfect pass possible!

5. 2 vs. 2' with 2 balls.

   All the above mentioned games, with 2 or 3 balls per rally. Now the team that won two out of three rallies will be the winner. The second and third ball should be thrown between the players with a service-like trajectory.

Hints

- **Receiver**: Never use the back roll/ side roll-techniques of the indoor game while passing!
- Be prepared to sprint and play immediately after your playing action!
- The passer positioned diagonally to the server always takes the middle or the so-called 'husband and wife area'!

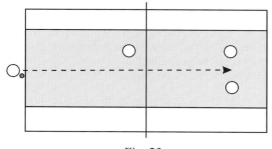

Fig. 23

6. '2 vs. 2', played out of the 2-man reception formation.

   This game is played on a 6 x 9 m - court to make communication between the receiving players more difficult (see Fig. 23).

Hint

- **Receivers**: Communicate early!

Variations:
(1) '2 vs. 2' on 4,5 x 9 m with 2-man reception formations.
(2) Diagonal arrangement of these mini-courts (see Fig. 62).

TRAINING WITH FIVE OR MORE PLAYERS

Depending on the certain training goal, game variations with five or more players could be organized as follows:
If the goal is the improvement of the server's or passer's individual tactical skills, the fifth and/ or sixth player could concentrate on practicing their serves. Meanwhile, the other four players just would have to fulfill their other training goals. Depending on their caliber of play and the surrounding conditions, one or two players could practice different elements of play for a longer duration of time.
Practicing with more than four players, can contribute to psychological training as well. The player will be trained that, if he commits a fault, he will be eliminated from the game. He will be allowed back into the game, only when another player commits a fault. When practicing with an uneven number of players, it is entirely possible that team partners will change often.

1. '3 vs. 3' with predetermined (specialized/ constant) setter.
Preceding all other forms of play, this game can be played with a complete beach team on the whole court. The simplification consists of the elimination of the open (undefined) action situation, thus the setting, passing and attacking assignments are exactly distributed to each of the players.
Moreover, the defined setter simplifies the communication between the receivers and therefore the transition to the attack.

Variations:
(1) '3 vs. 3' with one player permanently serving.
Again, this is a suitable game for practice, because the passers just have to receive one player's serves.
(2) A synthesis of the actual game and its variation (1), with one setter at the net and one constantly serving, is played over a certain period of time or until a certain number of points has been reached.
(3) '3 vs. 3' following the French beach rules (see chapter 3.5.1).

2. '1 vs. 1 with predetermined setter - **'Beach Volleyball Player's Game'** on the 4,5 x 9 m - court.
When practicing with six players, this type of game is recommended.

Variation:

(1) '2 vs. 2' and '1 vs. 1' on each half of the court.

Four players are playing a '2 vs. 2' game, on one half of the court, following the beach volleyball rules, while two players keep playing '1 vs. 1' with 2 or 3 ball contacts on the other half of the court.

3. '4 vs. 4' with 3 front row players and 1 backcourt defender.

This game follows the beach volleyball rules and the rotation order rules of the indoor game. The backcourt player can fulfill the setter's functions simultaneously. This game represents a very good transition to the '2 vs. 2' - game, since it connects a familiarization, with beach volleyball, with playful fun. Moreover, it consists of many elements from the indoor game and is therefore, in conjunction with the subsequently detailed variations, a good alternative to beach volleyball, too. The 2-man reception should be used all the time.

Variations:

(1) '4 vs. 4' with 2 players at the net and 2 backcourt players.

This game is also recommended for indoor players who want to make the transition to beach volleyball, or use the beach game as a preparation for their indoor season. It only allows the back row players to receive and perform defensive functions. While the net players only pursue blocking, setting and attacking tasks.

(2) '4 vs. 4' following the rules of the American Beach Volleyball League (see Chapter 3.5.2).

6 SET AND ATTACK SITUATION

6.1 ANALYSIS

The attack is built up according to the particular situation. Therefore, the opponent's service strategy determines the action sequence of the attack build-up during each rally. Thus, it becomes clear, that, in beach volleyball, no player can specialize as a setter or an attacker. On the contrary, both players must be able to convert setting and attacking actions successfully.

That is why a beach volleyball team must consist of two players who are as versatile as possible. Each with excellent skills in the passing, setting and attacking situations. Consequently, there will be no differences between the primary and secondary setter or primary and secondary spiker, as is common in the indoor game. Likewise, there can be no differences made between an attack build-up over front row or over back row players, since both players are the front and back row players simultaneously. In beach volleyball, however, the set from middle or deep court is more important.

The effect and the importance of the attack on two by the setter is not as crucial as in the indoor game. This becomes clear when the rules are considered. The open-handed trick attack by the setter, like the tip in the indoor game, and the side (lateral) set to the opponent are not permitted. Otherwise, the attack on two has rarely been used, due to two further reasons:

a. The perfect indoor game pass must be avoided on the beach since it is likely to lead to further mistakes.
b. For the benefit of set precision, the players do not use the jump set.

Two-man reception, attack build-up and -completion can be seen as one unit, in that they are the first basic game situation. Therefore, this situation will subsequently be called complex 1 (C 1). Complex 2 (C 2) means the consecutive attack build-up and -completion from the defensive situation. The superiority of the C 1 versus the C 2 is much higher in the beach game than in indoor volleyball. Unfortunately, as of now, not all indoor volleyball rules have been adapted in order to decrease the superiority of the attack. It is actually unbelievable that in beach volleyball the block touch is still counted as a team's first ball contact. This simply means that the blocker and the backcourt defender face even bigger odds than the six defending players in indoor volleyball. The adaptation of the indoor rule, not to count the block touch as the first ball contact, would definitely lead to a stronger block and backcourt defense in beach volleyball, since new defensive strategies could be developed and introduced.

> The following demand is presented in order to make the beach volleyball game even more attractive: **No later than after the Olympic beach volleyball tournament, all the rules of the indoor game that have led or would lead to a strengthening of the block and the backcourt defense must be adapted to beach volleyball.**

A comparison of the C 1-situation between men and women shows the following differences:

– The set from middle or deep court, which shall be understood as a set resulting from a bad first pass or after a save, is used more often in the women's game.
– Because of the following situations, women also use the setter's trick attack more often:

a. Consciously and intentionally, when one of the opposing players clearly demonstrates her blocking intention very early,

b. unplanned, in order to avoid faults during subsequent actions. Especially, when the first pass has been played too close to the net,
c. planned, if the partner is not able or not ready to play the attack after the pass.

– Moreover, it can be observed that the attack '*on two*' is intentionally played only after good or very good passes. Most of the time, in this case, the female beach players use a spin spike from a standstill. A jump attack can only rarely be seen.

6.2   ATTACK BUILD-UP

The attack build-up out of the service reception formation is described in chapter 5.2.

Fig. 24a+b

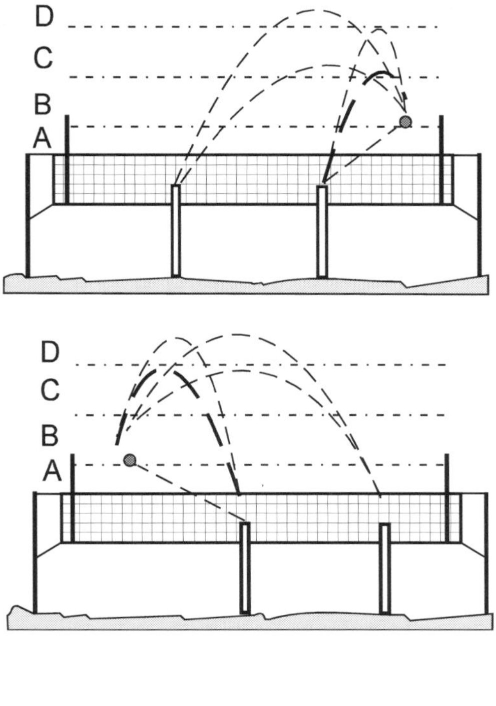

Since there is only one attacker available, there are basically no combination attacks in beach volleyball. Most of the time, the attacker has very long approaches to the net. More importantly, he must only act against a single block, independent of the transition speed from reception/ defense to attack. Considering these facts results in the subsequently mentioned set and attack possibilities. Regarding the length, height and speed of the set, the following categories can be listed (Fig. 24a+b):

Area **A**.: Fast and low sets (up to 0.4 s and app. 60 cm over the plane of the net) are **not used** in beach volleyball since they can only have negative repercussions for the attacking team.

Area **B**: **Medium high sets** (0.4 - 0.8 s, 2 - 2.5 m high) with a **medium distance** (app. 2 m) between setter and attacker. These are the **optimum sets** in the game of beach volleyball, because,

- the **wind influence** on the ball is **minimized**,
- the harmonization of the setter's and the attacker's actions, regarding timing/ space, can always be organized similarly.

Area **C**: **Medium high sets** with a **long distance** between setter and attacker (0.8 - 1.2 s, more than 2.5 m high) are **only used in case of bad first passes**, thus the ball must be set more than 3m away from the originally intended setting spot.

Area **D**: **High sets** (more than 1.2 s, more than 4 m high) from a **medium or long distance** are used **after bad service receptions**, most of the time, after an emergency reception.

The hand backsetting action is only used in the context of a trick attack with both hands, and almost never as a "real" set to the attacker. If the setter is forced to use a backset he will basically play a lateral set or a backset with his forearms, thus with the bumpsetting technique. This fact urges the indoor player to make a transition to the bump set and to relearn this technique.

In indoor volleyball, the backset with the bumpsetting technique has only been used in emergency actions as a third ball contact, whereas in the beach game, the bump set must be executed very accurately as a setting action. That is why the bump set, as backset or side (lateral) set, must be mastered and practiced by every beach volleyball player.

Actually, the bump set is used almost as often as the hand set and is therefore of equal importance. The reasons for the frequent use of the bump set are:

1. The non-receiving player is very often not able to reach the perfect position to set the ball,
2. the hand set is strictly judged at the international level.

USA: The second reason is more effective in US-professionals' game than in the European arena. Until 1990 for example, a hand set that traveled with more than one rotation had been called a technical fault by the referee. In order to avoid these calls and technical faults, the bump set was preferred and therefore intensely practiced.

Another explanation for the frequent use of the bump set exists with respect to the timing of the non-receiving player. This player starts his movement towards the setting spot not before he is sure about the quality of his partner's pass. This late movement and his observant timing enables the setter to run down passes of mediocre or bad quality. However, this perfect running timing forces the setting player to have a long wait in the middle of the court, app. 2 steps in front of his passing partner, and to subsequently run down the first pass. Low first passes in strong wind conditions have to be reached as well. The running movement of the setting player can almost be described as an overtaking of the ball traveling towards the net. Many players, especially at medium levels of play, and also at the top national level, have not yet recognized the importance of the observant running timing of the setting player, in order to build-up the attack perfectly. They often commit a **substantial error** in that they tend to move to the setting spot too early, at the moment at which they recognize that they do not have to play the pass.

The medium high set from a short or medium distance, as the perfect set in beach volleyball, requires very good communication with regards to the setting and the attacking location. Three communication possibilities are employed:

1. Without regard to the setting location, the attacking location will always be the same, for example at a predetermined position, even in the case of a medium quality set.
2. The attacking location will be relocated depending on the setting location. If, for example, the setting location is more than 2 m away from the usual position, the attacker will move in the direction of the new setting spot in order to receive the **same** set.
3. The attacker clearly identifies his attacking location verbally.

For the game of beach volleyball, the second communication possibility in conjunction with the third, in the case of medium or bad quality pass, is recommended.

Coverage of the attacker can not be neglected. The attack coverage has, of course, only a very small share of all team defensive actions. However, when taking into consideration that a successful coverage of one or two balls rebounding from a block can decide a game, it will become clear that the attack coverage must be practiced in training.

Systematic observations show that the execution of the attack coverage is *the* tactical part of the beach game, as well as in indoor volleyball, that has been neglected the most so far. Although players and coaches are convinced of the necessity of the attack coverage, they do not convert it effectively in training or in competitions. This behavior can be explained by the attack's dominance in beach volleyball, particularly out of the service reception. The players expect successful attacking actions and therefore do not pay enough attention to the actually necessary coverage.

Both players have coverage functions. The attacker must cover himself, thus he should save balls that are rebounding in front of him, directly behind him and beside him. The setter is responsible for all rebounding balls that are on "his" side of the attacker and for all balls further behind the attacker. Since the sets are played over medium distances most of the time, the setter should try to reach a medium-low coverage posture with one step at the most. In case of a blocked ball, the attacker tries to turn his body during the landing in order to cover himself. All covered balls must be played high to the front center of the court, in order to make for an easy next set for the partner as well as be able to again approach for the following attack.

6.3 INDIVIDUAL TACTICS OF THE SETTING BEACH VOLLEYBALL PLAYER

Observations at the German top level men's tournaments and at the US-professional level of play show the following results:

–   In terms of the numerical (quantity) distribution of all techniques, the set maintains the second position behind the attack with 20% of all playing actions.
–   At the German national level, about 73% of all sets are executed on the third of the court that is close to the net and app. 27 % are played as a set from middle or deep court. Here, almost 20% of the passes are set from the court's center. More than one half of all sets (52%) are executed in the Pos. III area. Less than 0,5% of all sets are played from outside the court's boundaries.

–   With 72%, the hand set has the highest significance, whereas only 26% of all sets are executed with the bump set technique (see table 9). One-hand sets are only used in emergency situations. The male US-professionals however use the bump set with a share of 55%, the hand set has only a percentage of 45%. An even higher share of the bump set (64%) has been observed in the female professionals' game (hand set 36,3%, see table 9). The reason for the overall more frequent use of the bump set in the United States is the stricter interpretation of the rule regarding the hand set (see also chapter 3.1 and 6.3.1).

Photo 31

- In the C 2 situation of the professionals (male and female), the bump set outweighs the hand set with a ratio of 3 : 1.
- At the national German level, many more sets are played in a standing position (62%) than in motion (about 26%) or in a falling motion (app. 12%).

| | AVP Pros | | | WPVA Pros | | | German top level men |
	overall	C 1	C 2	overall	C 1	C 2	overall
hand set	45%	50%	27%	36%	42%	25%	72%
bump set	55%	50%	73%	64%	58%	75%	26%

Table 9: Setting techniques

- Almost one half of all bump sets are executed in motion, whereas only about 30% are played in a standing position and app. 23% are played in a falling motion.
- About 76% of all hand sets are played from a standstill, app. 19% are played while moving and about 5% are executed in a falling motion.
- At the German top level, almost 92% of all sets are played with the setter facing his setting direction. Only 2% are played as lateral sets, and about 6,1% are played as backsets. The backsets are mostly played with the bump setting technique. This very high percentage of frontal sets can not be observed at the professional level, since the professionals perfectly and attentively time the running for the setter in beach volleyball. This often forces them to set laterally (see chapter 6.2).
- Almost 56% of all sets are played with optimum quality. Another 36% are played with good quality, so that a jump attack is still possible. Less than 6% of all sets have medium quality, where no jump attack or no attack at all is possible (see table 10).
- All handsets are of optimum or good quality. About 86% of all bump sets reach these quality levels, whereas the good quality sets (50%) overweigh the sets of optimum quality (36%). About 12% of all bump sets are of medium quality, 2% result in direct faults (see table 10).

| | Quality | | | |
	optimum	good	med.	fault
overall	56%	38%	4%	2%
hand set	65%	35%	-	-
bump set	36%	50%	12%	2%

Table 10: Quality of sets

The setter's primary task is to compensate for inaccurate first passes and to know the partner's peculiarities, so that the attacking partner will always get "his" perfect set. Each beach volleyball player must have perfect skills with respect to the frontal hand set from a standing position and the bump set. The jump set, frontal or lateral, has no significance.

The bump set frontally (Photo 32a), laterally (Photo 32b) and as backset (Photo 32c) is much more important.

Photo 32a: Frontal bump set

> In beach volleyball, each player must be able to set a perfectly accurate set for his partner in any type of wind condition and **from any position on the court** without any technical difficulties or even faults.

The beach volleyball player constantly tries to use the hand set since this technique will allow the most accurate sets. Especially in light and "medium" winds, the hand set is more precise than the bump set because the ball can be "accompanied" into the intended direction for a longer period of time. The wind must always be considered, particularly when executing a set from medium or deep court. Thus, the setter must push the medium high set more or less against the wind, so that the ball does not travel

Photo 32b: Lateral bump set

– across and beyond the attacker when setting with **headwind**,
– across the net to the opponent when setting with **tailwind**.

Photo 32c: Bump set as a backset

Strong winds can lead to technical mistakes when using the hand set. Additionally, when the player can not reach a well-balanced position to play a hand set, the bump set is being used.

It becomes clear, that here the bump set is of much more decisive importance than indoors. With regard to the opponent's actions, the same may be said for the setter:

> Since the attacker must spike against only one blocker at most, the **precision** of the set, almost without consideration of the opponent's actions, is the **most essential precondition** for a **successful attack execution.**

The accuracy of the set must be seen as even more valuable, if one takes into consideration that the attacker will have great difficulties in the case of an inaccurate set. A change in the approach direction and the compensation for an inaccurate set is very difficult to execute.

Inprecise sets and sets that are too far off the net, may lead to attacks from mid-court (2 - 3 m) or to mistakes by the attacker (for example the attacker ending up too far underneath the ball). These attacks are less effective because the attacker's action height is reduced and thereby the opponent's possibility to defend with two backcourt defenders is increased.

The setter's trick may only be played frontally with two hands or as a backset. As a result, the one-handed set is **not** a part of the beach player's training.

In indoor volleyball, the observation of the opponent by the setter **prior** to his set is very important. In beach volleyball however, the observation of the opponent by the setter **after** his set is of even higher importance.

Immediately after his set, the setting beach volleyball player must observe the position of the opposing backcourt defender in order to call to the attacker concerning the best attacking direction. By doing that, the setter makes the decision for the attacker easier. However, the call is given directly before the attacker's spiking action in order to compensate the backcourt defender's faking actions. If necessary, the setter must change his call once again shortly before the spike.

Accordingly it can be concluded that the individual tactical actions of the setter are reduced to an optimum set and a subsequent perception of the intended defensive position of the backcourt defender.

The most significant factors of the setter's individual tactics as well as special forms of training will be discussed in chapter 6.3.2.

6.3.1 SETTING TECHNIQUES

Motion sequence of the overhand set

To a large extent, the technique of the overhand set is similar to the indoor technique. The following differences, particularly regarding the movement prior to the set, the setter's balance and ball contact, have to be observed:

The non-receiving player waits a long time, until the moment of the pass, before he moves to the setting spot. Before the moment of the pass, the setter can not be sure about the quality of his partner's pass. By being patient and using attentive running timing he will be able to run down passes of mediocre or bad quality. As a result of this optimum running timing by the setter, the bump set, very often played laterally, as well as the knee-drop technique when using the hand set, are especially important for the non-receiving beach volleyball player.

Any movement, no matter if the set is being executed from a standstill or in a falling motion, should be either concluded before the ball contact or in the phase of optimum balance (see chapter 3.1 and 5.3.1). For example, at the lowest (culmination) point of the knee drop set, the body comes to rest for a split second of perfect balance. The elementary actions "run-turn-posture (or. reaching the culmination point or the point of perfect balance)" are therefore concluded before the ball contact.

USA: At the US-professional level, hand sets that are played in motion are very often punished as a tactical fault by the umpire. A sideways positioning of the setter relative to the ball, which can often be seen in indoor volleyball, is indicating balance problems and therefore also likely to be treated as a technical fault at the professional level of play.

Photo 33: Hand set

Ball contact (Photo 33): During first contact, the ball's speed is slowed down. The hands receive the ball elastically and are brought back app. one inch towards the forehead, the elbow angle decreases slightly, the elbows point outwards. Immediately after this receiving motion, the ball is sped up with the extension of the whole body, the arms, wrists and fingers. By turning the wrists and therefore the thumbs forwards and outwards, the ball is directed into the new direction. In any type of hand set, the wrist or hand extension as well as the arm extension should be used.

USA: The common setting technique known from indoors, where the power is created mostly by wrist and finger action, is likely to be punished as a technical fault in the U.S.

In contrast to indoor volleyball, the ball contact is slightly longer. However, although the whole motion resembles a quick catch and a throw, catching, holding or throwing the ball will be punished and must therefore be avoided. As a result, it is critical to execute the whole motion very quickly.

The **side set or lateral hand set** is almost identical to the indoor technique. Only the setter's position at the target relative to the ball and the arm extension show differences to the frontal hand set. When the setter is late getting into position, or when the setting spot is too close to the net to allow a turn towards the attacker's direction without touching the net, the setter must use the lateral set with his shoulders parallel to the net.

Photo 34: Knee drop set

> In beach volleyball, the common indoor setting techniques with a **side roll** or a **back roll** should be **avoided** as far as possible.

The direct playing readiness of both players is more important than indoors, where 5 other players can take over subsequent actions. That is why the previously mentioned types of sets are only used in emergency situations. Such is the case when the pass is traveling too high across and behind the setter. Here, the setter uses the back or side roll following backward or sideward steps. An optimum, well-balanced player position underneath the ball is only possible using the roll techniques. That is why the roll is the best technique in the described emergency situations:

Because of the above mentioned reasons, the knee drop set (Photo 34) should be used much more frequently than the roll techniques. Moreover, it allows a better balanced set.

As in all situations, in which the player must reach a well-balanced position underneath the ball under time pressure, this technique should be used. Many American professionals make the shift to this type of set at the moment of ball contact, even when they are setting from a standstill. By doing this, they can keep a low body center of gravity and can therefore keep their balance during the entire setting motion. This technique can be unconditionally recommended since it guarantees optimum balance and therefore minimizes the possibility of a technical fault (improved ball control). The much faster stand-up movement, as compared to a roll set, along with immediate readiness for the next play is another reason for the recommendation of this **optimum** technique.

Motion sequence of the knee drop set (Photo 34)

The preparation for this playing action (movement to the ball, movement to setting spot etc.) is similar to the previously described setting techniques.

At the moment of initial ball contact (cushioning ball reception by the hands), the player drops to the ground by increasingly bending his knees. Actually, there is almost no or minimal (toes) contact between feet and ground during the ball contact. This, as well as the low center of gravity of the body, leads to a perfectly balanced set without being negatively influenced by the uneven sand surface. The upper body remains *upright* during the entire motion.

The following sequence of the movement resembles a usual hand set. Only the lack of leg extension is compensated for by an intensified arm and wrist impulse. The player lands on his lower legs and knees, his rear end does not touch the surface of the sand.

The entire motion also allows a body *turn* toward the setting direction. This turning motion is initiated shortly before ball contact and ends with the setting of the ball toward the new direction. This is not considered to be a rule violation..

Motion sequence of the bump set

The various types of bump sets are, to a large extent, similar to the techniques that are used for the service reception pass. Differences exist in the intensity of the arm's impulse, since the ball is traveling at the player with a much lower speed. Consequently, the bump set may be played more actively than a service reception pass (Photo 35a). Most of the time, the setter must play from a lower body posture. This is due to the fact that he often does not reach his setting location in time.

However, the setting player attempts to reach the setting spot rapidly and to position himself behind/ underneath the ball. The position must be so far underneath the ball that the player is able to set with arms positioned horizontally enough to give the ball a high-angle ball trajectory (Photo 35b).

The body extension and arm impulse will be intensified through the forward pushing movement of the shoulders, at the moment of ball contact. The arms follow through from their horizontal position up to almost near shoulder level, which allows for a long ball contact.
Moreover, the ball's direction is controlled by turns of the playing platform and the dropping motions of the shoulders:
If the first pass is too close to the net, the setting player must set the ball laterally from a position frontally facing the net (see Photo 32b). Again, the principle "angle of incidence=angle of deflection" applies.

Photo 35 a+b:
Bump set

This is of course also effective when the setting player must execute a backset without visual contact with his partner. Here, the arm's impulse must be severely intensified, the arms should "accompany" the ball up to head level. Consequently, the ball will travel backwards, beyond the setter (Photo 32c).
The late arrival to the setting location, a low pass or other emergency situations can force the following emergency techniques:

- Setting during a running motion;
- jumping into a low body posture for example the one-legged knee drop;
- setting in a falling motion;
- diving set.

6.3.2 INTRODUCTION OF SPECIFIC BEACH VOLLEYBALL SETTING TECHNIQUES

The following prerequisites, originating from the **indoor game** are required for these methodical training steps:

- the frontal overhand set, especially as a high set over a long distance,
- the forearm pass as a service reception,
- the spin spike,
- the wrist spike,
- the trick attack as a spike.

The following contents and techniques will be introduced and pursued in the following, prior to the methodical training steps regarding individual tactics:

- the half-high set from a medium distance, as a hand set as well as a bump set,
- the spin spike longline as well as cross-court (in chapter 6.4.2),
- the trick attack as a spike (in chapter 6.4.2).

Exercises for two players with respect to hand sets and bump sets from medium distance:

1. Player A is standing 3 - 4 m off the net, player B is already waiting 1 - 1,5 m off the net at his target (setting spot).
2. The attacker (A) tosses precisely to the setter (B), later inprecisely. At first, the setter

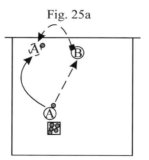

Fig. 25a

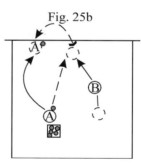

Fig. 25b

should set the ball without prior movement. The inaccurate tosses however should force the setter to move before his setting action. The attacker makes his approach, gets the set, executes his spiking motion and catches the ball at the highest point of his reach. The player's functions alternate after six tossed balls (Fig. 25a).

Hints

- Turn to your target (attacker) direction before executing the hand set!

- Always take a perfect position relative to the ball, namely underneath the ball for a hand set and behind/ underneath the ball for a bump set!
- Precisely set the ball half-high, app. 1 m off the net and about 2 m from yourself into the attacker's line of approach!
- Consider the wind with regard to the height and direction of your set!
- Push the ball more or less into the wind - depending on the wind's force!

Observation aid
- Can an intensified arm impulse out of a lower body posture be observed?

Variations:
(1) Similar to the basic exercise, but now the court player (A) uses volleyball techniques to play the ball to the setter. The setting player (B) makes an additional movement at the moment of the pass, f. e. he
- touches the ground with both hands or
- makes a 180° turn or
- touches his heels etc.

Hints
- Move to the target during or *with* your additional movement!
- You will not commit a technical fault, if you set from a perfectly balanced position!
- Do not let passes with high trajectories cross over you!
- Always try to see the ball!

(2) Similar to the variation (1), but now the setter starts from a position which should initially be 4 m off the net, and later further off the net. The setting player may start his movement when A tosses the ball for himself in order to pass it to the net (see Fig. 25b).

Hints
- Start late - when you are the setting player - to a position **shortly** in front of the anticipated target (setting spot), in order to avoid being outplayed by a high pass that would travel across and beyond you!
- Try not to play in motion, but from a well-balanced standstill!

Observation aid
- Does the setter maintain a position underneath and behind the ball at the moment of his set?

(3) Similar to the basic exercise **1** and its variations, now from different setting spots at the net. Particularly the main setting spots III (for the set to position IV) and II/III (for the set to position II) must be included more often in this exercise.

(4) Similar to the basic exercise **1** and its variations, but now the set should be a set from middle or deep court, thus the attacker has to pass or toss the ball inaccurately to the court's center. However, a hand set should still be possible.

Observation aid
–   Are leg and wrist impulse clearly supporting the arm extension/impulse during the set from deep court?

(5) Similar to the basic exercise **1** and its variations, but now the setter tosses a ball with a lot of rotation to the setter.

Hints
–   Use the hand set as often as possible!
–   If you are anticipating technical difficulties, use the bump set!
–   Play the ball with both forearms simultaneously in order to counteract the ball's rotation!
–   Compensate the ball's rotation and reverse its spin by pushing the playing platform "underneath and through" the ball!

2.   Two players bump-pass the ball to each other, at first as accurate as possible and without changing their position (half-high pass, medium distance).

Variations:
(1) Similar to exercise **2**, but now as a lateral bump set (as a 2 m-high set, from a 2 m-medium distance).
(2) Similar to the exercise **2**, but now as a backward bump set. The players are positioned 1 m apart from each other in order to deliberately force the backset.

Hints
–   Pay attention to the fact that the arms must be positioned a little higher than horizontal at the moment of ball contact!

3.   Bumping the ball up as a bump set action, initially without, then later with a change of the players position.

Variations:
(1) Similar to exercise **3**, the player changes his position by lengths of app. 2 m, both the hand set and the bump set should be practiced.
(2) The variation (1), but now the player must carry out an additional movement after his set. Immediately afterwards he should use the appropriate setting technique.

Hints

- Choose your position in such a way that you will face the ball frontally, while it is traveling at you!
- Compensate for changes in the ball trajectory caused by wind, through additional footwork. This will enable you to take the optimum position relative to the ball at all times!
- At the moment of the set, the arms are almost parallel to the ground!
- A follow-through with your arms up to shoulder level leads to more ball control!
- When playing a bump set from a very low body position, the arm impulse is much greater than it is from a service reception pass!
- Do always observe that a conscious forward pushing motion of your outward shoulder, as well as the turning of your playing platform will direct the ball into the desired direction. Pay attention to the *deflection angle principle*!

(3) The attacker at the net jumps and plays a trick attack (poke or any off-speed attack) to his setter who will play a bump set.

(4) Similar to variation (3), but now the trick attack is played to either one of the setter's sides.

4. The basic exercise **1** and its variations, but now the toss/ pass should force the setter to use the bumpsetting technique.

6.4 INDIVIDUAL TACTICS OF THE ATTACKING PLAYER

The following observation results can be given regarding the frequencies of the various attacking techniques, their qualities and the attacking locations:

- With a share of about 22%, the attack is the most frequently used element of play in beach volleyball.
- Only 6% of all attacks on the German national level are played from positions that are further off the net. Almost 94% take place at the net positions II, III and IV. The distribution of this high percentage is: 41% on pos. IV, app. 31% on pos. II and app. 23% on pos. III.
- 53% of all attacks are hard-driven spikes. The share of tactical attacks is app. 40%, another 7% are played from a standing position. With almost 65%, the share of hard-driven attacks is even higher on the male professional level. Only about 35% of all attacks are tactically played as spin spikes or trick attacks. A balanced ratio hard-driven attacks and spin

spikes/ trick attacks has been observed in the US-women's professional game (see table 6 in chapter 3.2.3).

– The quality of attacks that has been observed at the German national level is as follows (men): about 56% of all attacks are successful, without the opponent being able to play any counter-attack. The share of direct attacking faults is almost 15%. After 25% of the attacks, the opponent is able to play a counter-attack out of a jump. In terms of effectivness, no further differences have been observed between hard-driven and tactical attacks.

Photo 36 a - d

The explanations of the attack build-up and the individual tactics of the setter show, that in beach volleyball, quick attacks and high sets are to be avoided as much as possible. The most important attacking techniques are wrist-controlled attacks, spin spikes and trick attacks. The trick attacks may not be played with an open hand, but as a spike motion with the fingers closed. Until 1995, the difference between hard-driven balls (straight ball trajectory) and tactical attacks, the so-called shots (arch-like ball trajectory), had an effect on the type of digging techniques used. A hard-driven ball might have been defended with multiple ball contacts, for example, as a hand set motion with both hands. This defensive action was not allowed while defending against shots or spin spikes or trick attacks. Now, the open-handed digging of an off-speed attack

during the team's first contact is allowed (see also chapters 7.5 and 7.5.1, here especially the **"rule considerations"**).

USA: An attack whose speed has been clearly reduced by a net touch is not considered to be a hard-driven ball in the US-professionals' rules. This type of attack is treated as a shot, therefore, the defensive action may not be carried out with multiple consecutive ball contacts. However, a hard-driven ball rebounding from the block is considered to remain a hard-driven ball.

Compared to the indoor volleyball attacker, the individual tactical actions of the beach attacker are apparently more simple. He must act successfully against **one** blocker and **one** backcourt defender. Of even more decisive value than the tactical behavior is the precise execution of the attacking action. The attacker must be able to hit the ball to almost any area of the opposing court. The power put into the attack is not as decisive, compared to the ability to accurately hit the ball at uncovered areas of the opponent's court. Moreover, spikes that are hit off the blocker's outside hand should be preferred over spikes that touch the blocker's fingertips.

These explanations clearly show that the attacker must primarily be able to hit wrist-controlled spikes *past* the block or spin spikes and trick attacks *over* the block toward the uncovered court areas. When one takes into consideration that at the highest level of play, the blocker and backcourt defender form a highly efficient co-operative unit, the attacker is forced to hit the ball with the shortest possible flight path to the uncovered area.

In order to be able to do so, the setter must give his attacker a call concerning the best direction of attack. As has already been mentioned, the setting player must observe the opponent directly after his set in order to give his attacker the information,.

a.   regarding the attacking direction,
b.   if the block is up.

With the initial information, the attacker is assisted in choosing the direction of attack, which depends upon the position and the direction of movement of the backcourt defender independent of the block. Consequently, the attacker can play an arched tactical attack over and across the block toward the called direction.

Particularly in the case of deep court sets, the information whether the block is up or not is very important. The professionals consider these calls to be supportive measures, which means that they do not rely completely on their partner's call. Primarily they use their own anticipation abilities. Calls will be critical if the attacker has no or only a limited chance to observe the opponent's defensive movements. This does for example apply in the case of a deep court set. Accordingly, the attacker then has two possibilities. Depending on his own observation and his partner's call, he may either hit a **hard-driven ball into the court area not covered by the block** or a **tactical attack, meaning a trick shot, towards the court area not covered by the backcourt defender**.

USA: Besides the numerous individually arranged calls, the three most common helpful calls are:
   –   "Angle" or "cut" mean, that the attacker should hit cross-court;
   –   "Line" means that the attacker should hit down the line;
   –   "No one" means that the blocker is not up.

All calls must be short and unmistakable. Therefore, the positions "**I**" and "**V**" from the indoor game could be used instead of shouting "line" or "Angle".

The attacker's actions require very good skills in terms of mental attention, his coupling-, as well as transition-abilities. Therefore, these skills must be adequately trained.

The immediate transition from attack to block, or backcourt defense when the player is fulfilling his primarily court-defensive tasks, is the most important team-tactical precondition. This is aside from the team's own attack coverage, which is also necessary to co-operate successfully as a team.

Compared to the indoor player, the beach volleyball player must not only have mental strength. Moreover, he must express this mental strength. The fact, that the opponent can choose the passer and therefore the attacker, already shows the need to be able to withstand mental stress. In contrast to indoor volleyball, the beach player can not escape this stress through player substitution. Eventually, he must take responsibility for own faults or ineffective actions. Consequently, dealing quickly with mental pressure is critical for the beach volleyball player. Therefore, he must have high physical and mental stability as well as good deal of self confidence.

Individual tactical factors

The following factors have an effect on the receiving and therefore attacking beach volleyball player. They are listed following the sequential order in which they occur:

1. Prior to the opponent's serve:
   - Wind and sunlight conditions,
   - current score or, for the US-pro-level, remaining rally clock time,
   - referee and linesmen attitude/ performance, spectator behavior,
   - one's own as well as one's partner's and opponent's mental and physical condition,
   - the opposing blocker's strengths and weaknesses,
   - the opposing server's effectivness, anticipation of the type and direction of the serve.

2. After the opponent's serve:
   - Service type and direction, possible difficulties implied by the serve,
   - one's own passing strengths and weaknesses,
   - communication with the partner.

3. After the service reception:
   - pass quality in terms of height, distance from the net and the target (setting spot),
   - performance of the setting partner relative to time and space,
   - consideration of the individual tactical skills of the partner as a setter,
   - anticipation of the set.

4. After the set:
   - set quality in terms of height, speed, distance from the net and from the attacking position,
   - blocker's starting position and anticipation of his blocking action,
   - backcourt defender's movements.

5. Prior to the attack:
    –   quality of the block in terms of aggressiveness, arm positioning towards ball and timing,
    –   one's own timing,
    –   perception of the setter's call,
    –   choice of attack type and direction.

6. After the attack:
    –   attack effectivness,
    –   anticipation of further rally development,
    –   immediate transition to the block or court defensive position, or another attack.

Here, the individual tactical actions of the beach volleyball player consist of the ability to determine and to consider the decisive factors for a certain game situation. The significance of individual tactics can not be emphasized enough.

> Because of the above mentioned reasons, training must be structured in such a manner, that the player is forced to make observations and decisions in every form of training and exercise.

6.4.1 ATTACKING TECHNIQUES

Motion sequence of the spike

To a large extent, the technique is identical to the indoor spike. The following differences in the beach technique have to be observed:

The player makes the transition to the attack from the passing or defending action. If he (right-handed) attacks on the right court side, he will choose a *straight approach line*. When attacking on the left court side he will choose an *arched approach line*. There are two different ways to initiate the approach:

–   running steps are *fluently* transformed into run-up steps and hop-step;
–   the player runs toward the net, and *holds out* for a short moment at a distance of 2 - 3 m from the net and then starts his run-up steps.

Even though the hop-step (last step) is shorter than indoors, the takeoff is identical to the indoor technique. Also similar to indoor volleyball are the arm swing, the ball contact and the spacial relation of the body to the ball.

The spiking direction is controlled by wrist (hand) rotations to the left and right. Moreover, those rotations are initiated through inward (pronation) and outward (supination) turns of the lower arm (Photo 37a).

The follow-through and landing are similar to the indoor technique. Some players use an upper body rotation in order to develop a straight powerful arm swing while varying their spiking direction (Photo 37b). In this case, the body rotation will be initiated by a more powerful jump-off motion from the right or left leg. The remaining motion sequence is identical to the usual spike. The rotation of the upper body still allows wrist turns in order to again change the spiking direction.

Photo 37a: Control of spiking direction by wrist and lower arm rotation

Photo 37b: Spike with upper body rotation

Motion sequence of the spin spike

The different American terms for the attacking technique variations are listed in the glossary.

> With the exception of the arm swing and the wrist action, the motion sequence must be identical to that of a hard-driven spike.

Therefore, the motion may be called identical to the usual attack. Only less power is put on the ball. The ball is contacted from behind and underneath its center and the arm swing is slowed down as late as possible. In both variations described below, the hand action ends with the hand clearly roofing the ball.

The length and height of the ball's trajectory depend on the amount of power put on the ball, the duration of the ball contact, the first contact point and the length of the contacted ball surface:

a. If the ball trajectory is to be similar to a high arch, the first contact point should be far underneath the center.
b. If the ball is to fly lower, the first contact point is slightly underneath its center.

Particularly in beach volleyball, the spin spike is executed straight forward as a line shot, as well as cross-court and extremely cross-court (cut shot), with or without turning the body toward the hitting direction.

Photo 38a: Cut Shot right to left

The **cut shot from right to left** is a spin spike, during which the player (right handed) contacts the ball underneath the center/on the right side of the center. He "wraps" his hand over the right side of the ball (Photo 38a). The palm of the hand turns around the ball and is finally pushed down by the wrist's action until the thumb points straight up. The ball will then fly with an inside spin. It will fly sharply cross-court to the right front corner of the opponent's court.

Executing **the cut shot from left to right**, the player must contact the ball on the left side, underneath its center. Again, the palm will be wrapped around the ball and finally pushed down. Now, at the end of the motion, the thumb should point straight down. The ball will then be flying with an inside spin sharply cross-court to the left front corner of the opponent's court (Photo

38b). If the above described techniques of wrist rotation are used for off-speed spikes along the line, they will be called **line shots**.

The importance of spin spikes, normal spikes and shots with wrist rotations has already be pointed out. The reasons for the frequent use of these techniques is the prohibition of the open-handed dink and the necessity to be able to precisely hit any point of the opponent's court. In order to have another precise attack variation, other than the spin spikes/ shots, the so-called poke shot is used as an equivalent shot to open-handed dinks.

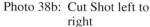

Photo 38b: Cut Shot left to right

Photo 39: Poke Shot

Motion sequence of the trick attack (poke shot)

Approach, takeoff and arm swing are similar to other off-speed spikes, such as the spin spikes/ shots.

Shortly before ball contact the arm's swing is slightly slowed down.

The fingers then will be bent at the middle joints of the hand. The player contacts the ball with the middle joints (Photo 39).

The ball is hit with wrist action. The length and direction of the ball and its trajectory can be well co-ordinated through wrist rotations or through controlling the power of the wrist action.

6.4.2 INTRODUCTION OF SPECIFIC BEACH VOLLEYBALL ATTACKING TECHNIQUES

The spin spike toward any attacking directions (cut shots as well as line shots) and the trick attack with a spiking motion (poke shot) will be introduced here:

> Principally, the entire motion of these off speed attacks should not differ from the execution of a hard-driven spike.

Exercises:
1. Spin spike over the net to different court areas. The practicing player should stand on the ground and should keep his court position. He should practice particularly line, cross-court and extreme cross-court shots (cut shots) or spin spikes. If only two players participate in this exercise, the second player should be the target and catch the ball after a defensive action.

Variations:
(1) Similar to the basic exercise, but the player should hit the ball from different court positions.
(2) Similar to the basic exercise and its variation (1), but with a ball tossed higher and a jump from a standing position.

Hints
–   Always pay attention to a safe and well-balanced takeoff from a balanced position!
–   Wrap your hand around the right half of the ball in order to hit a cut shot from right to left! Check your motion by observing whether or not your thumb points straight up after the ball contact!
–   Your thumb should point straight down after hitting a cut shot from left to right!

2. The first exercise and its variations but with a poke shot.

Hints
–   The arm swing is identical to all the other attack techniques!
–   Slow your arm swing at the last second before ball contact!

- Contact and hit the ball with the middle joints of your fingers!
- Place your finger's middle joints behind and underneath the ball while making first contact, then follow through with wrist action!
- Avoid any kind of pushing motion!

Variation:
(1) The exercises and their variations but with arched shots over the block.

Hints
- Poke the ball app. 2 m behind the blocker!

3. The attacker should hit spin spikes to different targets.

Variations:
(1) Similar to the basic exercise, but the player should hit his spikes from different court positions.
(2) The player may not choose another target before the successful execution of three spikes to the same target.

4. Similar to the basic exercise and its variations, but now the player should practice poke shots.
After a good adaptation of the technique, the setter should determine the attack targets through **calls**. However, initially the call should be made at the time of the set, later directly after the set and lastly at the last second before the attacking action, as in beach volleyball.

6.5   SELECTED FORMS OF TRAINING

The explanations pertaining to the following exercises and forms of training refer more to the pragmatic execution and organization aspects of everyday training and less to theoretical-didactical principles:

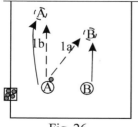

Fig. 26

EXERCISES AND GAME FORMS WITH TWO PLAYERS

For the attack build-up after the service reception

Exercises:
1. One of the players tosses a ball either between himself and his partner (Fig. 26/ 1a) or more or less to each other's sides. (Fig.

26/ 1b). Basically, communication should be done through a call or an unmistakable movement to the ball.

The non-receiving player must orient himself toward the setting spot direction and play the set according to the quality of the pass, either as a hand set or a bump set.

Hints

– Setter: Try to reach your setting spot after an evaluation of the pass quality!
– Do not move too early toward the setting spot to set passes of mediocre quality or to save passes of bad quality without the necessity to run to the backcourt again!
– Always check the quality of your set and ask for information from your partner regarding your setting quality!
– Attacker: Always use the same action pattern related to court space and timing while approaching the net after your pass (approach, direction of approach, distance to the setter, takeoff timing etc.)!
– Try to inform your partner as to the conditions of your readiness, or non-readiness, through calls!

2. First, the setter acts as an attacker from the other side of the net. He hits a spin spike from a standstill to his partner's court side, changes courtsides underneath the net and moves into the range of the anticipated target of the pass, his setting location. The setter determines the attacking direction and therefore the type of attack through calls. Depending on the different levels of play, the setter should call, f. e. "One"! as late as his opponent, who does not yet exist here, is observed. Therefore, the call should be given as soon as possible, before the attackers spiking motion. If necessary, the call may even be changed split seconds before the attacker's arm swing (Fig. 27).

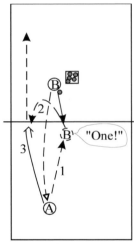

Fig. 27

Hints

– Receiver/ attacker: Do not play the perfect beach volleyball pass too close to the net!

Variations:

(1) Similar to the basic exercise, but with varied setting spots and attacking locations.

(2) The spin spike should be hit from a jump, 5 m from the net.

3. The player at the net hits a trick attack to the reach of the passing player or a spin spike into backcourt so that a passing action becomes necessary. The receiver tries to play a perfect pass and to make an approach from medium distance which has the correct temporal and spacial timing and motion pattern. The setter determines the attacking direction.

For the attack's precision

Game forms:
1. '1 with 1' on the 4,5 x 9 m - court.
    The attacker always hits a frontal spin spike (line shot) deep into the backcourt. After his dig, the partner catches the ball, moves to the net, tosses the ball himself and plays a precise shot to the partner.

2. '1 with 1'; attacker with defender.
    The backcourt defender determines the attacking direction,
    a. by taking his defensive position and covering a specific area early,
    b. by call.

Variation:
(1) Determining the attacking direction only through the early positioning of the defending player.

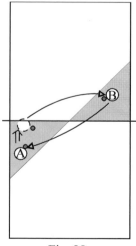

Fig. 28

Hint
–   Try to watch the opposing defender immediately after your set in order to spike a hard-driven ball if necessary!

3. Similar to the basic game form **1**, but with three ball contacts on each side of the net.

4. Similar to the basic game form **1**, but on extremely diagonally arranged courts (Fig. 28).

5. Similar to the basic exercise **1** on 4,5 x 9 m with diagonal arrangement.

Variation:
(1) All the mentioned games as games against each other.

Considering and overcoming the blocking player

Game forms:

1. '1 vs. 1' (Photo 40).
   The attacker tosses or sets the ball himself and hits past the block or over the block. Initially, the blocker clearly shows his intended blocking direction, then later he will act in a game-like fashion. At first, the attacker must hit hard-driven balls past the block, later line or cut shots and lastly poke shots over the block.

2. Similar to the basic game form 1, but now the attacker deliberately tosses the ball close to the net and hits a cut shot or 'pokes' past the block.

Photo 40: '1 vs. 1' (Bruk Vandeweghe and Bob Vogelsang)

3. '1 vs. 1'; but now game-like, where the blocker can act free of restrictions.

4. '1 vs. 1' on the 4,5 x 4,5 m - court with three ball contacts, whereas each attacking action must be defended with a block.

Hints

- Try as an **attacker**, to cover balls rebounding from the net by yourself!
- Try as a **blocker** to reach for the poke shot first or, only as a second priority, cover yourself and save this shot within your close range!

FORMS OF TRAINING WITH THREE PLAYERS

For the training of the attack build-up after the service reception

Forms of training:

1. '1 vs. 2' in the sense of the '1 vs. 1' - game.
   The server/ backcourt defender executes all his actions to the reach of one certain attacker/ passer, consequently, each player has a clearly defined function.

134

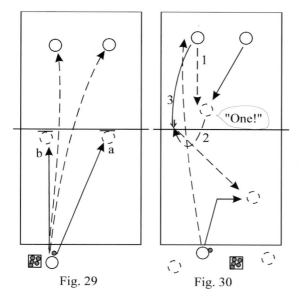

After 5, 8 or 10 serves, the server becomes setter, the receiving attacker rotates to the service position and the setter takes the pass and attack function.

Variations:
(1) Similar to the basic game **1**, but now with the server as a blocking player on the right half of the court (see Fig. 29a), later on the left half. The attacker may not use the poke shot.

"One!"

Fig. 29   Fig. 30

(2) The attacker must only play a hard-driven ball.
(3) The attacker plays an extremely angled cut shot or a short poke shot.

2. Server/ backcourt defender against one beach volleyball team.
The single player serves from all possible spots behind the baseline (see also Fig. 22) and defends one half of the court. Directly before the attacker's hitting motion, the setter must give his attacker a call with information regarding the defender's position. The attacker should try to hit the ball to the reach of the backcourt defender. Although this is not like the "real" game, it is highly recommended because it improves training execution. The defender tries to build up a successful counter-attack with, no more than, four ball contacts (Fig. 30).
At first the defender should act at a longer distance from the attacker, then later closer to the net.

Hints
– **Setter**: Move to the anticipated setting spot in such a manner, that you will always be able to run down any passes of medium quality and that the ball will not overtake you! Take the service quality and your partner's passing abilities into consideration!
– Try to cover the subsequent attacker following the set!

135

–   Always give an informative call to your attacker regarding the court area which is not covered by the opponent's backcourt defender. This call should always be given following your set, but directly before the attacker's hitting motion!
–   **Attacker**: Inform your setter if he even has more time to call!

Variations:
(1) Similar to the training form **2**, but now according to the "real" game. Here, the attacker hits the ball into the opponent's open court area, with the informational support from his setter. With the exception of the short poke, all types of attacking techniques may be used. Even a simple ball touch by the defender will earn him a point.
(2) Similar to the training form **2**, but now the server acts as blocker. Again, a touched ball will earn him a point.
(3) Similar to the training form, but now the server acts in a game-like fashion, according to his anticipation. Depending on the quality of his serve and the opponent's pass, he will decide whether to play at the net or in the backcourt. Of course, he will attempt to irritate the opponent through faking certain moves.
(4) Similar to variation (1), but now the backcourt defender fakes his moves in such a manner, that the setter will be forced to change his call shortly before the attack.

Hints
–   **Setter**: Observe the backcourt defender as long as possible. You must be able to change your call in order to give your attacker the correct information!
–   **Attacker**: Do not rely solely on the call, use it as an aid supporting your decisions!
–   Try to convert late call changes!

For the improvement of the attacker's individual tactical skills
Forms of training:
1. '1 vs. 2'.
   The attacker himself tosses the ball and tries, considering the blocker and the backcourt defender, to attack successfully. Each attacker hits 5, 8 or 10 balls in a row.
   The defending team will be awarded a point if the attacker commits a fault or if they execute a successful counter-attack. The backcourt defender simplifies the situation for the attacker by leaving out all faking moves once the attacker has tossed the ball. Then, the defender should not move and should clearly show the area he is covering.

Hints

- Try to attack successfully, given your knowledge about the defender's position and particularly the blocker's actions!
- Hit to the uncovered areas by using a spin spike over the block or a cut shot past the block!
- Use the poke shot!

Variation:

(1) The blocking player clearly shows his blocking direction, the area that he will be covering, and the defender acts accordingly.

Hints

- Try to determine the defender's positioning shortly before your spiking action!
- Spike hard past the block toward the area not covered by the block!

FORMS OF TRAINING WITH FOUR PLAYERS

Forms of training:

1. '2 vs. 2' with predetermined functions.

   One team always serves, while the other one tries to sideout.

   At first, the players on the receiving team always have the same function - either as passer/ attacker or as setter. It becomes clear that with regard to the reception, the receiving team must only cover one half of their court. After 10 serves the players change functions, at first within their team, then later they shift from one to the other situation of play.

Variation:

(1) The basic exercise form on the beach volleyball court, following the special rule that the defending team will be rewarded with a point just for touching the ball and with 3 points for a successful counter-attack. This "one touch-one point" rule does not apply to hits off the block.

Hints

- **Setter**: Play a perfect set for your partner!
- Try to maintain your balance at all times, even while playing a ball in a falling motion!
- Avoid any kind of back roll or side roll!
- After covering your attacker, move to the net in order to block, or back off the net in order to play backcourt defense!
- **Attacker**: Never change your motion sequence with respect to your approach, takeoff and arm swing!
- Consider that a differing motion pattern will signal your opponent that you are planning another kind of attack!

- Hit a hard-driven ball past the block or a tactical shot over the block, or hit an extremely angled cross-court shot, the cut shot!
- If the blocker does not block over, increasingly attempt to hit off his outside hands!
- When hitting a bad set with no block up, try to spike hard between the defenders!
- If the blocker backs off the net too late, play a long spin spike or poke shot far over his head to the baseline!
- Try to master co-operation with your partner, in particular with respect to information exchange and its special conversation!

Observation aid
- Is it necessary to practice some attacking techniques under simplified conditions?
- Does the player reach the same setting precision when using the bump set instead of the hand set or is special practice for the bump set necessary?
- Are sloppy footwork and an unevenly balanced posture the reasons for technical deficiencies while executing the set?

2. '2 vs. 2' on the half court (4,5 x 9 m), following beach volleyball rules (Fig. 31).
   Both players are responsible for the pass. Special rule: The whole court (9 x 9 m) is the effective playing area for balls which are deflected back

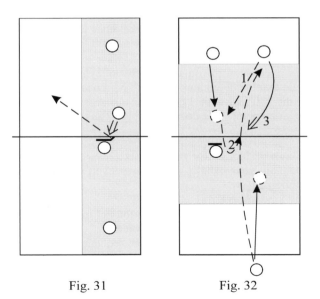

Fig. 31   Fig. 32

from the block toward the attackers court. This is the case so that an automatization of technical faults may be avoided, especially regarding the blocker's hands- and arms-position.

Hints

- **Attacker**: Consider that a hard-driven ball and a wipe-off attack could be more successful than pokes or other off-speed tactical attacks!
- **Setter**: Since the block will probably be more successful in this form of play, the coverage of your attacker is your most important task after the set!

3. '2 vs. 2' on a 9 x 5 m - court following beach rules (Fig. 32).
    The effective playing area for the reception situation is the whole court (9 x 9 m). The attack and the block/ court defense is played on the 9 x 5m - court.

Hints

- Try to hit hard and extremely angled cross-court, in order to play a shot or to hit a ball off the block!
- If the backcourt defender moves behind his blocker, use an extremely angled cross-court shot (cut shot)!

FORMS OF TRAINING WITH FIVE OR MORE PLAYERS

Forms of training:
1. All games with four players and three balls per rally.
    Thus, after the first rally has been played with a serve/ service reception, each team will receive a down-ball. The team that wins two or all three rallies will get the "big point".

Variations:
(1) Similar to the basic form **1**, but the down-ball will always be thrown to the team that committed the fault. Later, it will be tossed to the team that won the previous rally.
(2) The same with five balls.
(3) The same, but the fifth player permanently serves. The players change their positions or teams after 5, 8 or 10 serves.
(4) Like the basic form, but now the player that committed two faults will be substituted. A fault is an attack which has been defended and successfully counter-attacked. The substitution can also take place after a player has committed two faults in a row.

2. '3 vs. 3' as a special form of beach volleyball (see chapter 3.5.1).
   Each team has one player acting as their setter without passing tasks for the duration of one set.

3. '4 vs. 4' with three front row players and one backcourt player (see chapter 3.5.2)
   The reception should be played with a 3-man formation at first, later with the 2-man formation.

Variation:
(1) Similar to the training form **3**, but with 2 front row players and 2 backcourt players.

The beach volleyball player faces simplified situations of play in all types of volleyball games with more than 2 players on the court.
Therefore, the '3 vs. 3' and '4 vs. 4' - games serve as a **preparatory** or **introductory** games for the '2 vs. 2' beach volleyball game. For the indoor player, who wants to become a beach volleyball player, it makes sense to start with the '4 vs. 4' game prior to the "real" beach game, first following indoor rules, then later beach rules. The '3 vs. 3' game is a perfect transition form of play and the last step before completely adapting to the beach game. These explanations show that, for didactical-methodical reasons, the '4 vs. 4' - game should initially be the first learning stage before - by playing '3 vs. 3' - the transition to all types of play and of practice of the '2 vs. 2' - original game is made.

6.5.1 SPECIAL FORMS OF TRAINING

The following forms of training serve as drills for the improvement of the coordination of the setting player, as well as the passing and then attacking player. Especially the transition-, coupling-, orientation-abilities and the speed in ball handling actions will be practiced. These drills resemble game-like action sequences and should not be practiced longer than 6-10 s (see chapter 11.2 and 11.3). Depending on the duration of the action sequence, up to 3 repetitions may be executed. Afterwards, the player will collect balls or will take supportive functions. The actual break for recovery shall not be shorter than 2 min. These forms of coordination training must be performed at the beginning of a practice, in a fresh/ rested physical condition. However, prior to these drills the player must warm up to an appropriate level, moreover he should only include the motions into these drills that he has already mastered. If the player shows signs of fatigue, the drills must be stopped.

It becomes clear that the performance of these drills should be done following the so-called repetition method. They are suitable for the special preparation period and for the competition period (season).

Passing and attacking beach volleyball player

- 3 attacks vs. block after a pass.
- Attack vs. block after pass→blocking action→backing off the net→ attack.
- Block→digging a ball as own block coverage→attack of a half-high pass from medium distance.
- Attack vs. block after pass→fake block→backing off the net to play backcourt defense→attack vs. block.
- Fake block→backing off to defense→attack→block.
- Block between positions III/IV→block between pos. II/III→attack between pos. II/III.
- Attack vs. block after service reception between pos. III/IV→block between pos. II/III→digging a trick attack as own block coverage→ attack between pos. II/III.
- Pass→attack vs. block→2 attacks vs. block.
- 2 attacks in a row with a half-high set from medium distance and long approach path (app. 7 m).

In all the above mentioned drills for the passing attacker, the setter should start his actions from a deep court position, app. 6 m off the net.

- Depending on the type of drill, the setter should act appropriately after perfect, good and bad passes.
- The setter should perform blocking actions between sets.
- He should try to play the perfect set to his partner. It should be a half-high set from a medium distance or a high set from deep court, and always into the "approach set-up motion" of his partner.

The following forms of training are aimed at improving the setting beach volleyball player. They shall be performed with the hand set as well as the **bump set**.

Setting beach volleyball player

- Non-(service) reception→block→set→coverage.
- Non-reception→set→backcourt defense→set.
- Non-reception→set→coverage→backcourt defense.
- Non-reception→set (half-high, from medium distance)→block→set (high, medium distance).
- Non-reception→set or attack on two (setter's trick)→block→setter's trick.

- Non-reception→3 half-high sets from a medium distance with attacker coverage between sets.
- Non-reception→3 high sets from middle or deep court with digging action between sets.
- Set after a perfect pass→block→deep court set.
- Deep court set→coverage→block→deep court set.
- 3 setting actions from middle or deep court with subsequent coverage all the times.
- 3 setting actions to the same target following different first passes.
- Non-reception→set→block→deep court set→attack→set.
- Non-reception→3 setting actions with different techniques.
- Non-reception→deep court sets from varying positions with various techniques and several different ball trajectories.

All the above mentioned drills for the beach volleyball player, acting from the service reception situation, may be arranged into any combination. However, they must be appropriate for the caliber of play of that individual player.

Photo 41

7 BLOCK AND DEFENSE SITUATION

7.1 ANALYSIS

The fact that blocking over was not permitted before 1986, resulted in attacks being played very close to the net. This led to the development of special beach-techniques for the backcourt defender. The tight attack also led to a forward relocation of the backcourt defender's court position in order to be able to defend hard-driven balls from an optimum position. This practice was first adopted and successfully incorporated into the defensive tactics of the US men's national team. At that time, it consisted of many players with beach volleyball experience. Thereupon, other national teams moved their basic defensive positioning forward and adopted the new techniques.

Inevitably, the '2 vs. 2' beach volleyball game, where the block and the backcourt defense is performed by only two players, led to the development of communication between blocker and defender through signals. This kind of communication prior to the opponent's attack, has also been successfully adopted by indoor volleyball teams.

The block and backcourt defense aspect of the beach game has gone through immense maturation, since blocking over was allowed in 1986. Since then, the effectivness of the whole defense has been increased enormously. It is understandable that the new beach volleyball blocking over rule again led to a slight backward relocation of the backcourt defenders' basic position. This is because now the attack had to be played farther from the net.

However, compared to indoor volleyball, the block and the backcourt defense's inferiority is still immense. Therefore, it is incomprehensible, that the touch of the ball during a block is still counted as a team's first contact. The whole defensive situation, especially because of the subsequently extensive limitation of the attack build-up, is made much more difficult. Hopefully this rule will be altered within the next several years, so that the ball contact during the block will not count as the first contact.

A defensive strategy will only be effective if it meets the following demands:

- Taking into account the varying abilities, strengths and characteristics of the opposing attackers.
- Numerous alternations of block and backcourt defense strategies, in order to make recognition of the defensive formation, and especially the intended movement of the backcourt player, more difficult.
- Mastering of fake blocker actions, with respect to his intention whether to block or not, as well as by the backcourt player.

- Planning a defensive strategy according to one's own strengths and weaknesses, particularly with regard to the possible specialization of blocker/ backcourt defender.

The aims of the defending team should be:

- Winning a point or a sideout through an aggressive block.
- Making a counter-attack possible by weakening the opponent's spike by blocking a zone.
- Perfect co-operation between the blocker and backcourt defender in order to save every ball.

Observations at Germany's top level of men's beach volleyball show the following percentages for different defensive actions with the block relative to actions without a block:

- app. 67% actions with block,
- app. **33% actions without block**.

Figure 33 shows the distribution of blocking actions to the three main areas at the net. In international

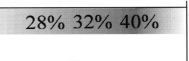

Fig. 33

tournaments, it has been discovered that the best teams clearly had a better blocking efficiency. This shows the significance of the block with regard to a game's final result. The backcourt defender's successful play depends decisively on the effectiveness of the block, especially with respect to its ability to screen certain areas of the court (zone block). This will allow the setting up of the defense and makes the backcourt areas smaller.

7.2   BLOCK- AND DEFENSE-FORMATIONS

Two basic formations are used in beach volleyball:

1. Defense without block, with two backcourt defenders and
2. single block with the backcourt defender in the court's center.

Many more situations without the block may be observed in women's beach volleyball. This can be traced to their limited athletic and individual tactical abilities. For example, a pass of mediocre quality from deep court is more likely to create a down-ball situation in the women's game than in the men's beach volleyball game.

It is clear that the player's abilities play a decisive role in determining the choice of defensive functions. The defensive situation is the only area in the game of beach volleyball in which a specialization with respect to the player's main function can make sense.

Consequently and in principle, each beach volleyball player must be a superior all around-player. However, if he plays with a partner with better or worse block qualities, a specialization shall be attained. This does not mean that the weaker blocker may neglect his own block training, though. On the one hand, he will play with different partners, and on the other, situations where he is forced to block, occur in every game. Block training, for the weaker blocker, is even more important. This is obvious when considering that the partner, who constantly jumps for the block, may become fatigued, during the course of a tournament. Therefore, the functions may sometimes have to be shifted. Very well functioning teams start a tournament without specializing a blocker or a backcourt defender. This allows them to be able to play decisive situations or games with specialization and without physical overload. The above mentioned explanation clearly show the necessity of block training for a player weak in that technique.

7.2.1 BASIC DEFENSIVE STARTING POSITION

If both players act **equally as blockers and as backcourt defenders**, the starting formation may be described as follows:
The blocker waits at the middle of the net, 1 m behind it. Here, he can move to the attack location or attack bad first passes that travel directly across the net. Moreover, this starting position does not make the intended serving and blocking strategy obvious to the opponent. The position will also help in down-ball situations. This happens when the blocker must back off the net in order to reach his backcourt passing, defending or attacking position, while covering the shortest possible distance (Photo 42).

Photo 42: Basic starting position of the blocking player

In case of an arranged play, with respect to the service strategy, it may sometimes be observed that the blocking player will tend to move towards the anticipated attacking location. This starting position must be **rejected**,

–   because the receiving team can consciously change its attacking tactics in the case of a very good first pass and hit the ball *on two* and/ or
–   the passing player can deliberately play a fast and precise bump pass toward the uncovered court area.

In women's volleyball, the blocker starts 2 m off the net. This makes sense for the following reasons:

–   The service reception often leads to deep court sets or to down-ball situations,
–   the distance to the backcourt position is kept shorter,
–   in order to run down bad first pass or passes which were deliberately played *on one* across the net,
–   since the women's attack is quite often not as hard, the defensive formation with two backcourt defenders seems to be more promising.

At the medium international level of women's beach volleyball, it can frequently be observed that teams will start with a "two backcourt defender formation", regardless of the quality of the first pass.

It is highly recommended that teams at a medium or low international level should more frequently use, the fake block and a direct positioning without a block (see chapter 3.4, factors determining performance).

Immediately following the serve or his own attack or attack coverage, the backcourt defender takes his basic starting position 5 - 6 from the net in the center of the court (see Photo 42). This starting position is very important since the defender is equidistant to all court areas. Above all, it does not give the attacking team any indication as to the intended defensive position.

Some players tend to reorientate themselves after the serve to either one or the other of the two courtsides. However, inquiries at the professional level show that this starting position for the backcourt defender should be rejected unless it has already been arranged to defend without a block.

Teams with a **specialization in blocking and backcourt defense** should take the following starting positions:

If the blocker serves, he will quickly move toward the net. In this case, he will move near the anticipated attacking location and blocking position. Depending on the service location, the backcourt defender takes a position that will not interfere with the running path of the server/ blocker. If, for

146

example, the server/ blocker serves from the center of the baseline, the backcourt player will be standing to the right or the left half of the court. It must be noted that the non-server (blocker or backcourt defender) is not standing in front of the server (Photo 43).

According to the rules, the server's partner may not obstruct the view of the players receiving the serve. Neither the view of the server nor of the ball may be covered through screening. The screening player must move to the side upon opponent's request.

Photo 43: Basic starting position (block specialist serving)

7.2.2 DEFENSIVE FORMATION WITH BLOCK

The blocking player waits 1 m from the net, the backcourt defender about 5 - 6 m from the net. Prior to the serve, the blocker signals the server/ backcourt defender, as to which area of the court he is going to cover and in other words, to take away from the attacker. However, the blocker's decision does not limit the backcourt defender's freedom of action, with respect to individual tactics.

Maintaining his position, the blocker watches the opponents' attack build-up. In the case of a good or very good set he will quickly move to the probable blocking location. This movement toward the net is made very late. This is done so that he can set up his jump with a step toward the net. Depending on the net distance and on the set's quality, the blocker will assume his takeoff position early. He could also initiate his takeoff with a quick hop-step (set-up step) into the squat position.

> Basically, the blocker should **not change his intended blocking direction**, once he has communicated it to his partner.

However, he constantly tries to hide his intended blocking direction by either showing it very late or changing it at the last moment in order to deceive the attacker (preplanned sweep-block).

> The decision of the backcourt defender, as to which area of the court he is going to move at the moment of the attack, depends on the arranged **tactical plan**, his knowledge of the **attacker's tendencies, strengths, and weaknesses** and on his **anticipation**.

These explanations result in the following possibilities for defensive formations (see also the following chapters referring to the individual tactics of the blocker and the backcourt defender):

– If the blocking player is blocking line, at one of the main beach volleyball blocking locations between pos. III/IV, the backcourt defender will cover the right court side against hard-driven balls and the rear left side against tactical shots (Photo 44a).

Photo 44a: Block longline - running down the poke shot

- If he is blocking between pos. III/IV and covering cross-court, the backcourt player will move to the left court side and take a medium low to low body posture in order to defend against hard-driven balls or to run down tactical shots heading cross-court (Photo 44b).

Photo 44b:
Block angle - running down the cut shot

- If the blocker acts at the other main beach volleyball blocking location between pos. II/III, covering line, the backcourt defender will defend the left side of the court against hard-driven cross-court attacks and the rear right area against tactical shots (Photo 44c).

- If the net player blocks cross-court between pos. II/III, the backcourt player will take the right court side. He will then defend the left side against tactical attacks (Photo 44d).

Photo 44c: Block longline - running down the line shot

Photo 44d: Block cross-court - backcourt defender in the court's center

- If the blocking action takes place at the net's center, the backcourt defender will move according to the prearranged plan with his partner, outside of the screened area to either to the left or right (Photo 44e).

Photo 44e: Block in the net's center

- If the block takes place on the outside positions, the backcourt defender will act accordingly. He will follow the tactical plan, in the same manner, on the right or the left side of the screened area (Photo 44f).
- If the blocking player uses the spread block or open split block and he has given this information to his partner, the defender will act between the two one-hand-screens (Photo 44g, see also Fig. 51a).

Photo 44f: Outside block -
backcourt defense
according to the tactical
plan, here longline

If the blocking and defense formations are to be compared with a single player's actions in indoor volleyball, it may be said that the blocking player's action resemble the indoor middle blocker's behavior. The actions of the backcourt player are similar to the behavior of the indoor player at pos. "VI in half-court".

Basically, the backcourt defenders' responsibilities and functions may be illustrated in Fig. 34a-c on the following page 152:

–   The blocker defends area A against hard-driven balls and those areas close beside and behind him (B) against trick attacks or shots. He covers his own block. The backcourt defender defends area C against hard-driven attacks and covers area D against long tactical shots. He has no chance against hard-driven and/ or precise spikes into area D. This example eventually shows a static formation in order to clearly separate the defensive areas and player functions from each other.

Photo 44g: Spread block -
defender between the
two one-hand screens

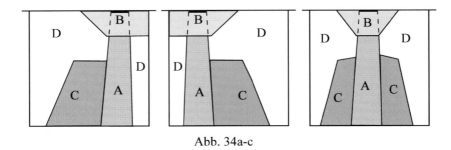

Abb. 34a-c

7.3 ATTACK BUILD-UP FROM THE DEFENSE SITUATION

Knowledge of the percentages and effectivness of actions with the ball is important for the evaluation of the counter-attack (see also "Individual tactics of the blocking player", chapter 7.4 and "Individual tactics of the backcourt defender", chapter 7.5).

The significance of the counter-attack will become obvious if taken into consideration, that, at the international and national level of men's beach volleyball, about 45% of all points result from a defensive play with a subsequent counter-attack and about 15% result from successful blocks. These numbers profoundly demonstrate the importance of the C 2 situation. Moreover, about 24% of all points are won by service aces and about 16% through attacking faults by the opponent.

The following player demands are set from these facts:

1. **Each beach volleyball player must have very good setting skills**. This demand has already been extensively substantiated in the chapters on structural analysis and the attack build-up from the service reception. A **precise set from deep or middle court** is critical for the attack build-up from the defense. The set must always lead to an increase in the quality of the pass. This will enable the team to initiate an effective counter-attack. The player must convert the set as a hand set, as well as a bump set to be able to play a proper and technically correct set following poor passes.

2. Since communication between the two partners is one of the most important preconditions for a successful defense and subsequent counter-attack, resp. the co-operation of the backcourt player with the blocker, and vice versa, **it must be included in each training session**. Basically, the *blocker* sets in the counter-attack, in the case where he *did not touch*

the ball. The counter-attack where the *backcourt player* sets, is the case where the blocker *touches the ball* first. The second form resembles the action sequence of an attack *on two* (spiking the 1st pass directly), as can be seen in indoor volleyball.

3.   Defensive training as well as the training of the attack build-up following defense, should at least be practiced **as intensely as** the training of the service reception and the attack build-up from the first pass.

Three basic situations may be distinguished with respect to the **action sequences of the attack build-up from a defensive play**:

a.   Situations, in which the blocker does not touch the spiked ball,
b.   Situations, in which the blocker touches the spiked ball,
c.   Situations without block and therefore down-ball situations (Photo 45).

Photo 45: Down-ball situation

a.:   Here, the blocker prepares himself for the set directly after his block jump. He immediately backs off the net in order to run down the pass. He is always prepared to run down saved balls and to set those high toward the court's center. The demand is: The **defense (block or self-coverage) has priority over the setting action**! Accordingly, the demand for the backcourt player: **Defense has the priority over attack**!

The following **action advice** applies for the backcourt defender under special consideration of the opponent's attack quality and his own abilities:

– Just try to keep the balls that are *very difficult* to defend, in play. This will enable your partner to reach them!
– Defend attacks, which are *difficult* to get at, high to the court's center in order to initiate a deep court set!
– Try to play balls, which are *easier* to defend, half-high or high, depending on the wind, into the range of the setting location. The pass should be 2 m from the net in reach of the blocker. This will simplify the set for him!
– Attacks which are *easy* to defend must be played half-high to a point 1 m off the net, slightly to the net's center, to make an optimum set possible!
– Always defend the ball at a lower height during windy conditions. Adjust the height of your defensive pass to the wind's strength!

Obviously, the boundaries between those actions described above are gray areas by nature. They depend on individual skills as well as on the certain situation. The backcourt defender in beach volleyball will act correctly, with respect to his individual tactical decisions, if he neither under- nor overestimates his abilities in certain situations.

Another main focus for the successful counter-attack is the perfect coordination of the conversion, regarding time and space, of the blocker's action to that of a setter, and of the defender's action to that of an attacker. Here, the following **action advice** applies:

– Be ready to execute an attack immediately after your defensive action!
– Attack toward the one side of the net that you can reach faster (the shortest distance from you)!
– Do not expect a perfect set after a defensive action, but a deep court set or a set of mediocre or bad quality!

b.:   In this situation, the blocker's abilities of transition, from block to attack, are of great importance. Depending on the quality and effectiveness of his ball contact, he will reorientate himself away from the net. In case of an effective block, he will back off the net in order to perform his approach to the attacking location. If he is expecting an emergency save by his partner, he will move nearer to his partner in order to keep the ball in play and hit it toward the opponent's court as effectively as possible.

Depending on how difficult the defensive action is, the backcourt defender tries to either play a half-high **set** toward the offensive range of the blocker/ attacker or to **defend** the ball toward his reach or to **save** the ball high into the middle of the court.

c.:   In these situations, two types must be distinguished:

1. The blocking player has backed off from the net after a faked block in order to play defense.
2. The opponent is clearly not in a position to jump and attack the ball.

1:    To a large extent, this situation is similar to the block and defense situation without the ball touching the blocker. The explanations made in point (a) apply. The following possibilities of backcourt defensive formations may be distinguished with regard to areas of responsibility:

–   **Prior to the set**, if the blocker decides to play defense instead of   blocking, he shall move backwards toward **his side of the court**.
–   If the blocker decides **after the set or** shortly before the attacker hits, to play defense instead of blocking, he will cover **the side of the court in which he finds himself at that moment (he will move straight backwards)**. Then, the backcourt defender will move to the other, free area (Photo 46).

Photo 46: Fake block situation

Basically, the blocker must take over the side of the court that he can reach and can therefore more quickly defend in that certain situation. The backcourt defender will act after communication signals on the other side of the court, or according to that certain situation. With respect to the choice of the court area to be defended by the net player, the following principle is still valid: **Defense has the priority over attack**, thus the net player shall not defend the side of the court from which he normally attacks but the side where he is likely to make the better defensive play.

2:     The areas of responsibility and the player functions, during the attack build-up in the down-ball situation, are similar to the service reception situation. Therefore, the net player is responsible for his usual side of the court and accordingly the backcourt defender for his side.

    – The latest moment the defensive position should be taken, is immediately following the set, depending on how clear the down-ball situation is.
    – The coordination will be called or signaled by the net player.

7.4   INDIVIDUAL TACTICS OF THE BLOCKING PLAYER

The following results are of critical importance for working out a block and defense strategy:

– In numerical distribution of various techniques, the block takes the 5th position with about 14% of all actions.
– At the German national men's level, almost 40% of all blocking actions take place in the area of pos. II, with a tendency towards the net's center (correspondingly, the main share of attacking actions take place at the opposite pos. IV). About 28% of all blocks are played at pos. IV and app. 32% at pos. III (see Fig. 33).
– Two thirds of all attacks are defended with a block.
– About 11% of all blocks are successful, therefore resulting in

Photo 47

a point or a sideout. App. 4% of all blocks are direct faults, where the ball is blocked "out" or the blocker touches the net.

- In half of all blocking actions, the blocker clearly takes away an area of the court from the attacker, who then is not able to hit a hard-driven ball into this area. The share of blocking actions, in which the blocker is not clearly taking away an area, and therefore not reducing his backcourt defender's responsibilities, is almost 36%.
- In about 11% of all jump attacks, the blocker fakes a block.
- Tendencies show that the American male and female professionals increasingly use a specialized block and backcourt defense; only 7 out of 20 observed teams played without specialization.
- On the contary, only 3 out of 10 observed teams in Germany played with a specialization in block and defense.

The improvement of the defensive performance is impossible without communication strategies between blocker and backcourt defender. Hidden behind his back, the net player can give the following hand signals to his partner:

- The blocker shows with his left hand how he is going to block the left attacker (of course seen from his viewpoint).
- Accordingly, with his right hand he shows how he is going to block the right attacker.

Photo 48a: Blocker's hand signals: line & cross-court

Because of the serving strategy, the blocker will, of course, know which attacker he must block prior to the serve, or no later than the moment of the serve. Even then he should basically keep both hands behind his back while giving signals (Photo 48a+b). This is done on one hand to avoid giving the opponent clues about the serving strategy and on the other to avoid the opponent's possibility to hit the ball *on two*.

- One straight downward pointing finger signalizes that the blocker will screen (cover) the longline-area (see Photo 48a).
- Two downward pointing fingers show that the blocker will take the cross-court (see Photo 48a).
- Showing a fist means that the blocker will play a fake block against this

particular attacker. This defensive strategy aims at making the opposing attacker insecure by confronting him with an unexpected situation (see Photo 48b).

– If the blocker intends to block the ball (to play a "kill or stuff" - block) instead of taking away an area, he will signal his intention with an open hand (see Photo 48b).

The last possibility mentioned may only be recommended for blocking players with very good anticipation and with superior athletic abilities, only rarely found. Here, the team consciously accepts the disadvantage, that the backcourt defender will not have an opportunity to orient himself with respect to his decision as to which area he is going to take.

The time for giving the hand signals depends profoundly upon the caliber of play. At all levels of play, signals are given prior to the execution of the serve. However, the best professionals are able to give and to recognize signals very late, immediately before the set or during the opponent's set (Photo 49). At the international level of play, the ability of players to communicate with signals *during rallies* has become very important since spies are informing the opponents about the intended defensive strategy.

Moreover, it is necessary that the server gives the net player a certain degree of feedback as to whether he has understood or seen the server's signals. Many players are not using eye contact for this communication, instead, the server gives a call to the blocker to show, whether or not he agrees.

If the blocker serves and then immediately runs to the net, the communication can be done vocally prior to the serve or with hand signals by the backcourt defender, or with hand signals by the blocker directly before blocking action.

Basically, the blocker is committed to his previously signaled blocking direction.

Photo 48b: "Fake & stuff block (ball)"

Photo 49: Hand signals during a rally

There are only two situations in which he has the right to change his intended block:

1. If the ball is set too tight toward the net, he will play a stuff block instead of blocking a zone and
2. if the ball is set far off from the net and he is not using the fake block, he will generally cover the cross-court.

However, the backcourt defender is not committed to stay on one side of his court, he always acts according to certain situations and will make the decision as to which area he is going to move to as late as possible.

The blocker may only act successfully if he has the following abilities:
With respect to his own performance, he must have perception, transition and coupling-qualities which are above average. Moreover, he must be very quick over short, middle and long distances. A high level of jumping endurance as well as discipline and a strong mental condition are other prerequisites. He must know the opponent's setting qualities and more importantly, he must be informed as to their tendencies, strengths and weaknesses as attackers. In a concrete situation of play he must be able to evaluate,

–   the **quality of the first pass** with respect to the possibility of an attack *on two*,
–   the **quality of the opponent's set**, especially under the wind's influence. While facing the wind (tailwind for the opponent) he must expect more tight sets or that more sets are blown over to his court. Reversely, with the wind at his back, he must expect more attacks played far off from the net and therefore a decreased necessity to block.
–   all the actions of the passing attacker with respect to the necessity of a fake block,
–   the alternation of attacking tactics and attacking directions.

7.4.1 BLOCKING TECHNIQUES

Motion sequences of active (aggressive) blocking techniques
Most differences between indoor and beach blocking techniques are observed in the footwork prior to the takeoff and to the landing. All other motion features are identical.
From his starting position, 1 m from the net, the blocker observes the opponent's attack build-up. In the event of a good set he will move very quickly to the probable takeoff spot. In any case, however, his movement takes place *very late*, thus shortly before his takeoff (Photo 50a-d). The ready posture is taken directly before the takeoff. It is similar to an indoor block. It

has been observed that most of the professionals lower their body's center of gravity extremely by bending their knees to an 90°- 60°- angle (or even deeper, see Photo 51).

The players refrain from a quick counter-movement, which would give them a better utilization of their muscle tension. Takeoff, jump and arm/ hand positioning are identical with the indoor technique; however an *immediate* and aggressive penetration over the net should be paid attention to (Photo 52).

Photo 50a-d:
Movement of the
net player to
block

Photo 51 (following page):
Low center of gravity
in the squat position prior to
the block

Photo 52: Immediate
penetration!

Photo 53: Immediate readiness to play!

The fingers are spread and the hands are kept so far apart, that a ball can not be hit by the hands or arms. The player tries to roof the ball with his hands. The hands should be placed correctly following the principle "angle of incidence=angle of deflection" so that the ball will be deflected toward the opposing court. The blocker turns into the direction of his own court prior to landing (Photo 53). If a ball is hit past him toward his right side, he will land in a *step-position* with his left foot in front. The right foot will then initiate the first step toward the anticipated and intended running direction. If the ball travels past the blocker on his left side, the left foot will land behind the player in order to start quickly (Photo 53).

161

The block may be played in a one-handed fashion if the jump did not bring the player near enough to the ball's trajectory or if the player had balance problems during takeoff. Generally, it can be said that "a one-handed block is better than no block!" (Photo 54).

Photo 54 & 55: One-handed block and sweep block

The **sweep block** is employed either **two- or one-handed**. The player follows the anticipated direction of the attacker's hit with his arms. He tries to compensate for changes in the hitting direction (the attacker's arm and wrist position) by using this technique. Again, following the sweeping motion, the blocker will fully extend his arms and penetrate (Photo 55).

In the case of simultaneous ball contact by the blocker and the attacker (**joust**), the ball is *pushed* with the open hand against the opponent's hand. As opposed to the prohibited open-handed trick attack, the rules do allow the open-handed ball contact during a joust.

The so-called **spread-** or **split block** is a special beach volleyball blocking technique. The player jumps with his arms wide spread open (Photo 56). Therefore he can hide his intended blocking type and direction until the last possible moment. At the last moment, the hands will either be closed and brought into the anticipated attacking direction or the blocker will hold on to the spread hand positioning to cover narrow court areas from the attacker.

Photo 56: Spread/ Split Block

Motion sequences of passive blocking techniques

Arm and hand positioning distinguish the passive blocking types and variations from active blocking techniques.

The penetration over the net is not as intense as in the active techniques. The arms are only brought forward a little, over the net, sometimes only extending up vertically over the head. The distance between arms and edge of the net is being kept as small as possible.

Again, the hands should cover an area as large as possible but not roof the ball. Short players bend their hands slightly *backwards* in order to deflect balls in such a way, that they can be kept in play inside the own court.

The **passive one-handed block** is used as well as the **passive sweep** variation. Specifically, the **passive spread block** is used by many top players.

Photo 57: Block against tactical shots

A special beach volleyball variation of the passive block is the block against tactical and trick attacks or shots that have been anticipated by the blocker *prior* to his takeoff.

In such a case, the timing of the takeoff as well as the hand and arm positioning will change. The blocker will jump *much later than usually*.

The arms will be extended straight up in order to intercept shots that are hit with a highly arched ball trajectory (Photo 57). If the blocker is able to get one or both hands *behind* the ball, he may even *hit* the ball back.

Action and motion sequence of the fake block

As previously mentioned, the blocker observes, then evaluates the quality of the opponent's set:

– In case of a good set near the net he will block.
– In case of a bad set further from the net he will block passively or he will fake the block and then back off from the net to play defense.

163

Until assuming the takeoff posture, the fake block is executed as a usual blocking action.

After the set or at the moment of the attacker's takeoff, the blocker will back off within a split second to play backcourt defense.

His body turns *toward his running direction* to start the movement as fast as possible. However, he keeps *visual contact with the attacker* during the whole motion (Photo 46, 58). The body turn is always executed towards the middle of the court, and never towards the sideline. Moreover the fake blocker always uses a forward run and never runs backwards or sidewards, since those running styles would be too slow. The running direction depends on his court position (right or left), on his current blocking position and on individual tactical arrangements (see chapter 7.2). The hands are kept at least above waist level, in order to be able to defend against spikes or shots with a high trajectory. He must always try to **avoid defensive plays while in motion.** Therefore, he should **stop the running motion at the moment of the attacker's hit.**

Photo 58 (**see also photo 46**):   Fake block

7.5 INDIVIDUAL TACTICS OF THE BACKCOURT DEFENDER

At the German national top level, the backcourt defending beach volleyball player acts in the following way:

– At only app. 10%, defensive actions are the lowest percentage in the numerical distribution of all playing actions. Here however, the backcourt defense has the biggest share at app. 9%, whereas the attack coverage share amounts to just 1% and the block coverage percentage is only 0.2%.

Photo 59

– Almost 26% of all actions take place close to the net at the pos. II, III and IV - areas. With respect to depth of the court, most of the defensive actions (64%) are played at the court's middle third. The fewest actions (10%) are executed at the rear third of the court. In regard to the width of the court, the largest share of defensive actions can be observed on the middle third (app. 43%; see Fig. 4 in chapter 3.2.1).

– By far, most defensive actions are executed with the underhand (forearm) dig (63%), followed by one-handed actions (28%). Special beach volleyball techniques like the so-called beach dig (open-handed dig) and the tomahawk only have shares of 6% resp. 3%.

– Regarding all defensive actions, about 41% are played in motion. At about 34%, actions in a falling motion have a relatively big share, whereas only 25% of all digs are played from a standstill or from a standing position. In most cases, the ball is played on either side of the defender's body (more than 62%). Only 38% of the digs are played in front of the defender's body (see table 11).

sideways	frontal	standstill	falling motion	in motion
62%	38%	25%	34%	41%

Table 11: Backcourt defense

- At the national level, almost 60% of all defensive actions are of a good quality. Therefore, a set and the subsequent counter-attack with a jump is possible (the defense of down-balls was also taken into account in this observation). About 26% of all attempts to defend an attack are unsuccessful. Following 14% of all defensive actions, the ball can only be played as a 'save' or a down-ball to the opponent.

The choice of the correct defensive area is the most important prerequisite for a successful defensive action. The backcourt defender's starting position is at the court's center, about 5 -6 m from the net. His ready posture is medium low. Because of the following reasons, the backcourt defender keeps the opponent guessing as long as possible, as to where he is going to defend:

- In order to make it impossible (or at least to make it more difficult) for the opposing setter to give the attacker an early call with the appropriate action directives,
- In order to take the setter's call into consideration while deciding which area he his going to cover.
- In order to make the opposing attacker uncertain.

This late movement by the defender again forces the opposing setter to give his informative call regarding the uncovered court area as late as possible.

If the call is given too early, the defender has the possibility to take this information into consideration for his own defensive movements.

> **Faking and irritating movements** by the defender are meant to misguide the opposing setter so that he will call to his attacker too early. This might result in possibly incorrect communication. Moreover the attacker's anticipation of the defender's movements will be made more difficult through these faking motions. The fakes, for example a quick misleading change in a running direction, are an essential part of **any** defensive action.

From his starting position the defender has the following options concerning the choice of the defense area. This will be under consideration of the expected attacking action:

- Usually, the defender will make the decision to go to the court area he is going to take following the set or the attacker's takeoff.
- If he is anticipating a hard-driven spike into the area not covered by the block he will reorientate himself shortly before the spike toward the unscreened area. However, he must try to defend hard-driven spikes from a still, balanced posture and to avoid defensive actions in motion. This,

of course, does apply to all defensive situations but especially to digs against hard-driven balls.

- If he expects a tactical attack toward the zone taken away by the block or into an area not covered by the block but far away from him, he will move at the moment of the hit or directly afterwards to run down this shot.
- If he anticipates his partner's faking of the block and subsequently backing off of the net, he will move towards the area not taken by his partner.

The knowledge of one's own defensive technical abilities as well as one's own physical and especially mental strengths is very important for the individual tactics of the backcourt defender. The right self-assessment and mental willpower are the keys for each successful defensive action. Anxiety and the lack of self-confidence guarantee failure.

The beach volleyball player as backcourt defender can only be successful if he acts under the full input of his willpower, concentration and concentrational endurance. Special attention receives his fighting spirit and will to win. In particular, he must have high tolerance toward any type of frustration since he has no chance to defend against most attacks. He must be mentally fit enough to be able to handle any unsuccessful action in order to keep on playing a "fired up" defense. In any case, the beach volleyball player as a blocker and/ or backcourt defender should refrain from blaming his partner for any team errors. Cheering each other up and giving positive reinforcement regarding the partner's actions, as well as changing defensive strategies are the preconditions for a successful co-operation of the beach team. Therefore, the backcourt defender's features are:

> Of paramount importance are superior anticipation abilities and **years of beach volleyball-experience**, proper use of specifically beach digging techniques in all situations of play, good transition ability from defense to attack, high speed over short, medium and long distances and **the will to never give up any ball (Photo 60a+b)**.

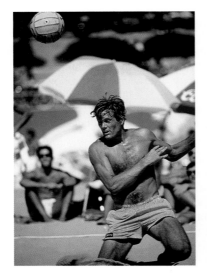

Photo 60a: Fighting spirit!

Photo 60b: Never give up a ball!

7.5.1 DEFENSE TECHNIQUES

Until 1995, the use of the defensive technique, that is suitable for a certain situation, has been influenced by the type of attack and indirectly by the rules.

Rule Considerations

Before the blocking over-rule was installed in 1986, the defenders faced many situations without a block at all. Therefore, open-handed digs were also used instead of the forearm dig, for balls hit low and short. Today, the open-handed dig for low traveling balls is not used very often. It remains to be seen how the latest rule changes will be interpreted by the referees and adopted by the players. Consecutive ball contacts are now allowed **during the team's first hit** or **in defending a hard-driven ball**. **A hard-driven ball may even be held momentarily**. These rules favor an increased use of open-handed techniques, and even underhand passes. However, this rule having recently been implemented and the fact that correct ball contact is still a judgment call, the rule's future development is still unclear.

Photo 61: Beach-dig

The rules allowed to dig a (hard-driven) ball with open hands (so-called **beach-dig**). This kind of attack is mainly used as an overhead dig (Photo 61).

USA: The rules have not yet been adopted by the American professionals, so that spin-spikes, shots or any off-speed attack may not been defended with open hands! Therefore, the tomahawk-technique still remains a necessary technique for the defense against shots which are to be defended overhead.

Because of the soft ground surface, the defender has the possibility to use acrobatic actions for his defensive attempt to make a play. In each defensive situation he will act appropriately, which means that he does not have to follow a rigid motion pattern or an unchangeable technical direction.

Motion sequence of the (forearm) dig

The sequence is similar to the defensive dig used indoors and to the already described pass in serve reception. The following differences regarding posture, arm position and arm motion must be observed:

Because of his ready posture (see chapter 5.3.1), the player has less time to form a platform and lower his body to a very low defensive posture, such as in indoor volleyball.

Therefore it can be observed, at the professional level, that the players do not fix or interlock their hands. Two types of arm positions can be observed:

- The forearms are *brought together* like in the serve reception, but without any fingers or hands gripping.
- The arms are held parallel at a distance of app. 10 cm from each other, and consequently form a larger platform.

These variations require perfect technical skills and are therefore only recommended for use during training or competition at the national/ international top level.

In contrast to the pass in serve reception, the following points must be paid attention to regarding the power input through the arms and the body:

- Retrieving a hard-driven spike, the arm and body input are very modest. Most of the times, the ball will only be cushioned in such a way, that the arms are pushed under and "through" the ball to give it backspin.
- The posture will be very low in the case of low or short traveling spikes that would land in front of the defender.

Besides the variations known from the service reception, the forearm dig can be played in a falling motion, in motion and in a jump. These variations are executed in different, acrobatic maneuvers that suit the certain situation .

Motion sequence of the one-hand dig

The one-hand dig with closed hand is used sideways and overhead. It will only be used if the player does not have enough time to bring both arms behind and underneath the ball In certain situations, this technique is preferred over two-hand digs, particularly when the dig is executed in a falling or in any other kind of motion (Photo 62).
The arm will be extended sideways, but still slightly bent. In the

Photo 62: One-hand dig

case of high traveling balls it will be extended upwards. The ball is played with the lower arm, the inside of the wrist or with the inside of a half-open fist. With this technique, the player can keep all balls that are traveling at him within a medium or long reach, in play.

If a player is threatened to be outplayed by a ball that is flying across and beyond him or to an area of the court which he is not covering, he will use the one-hand dig in a **falling motion**. This is done during a dive or any other kind of (acrobatic) **motion** (Photo 63).

A one-hand dig along with a side or back roll is avoided in the beach game. Instead, the dive is also used for balls that are either far to the right or left side of the body. The one-hand techniques enable the player to reach particularly balls in his long range. Additionally, the player benefits from the soft surface which allows acrobatic diving jumps (Photo 64a).

170

Photo 63: Outplayed?

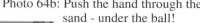

Photo 64b: Push the hand through the sand - under the ball!

Photo 64a: Acrobatic dive

As opposed to indoor volleyball, one-hand digs in a dive are played with the *inside of the wrist* and *not* with the back of the hand.

Since the hand may even be pushed "through" the sand or close to the sand, balls can be saved a split second before they touch the ground (Photo 64b). The "pan dig", with the flat hand on the ground from which the ball is deflected, is not used because of the uneven and soft surface.

Balls with a high trajectory, especially spin spikes/ shots are sometimes dug one-handed with a strong jump out from the basic defensive posture. The ball is then played with the inside of the wrist or the finger middle joints (as in the poke shot) of the extended arm at the culminating point of the jump, after a split second of "hang time".

Motion sequence of the open-handed dig (beach-dig)

The overhead beach-dig very much so resembles the overhead hand set. With the overhead dig, the defender may also play balls which are to the right or left of his head or body or balls at chest level. As already mentioned, it remains to be seen how the use of the open-handed digs will increase. So far the beach-dig is used against all hard-driven spikes, that come toward the player

- at or above head level,
- at shoulder or chest level,
- to the right or left of the body in close reach.

The defender starts the beach-dig out from the basic ready posture. The blocker sometimes uses the overhead beach-dig during his backward running motion after a faked block, consequently he is sometimes forced to play the beach-dig **in motion**. However, he should always try to avoid defensive play while in motion and therefore stop his running the moment of the attacker's hit, in order to play from a well-balanced posture (standstill).

The player turns his hands up, toward the ball trajectory. The hands are open as in the *setting* motion (Photo 61). The playing surface, the whole length of the fingers with cupped palms, is positioned at such an angle that the ball will be deflected toward the middle of the court or toward the partner.

At the moment of ball contact the hands cushion the ball as elastically as possible. While playing very hard-driven balls, this cushioning - with the hands brought closer together than in the hand set - will result in a momentary "holding" the ball". Again, depending on the speed of the ball and on the referees rule interpretation, the ball is played actively to the partner:

- **Hard-driven balls** are just *cushioned* and played with a very slight extension of the arms. The main impulse still comes from the ball's own kinetic energy. However, the above described momentary "holding" should give the player enough time to control his pass.
- **Off-speed attacks** should *more actively be played* with a an intense arm extension. The ball should be "accompanied" as long as possible in order to control the play perfectly. Moreover, the whole body can support the passing motion.

The ball may be directed through wrist turns. For example, a ball coming sideways to the body may be guided into the intended direction by turning the open palms upwards.

Depending on a certain situation, the beach-dig is also used **in a falling motion, in a jump** and **one-handed** over the chest or head level.

172

Motion sequence of the underhand beach-dig

The basic pattern of this technique is similar to the forearm dig. The following differences can be described:

Shortly before the spike, the player takes a very low and well-balanced broad squat position. The arms are slightly bent. The forearms are positioned next to or a little above the thighs with the hands above the knees.

The *open* palms (spread fingers) are held in a cupped shape and point upwards (Photo 65a).

Photo 65a+b: Underhand beach-dig

The ball is played with the whole inside of the hand. It is not deflected abruptly. Instead, the fingers cushion the ball's speed.

In any case, the ball is played actively. The forearms push through upwards and forwards by a forward pushing-through motion of the shoulders and by bending the arms. The wrists, held rigidly, support this movement (Photo 63b). This technique is mainly used frontally, sometimes to the right or left of the body from a standstill. Very fast balls which do not allow the player to bring both hands underneath the ball can be played **one-handed**. In such a case, the technique resembles the one-hand dig technique with the exception that the ball is now *deflected* by the stiff fingers of the open hand.

Motion sequence of the tomahawk

Until 1995, the use of open-handed digs for the defense against off-speed attacks, has been prohibited. Consequently, these attacks, especially over head level, were defended with closed hands and fingers. This technique is called "the tomahawk". The tomahawk enables the defender to play defensive passes with high precision and is mostly used against tactical attacks with a high trajectory.

173

Although the use of the open-handed dig against shots and off-speed balls has been permitted internationally, since the rule changes at the beginning of the '94/ '95-season, the tomahawk should still be a good technique against attacks of this type. However, balls traveling at low speeds above the shoulders or the head of the defender, can be played with the tomahawk, since this technique allows for very precise passes, almost as accurate as the hand set. It is still unclear, what developments can be expected concerning the open-handed techniques. Moreover, there has yet not been an official statement from the US-professionals (AVP), whether they are going to adopt the new international rules or not. As of now, the tomahawk should nevertheless be part of the repertoire of every beach player's defensive tools. This holds for whether they are beginners, national- or international-level players, or US-Pro level player.

With the exception of its use in backcourt defense, the tomahawk is used in the following situations:

–   For the reception of serves that travel very fast above head level,
–   for the faking blocker who has to dig a shot (high above him) that threatens to outplay him while he is backing off of the net,
–   for the attacker who must save a bad set after his executed approach. In this case, he saves the bad set with the tomahawk-technique while moving backwards.
–   As an alternative for the bump set, in case of a very high first pass in difficult wind conditions that make a hand set impossible.

Starting in the basic defensive ready posture, the hands will be raised app. 30 cm above the head, or as high as the anticipated ball. The arms are bent.

The hands will be put together with the fingers closed. The fingertips point upwards. As in the bump setting technique, there are many grip variations. They depend on individual preferences. The hand grip eventually determines the size of the surface playing the ball. A *large* and *even* playing surface is being created by all grip variations. The basic grips are the thumb-interlock grip (a) and the hand-overlap grip (b):

a.   The fingertips are brought together, and the thumbs are interlocked behind the back of the hands. The bases of the hands are app. 4 cm apart (This grip has a similarity to the "folding" of the hands for a prayer). Some players bend the middle- and the end-joints of their fingers. The ball is played with the outer *edges of the hands* (Photo 66a).

Photo 66a+b: Tomahawk hand grips

b. To form the more customary hand-overlap grip, the back of one hand is put into the palm of the other with the thumbs crossed behind the back of the hands and the palms pointing upwards. The ball is played with the *palms* (Photo 66b).

Ball contact is made by tilting the hands backwards while stretching the arms forward (Photo 67). The ball is played actively, thus with power put into the motion.

–   The more the hands are tilted backwards, the higher the ball's trajectory will be.
–   The stronger the arms are stretched against the ball, the longer the ball's trajectory will be.

Photo 67: Tomahawk-dig
–   The playing surface may be turned toward the intended pass direction by turning the wrists, according to the principle "angle of incidence=angle of deflection".

Similar to the different grip variations of the pass and the dig, the arms/ hands are unlocked and split apart immediately after the ball contact.

The attacker who must save a bad set while backing off from the net uses the fist-grip:

–   The left hand is formed as a "loose/ open" fist, the right hand is wrapped as an even "looser" fist around the left hand. The thumbs are interlocked. The fingers of the right hand reach down as far as the left hand's base joints (This grip resembles the grip used while swinging an ax). The hand *edges* are the playing surface (Photo 68, following page).

In contrast to the variations used in defensive situations, the ball contact is made by tilting the hands forwards.

Other than the hand set in beach volleyball, all tomahawk variations can also be used near the head and the shoulders. In such a case, no technical differences apply, the pass direction will always be controlled by the angle of the playing surface.

Photo 68: "Offensive" tomahawk

Gator-dig and chicken wing-dig

Other technical variations of digs are possible against hard-driven balls, as well as against shots that come at a defender under time pressure. The **gator-dig** is used to defend balls that travel at the player chest-high (Photo 69).

The triangle formed with forearm, upper arm and chest can be used in the same sense against chest-high balls under time pressure (so-called **chicken wing**-dig).

The beach volleyball player as a backcourt defender should learn to utilize all possibilities given to him by the rules. Consequently, the following principle applies for the digging of high-speed attacks from short distances which can not be defended with any other common technique (forearm dig, open-hand dig etc.):

Do not follow rigid technical direction. Instead, just bring a **large playing surface** (hands and/ or arms and/ or body and/ or legs) **behind and underneath the ball!**

Photo 69: Gator-Dig (Bruk Vandeweghe)

7.5.2 INTRODUCTION OF SPECIAL BEACH VOLLEYBALL DEFENSE TECHNIQUES

The introduction and further training of the so-called tomahawk-technique is taken as an example for the methodical steps that should be used for the introduction of defensive techniques. This digging technique is used particularly against tactical attacks (shots) with a high trajectory (higher than the defender's shoulder level). In almost every exercise offered, the ball will be tossed or hit to the defender.

Exercises:
1. (2-person exercise) Player A is positioned at the middle of the net, player B waits in defensive ready posture on the court at a distance of 5 - 6 m. A throws the ball to B, slightly above head level, so that B must pass/ dig the ball using the tomahawk.

While practicing this basic exercise and its follow-up variations, the defending player should dig the ball in such a way that he can catch the ball himself. This should be within his defensive reach, and done intentionally in order to learn **perfect ball control** *prior* to the practicing a precisely-aimed tomahawk-pass.

Hints
–   Test both grips of the defensive tomahawk and choose one of them!
–   Tilt your hands backwards in the moment of ball contact!
–   Keep the ball within your reach!

Variations:
(1) Player A throws the ball slightly toward the direction of the defender's (player B) left shoulder, later toward the direction of the right shoulder.
(2) Player A varies the throws by turning his body into the one direction that he is going to throw the ball to.
(3) Similar to variation (2), but without showing the throwing direction by a preceding body turn.

2. Similar to the basic exercise **1** and its variations, but now the player at the net plays a shot with an arched ball trajectory. The principle, that the defender must dig and afterwards catch the ball within his reach, still applies. Still, the important goal is to learn **ball control**.

3. Exercises **1** and **2** and the variations, but now the learning goal is the accuracy of the dig, as well as ball control. In order to dig/ pass the ball precisely over a certain distance, the player must put power into his action through an active arm stretch.

Hints

– Always keep visual contact with the ball!
– In the case where a ball travels at you with very low speed, use a leg extension in addition to your arm extension!

4. The exercises **1-3**, but with diagonally thrown/ spiked balls from longer distances (> 6 m).

5. Similar to exercise **4**, but now thrown/ spiked balls should force the defending player to change his position, within short or medium distances, before playing the ball.

An accurate dig requires a perfectly balanced posture. Difficult digs, especially those digs which require one to play the ball *in motion* should only be controlled, thus the digger should keep those balls within his reach or he should play them at a medium height toward the center of the court. In this case, the principle "**ball control has the priority over accuracy**" is effective! (Photo 70)

Photo 70: Tomahawk

6. The balls should be spiked in such a manner, that the defender is forced to use either the tomahawk or the overhead one-hand dig sideways.

Techniques using both arms must be preferred over one-handed digs!

Hints

– Try to find out suitable situations for every defensive technique!
– Always start your defensive motions from of a medium height ready posture!

7. Similar to exercise **6**, but now, by tossing the ball to himself, the partner acts as an attacker from the other side of the net.

8. Similar to exercise **6**, but another defensive technique should now be included into the drill. Later all defensive techniques are required and should be used. The attacker spikes balls with different angles, trajectories and speeds in order to force the defender to use the appropriate technique in the certain situations or to use the correct technique in every game situation.

> The **ready posture** should always be the same in order to react quickly to all kinds of balls: Close to the body, and away from the body, low, medium low, high and very high balls.

Variation:
(1) Similar to exercise **8**, but the partner attacks from the other side of the net.

Control exercise for the tomahawk:
The ball has to be played 10 times back and forth between the players using the tomahawk, without committing a fault.

Game forms:
1. '1 with 1' on a 4,5 x 9 m - court.
   The ball is brought into play with a spin spike instead of a serve. Player A hits a precisely aimed spike above shoulder level, so that his partner, B, must use the tomahawk. B should dig the ball within his reach in order to be able to set the ball to himself and spike it back across the net.

Hint

– Position your playing surface in such a way, that you will be able to control the ball perfectly, to cushion its speed and to dig it over your head!

2. '2 vs. 2' at first on 4,5 x 9 m, later on the volleyball court.
The spin spikes must be hit in such a manner, that the players use the tomahawk dig without blocking. One player of each team is a permanent setter, the other one acts only as a defender.

Hint
–   Play precisely to your partner!

Variation:
(1) Similar to game **2**, but now on the whole volleyball court, with two backcourt defenders. Well-aimed tactical shots should be hit toward the defensive reach of the backcourt players.

3. '2 vs. 2' following Beach-rules.
Special rule: Hard-driven- and fake attacks (short shots) are prohibited. Only medium and long range tactical attacks and shots are permitted.

Variations:
(1) Similar to game **3**, now tactical attacks into the whole court are permitted.
(2) All types of attacks, excluding short shots/ fakes, are now hit at close range to the defender.

Hint
–   Act from the basic ready posture in order to execute the appropriate technique instantly!

(3) Similar to the variation (2), but now the attacker may hit into the whole court.

Hints
–   Try to rate your skills correctly and play those balls, which are difficult to defend, medium-high or high to the center of the court!
–   Never dig/ pass directly to the opponent or too high/ long beyond your partner!

It must again be pointed out that, because of the limited volume of this book, methodical introductions can not be offered for all special beach defensive techniques. The above described exercises and exercise steps can be used accordingly for all techniques with slightly modified principles and action hints that can be looked up in chapter 7.5.1.

7.6 SELECTED FORMS OF TRAINING

Based on the usual training situation in beach volleyball, exercises and game forms for only two players will first be presented. They primarily serve to improve blocking and backcourt defensive techniques and to a lesser extent the schooling of individual tactics. Subsequently, exercises and game forms for three players will be offered in order to primarily train individual tactics and the attack build-up transition from defense. Additionally, for the individual as well as the team tactics, the forms of training with four players take defensive strategies into consideration.

The forms of training using five or more players, take into account on the one hand the defensive strategies of the '2 vs. 2' - game and on the other the special forms of the beach volleyball game '3 vs. 3' and '4 vs. 4'.

EXERCISE- AND GAME FORMS WITH TWO PLAYERS FOR THE BLOCKING PLAYER

Exercises and game forms:
1. Attacker vs. blocker.
   The attacker tosses the ball himself (half-high) and spikes longline from any attacking location at the net. Later he hits cross-court in prolongation of his approach direction. The blocker tries each time to block the area that the attacker determined.

Hints
- Do not block opposite to the attacker but in prolongation of his approaching direction!
- Penetrate immediately!
- Use the correct wrist angle to deflect ball to the court's center!
- Jump later than indoors!

Variations:
(1) Regarding the distance to the net, the attacker inaccurately tosses the ball on purpose.

Hint
- In case of tight tosses, block the ball with a "stuff" block. In the case where tosses are further from the net, block the approaching direction of the attacker!

(2) The attacker varies his toss direction and thereby his approach and hitting direction.

Hint
- Change your blocking direction at an early stage of the attacker's action and jump from an optimally balanced position!

(3) Not only does the attacker forcefully spike in prolongation of his approach direction, but in other directions as well.

Hint
- Block the attacker depending upon his arm swing and his position relative to the ball!

2. The exercise **1** and its variations, but now the blocker starts 1 m from the net.

Hint
- Initiate your block with a step toward the net and jump from a medium-low squat!

3. '1 vs. 1' on the 3 x 9 m - court (Fig. 35a).

Special rule: The attacker spikes only hard-driven balls. The whole court (9 x 9 m) is the effective playing area for all balls which are rebounding from the net. The attacker hits 10 times, afterwards the functions will be shifted. The winner is the player with the most successful actions.

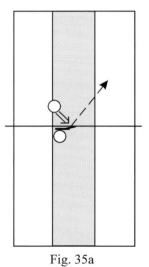 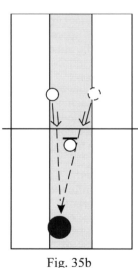

Fig. 35a   Fig. 35b

Hints
- Try to avoid having the ball be hit off of your outside hand by pushing your outside shoulder (arm and hand) forward or by pulling away both arms at the last moment!
- Your ready position is still 1 m from the net!

Variation:

(1) The attacker may play the trick attack to the close reach of the blocker. The blocker's action will be judged successful if he saves the ball using self-coverage.

Hints

- Observe the attacker's arm swing in order to recognize the poke early!
- If you recognize the poke after your takeoff, try to break off your blocking action with a body turn and transition to self-coverage!
- Try to cover and save each trick attack!

(2) The game form **3** and the variation (1) on 4,5 x 9 m.

4. The game form **3** and its variations with a spike toward predetermined areas (Fig. 35b).

EXERCISES AND GAME FORMS FOR THE BACKCOURT DEFENDER

1. Attacker vs. defender.
The attacker tosses the ball (half-high) and hits tactical shots toward a predetermined area (Fig. 36a+b). The backcourt defender acts in this area and tries to defend and subsequently to catch the ball. At first, the attacker spikes from a certain location, and then later from any location at the net. The organization and execution (counting) should be as in game form **3** for the blocker.

Variations:

(1) Similar to the basic form **1** on 4,5 x 9 m, without trick attacks and poke shots.
(2) The backcourt defender acts from his basic starting position in the middle of the court and defends tactical attacks toward the cross-court side (Fig. 36c).

Hints

- Always move as late as possible, following the attacker's toss from your starting position to the defense area!
- Observe the attacker's body position relative to the tossed ball in order to anticipate the direction of shots!
- Use the appropriate defensive technique in order to keep the ball in your own court!

(3) Similar to variation (2), but now the defender takes always the "line"-area of the court.

Hint

– Move quickly after the attacker's hit, in order to run down tactical shots!

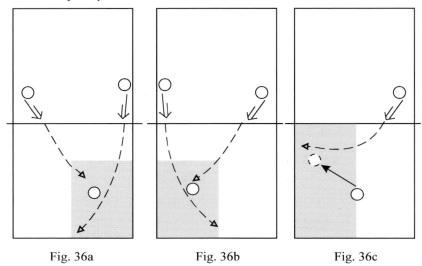

| Fig. 36a | Fig. 36b | Fig. 36c |

2. Similar to variation (2), but now the attacker spikes hard-driven balls into the determined zone. He may not toss the ball closer than 1 m to the net.

Hint

– Always choose your defensive position 5 - 6 m from the net in order to be able to defend short or sideways low driven balls with the forearm dig. Defend against balls that are driven at or above you, with the two- or one-handed beach-techniques!

Variation:

(1) The variations of form **1**, but only with hard-driven balls.

3. The attacker spikes hard toward court area C and plays shots into court area D (Fig. 37a).

Variations:

(1) Similar to game form **3**, but the attacker is located between pos. II and III.

(2) Similar to the game form and its variation, but now the attacker should hit hard toward the longline-zone C and tactically into zone D (Fig. 37b).

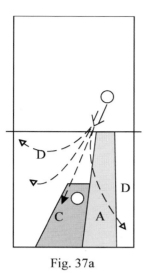

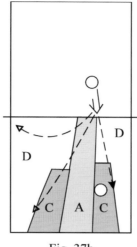

Fig. 37a   Fig. 37b

Hints

– Try to defend balls which are *very* "*difficult*" to dig high toward the center of your court and play *less difficult* balls in such a way that you are able to catch your dig yourself!

– Pay attention to your balance and make sure that you are always acting from a medium-high ready posture!

– Try to start your action with an open and relaxed arm position!

(3) Similar to the game forms and their variations, but now, after his spike, the attacker will cross under the plane of the net in order to set the defended ball and to make his partner's transition from defense to attack possible.

FORMS OF TRAINING WITH THREE PLAYERS

In the following forms of play, one attacking player plays against one defending beach volleyball team. Principally, the game can be decided by points after a predetermined number of attacks. Based on a usual beach volleyball situation, the two players, used to playing together, should form the defending team. A third player should play the supporting role as an attacker. It is obvious that the players must alternate their functions as blocker and backcourt defender in order to acquire universal skills. The attacker should choose different locations at the net for his spikes, as long as these locations are not specified by the exercise.

Advanced players as well as beginners should play the '1 vs. 2' - game, at first on the 4,5 x 9 m, 9 x 6 m, 6 x 9 m, courts and ultimately on the usual beach volleyball court. Advanced players as well as top-level players can play the below mentioned games as games with each other, prior to games against one another. The games with each other emphasize the improvement of technical skills and less significantly the training of the individual and team tactics. While playing games with each other, usually resulting in long rallies, intermissions should be deliberately held longer than normal.

1. Attacker vs. one beach volleyball team (Fig. 38a).
At first, the attacker should be informed as to the defensive strategy of the team (The net player will initially block the line area, the back row player will take the cross-court zone). The attacker will hit only hard-driven balls after he tosses the ball himself.

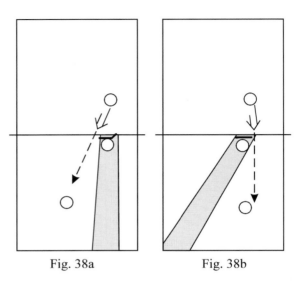

Fig. 38a   Fig. 38b

Execution and organization

– The defending team will be awarded a point after a successful block and/or if the counter-attack is caught or defended by the original attacker who played defense at that time.
– The team will get two points if it succeeds in playing a tactical shot which can not be touched by the attacker (defender).
– The team will be awarded three points if the counter-attack is carried out as an attack close to the net and the attacker (defender) can not reach the ball.

Hint

– All the so far given hints apply here and should still be observed!

Variations:

(1) The blocker takes the cross-court, the backcourt defender covers the other half of the court (Fig. 38b).

Hints

– **Blocker**: Be prepared to play the set after your blocking action!

186

- Try to obtain visual contact with your partner and the ball prior to your landing!
- Initiate your readiness to play the second ball with a body-turn before your landing and by landing in a step-like feet position.

(2) The attacker hits a hard-driven ball in prolongation of his approaching direction/ line. The blocker takes the main spiking direction and the backcourt player acts outside of the covered area.

Hint

- **Backcourt defender**: Be prepared to play the attack after your defensive action!

(3) The attacker either hits a hard-driven ball or plays a short shot.
(4) The attacker exclusively plays tactical shots or trick attacks.

Hint

- Be prepared as a **blocking player** to defend short shots within your reach, cover yourself!

(5) The attacker plays a hard-driven ball or a tactical shot.

Hints

- **Blocker**: In case the ball is touched by your block, be prepared to attack the defended ball with a very short approach!
- **Backcourt defender**: Try to play a ball touched by the block as a set to your blocker/ attacker or as a high save within his reach!

(6) The attacker may use any type of spike or shot.

Hints

- **Blocker**: Inform your partner about your zone block (about the area you are planning to cover)!
- Inform your partner early on, or, in certain cases, immediately before the attack, that you intend to fake the block!
- Always make sure whether your information has been recognized by your backcourt partner or not!
- **Defender**: Give your blocking partner a confirmation as to the status of his signals!
- Try to irritate the opposing attacker with the use of misleading/ fake moves!

2. Once in a while, the attacker deliberately plays an inaccurate toss for his own attack, in order to create a down-ball like situation. The attacking locations may vary between "close to the net" and "5 m from the net". In this latter case, the blocking player should back off from the net to play defense (Fig. 39).

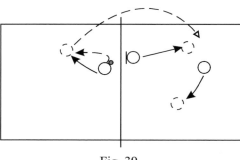

Fig. 39

Hints

- **Blocker**: Pay attention to the fact that you must make a fast retreat from the net to your usual passing/ attacking - half of the court, in the case of a down-ball situation!
- **Backcourt defender**: In case of a clear down-ball, you are responsible for your normal passing/ attacking, half of the court!
- In down-ball situations, recognized late, try to move straight backwards and cover the half of the court that you are currently occupying!

FORMS OF TRAINING WITH FOUR PLAYERS

1. '1 vs. 2' with one supporting player.
All the game forms with three players can be used. In the case of an unsuccessful beach team defense, the fourth player should hit a ball into the defensive range of the backcourt player. The defending team should get as many opportunities as possible to practice their attack build-up transition from the defensive situation. Later the fourth player should hit short shots toward the reach of the blocking player.

2. '2 vs. 2' following beach volleyball rules.
Special rule: The defending team hits the ball to the opponent as a down-ball, in order to practice several defensive situations in a row. At first the down-ball should always be played to the same player, later to any of the opponent's players. Finally the down-ball should be changed to an attack which is difficult to defend. In the beginning the attacking team should only use spin spikes and shots or short shots. Later all kinds of attacks may be used.

Hint

– Be prepared - as a **backcourt defender** or as a **net player** - to dig balls which are hit by the setter *on two*!

3. Attack under simplified conditions.
The attacking team may execute their attack after a an easy ball has been tossed to the passer by the setter. This leads to a perfect pass and a perfect set.

Variation:

(1) The attacker must execute his attacking motion following a spike by his setter and his subsequent dig.

Hints

– **Blocker**: The block will be necessary more often, if the wind is in your face!
– Always try to be a positive and motivating partner!

4. '2 vs. 2' as practice-game following beach volleyball rules.
Special rule: Each team has the side-out five times in a row without rotating the server. After these five serves, the other team gets the right to serve.

Variation:

(1) Game following beach volleyball rules.

FORMS OF TRAINING WITH FIVE OR MORE PLAYERS

1. The forms of training **1-4** with four players may be used without any restriction. The fifth player will initially play a supporting role as a server.

2. '2 vs. 2' following beach-rules as a power-game.
First, the fifth player puts the ball into play by hitting down-balls. The same team should receive 3-5 down-balls in a row. Later the team that committed the fault should receive the down-ball. Finally, the team that won a rally will receive the down-ball.
Special rule: The team that won two or three of three down-ball-rallies will be rewarded with a big point. Later the team that won two rallies in a row will get the big point and at last, the team that won three rallies in a row will be awarded the big point. In this type of power-game, the intermission time should initially be longer than 20-30 sec. Later 5/8/11 big points should be played without pause.

Hints

– Try to play accurately and to co-ordinate your actions according to certain game situations, ignoring the physically high demands, even when they become too great!

– Try to mentally prepare for a physical overload situation and try to keep up your fighting spirit, until the completion of all the rallies!

3.   Two players with supporting functions.
Game forms **1** and **2** are now played with six players. At first, the two supporting players act as servers from one side. Later, one player will serve from behind each of the baselines. After a while, power games may be played, where each supporting player hits the down-ball to just one team.

4.   '2 vs. 2' with three beach teams (Fig. 40).
Two players from the team that is not playing at that time (A) wait with a ball, behind each of the baselines. The serve (3) will be executed by the player who waited behind the court of the eliminated team, meaning the team that lost the rally (here: team B). As soon as the other server (A') recognizes, that the team on the opposite side of the court has committed a fault, he must drop his ball, run to the opposite court side (2) and join his partner. Subsequently, he will act as a blocker (A"). However, he will try to communicate with his partner (server/ backcourt player). The players of the eliminated team take a ball and move to their positions (2) behind the baselines. They will always be paying attention, careful to recognize their turn to bring the next ball into play (B') and to join the action again. The overall winner will be the team that first reaches 15 points. A point will be awarded for two won rallies.

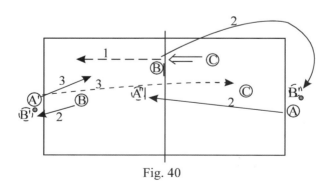

Fig. 40

Variation:
(1) For the duration of up to 10 rallies, one team will primarily receive and attack. Later that team will act as the serving and defending team.

5. '3 vs. 3' as a special form of beach volleyball
One player acts at the net to fulfill blocking and setting tasks, two players act as backcourt defenders and attackers.
The structure of the '2 vs. 2' beach volleyball game should be maintained, therefore the ball touch during the block will be counted as the teams first contact.

Variations:
(1) '3 vs. 3' following the mentioned French beach-rules (see chapter 3.5.1).
(2) '3 vs. 3' with seven players. In this case, the seventh player hits one down-ball to each team after the first rally.

6. '4 vs. 4'
The rules of the American Beach Volleyball League apply (see chapter 3.5.2). At first, the game is played with one blocker and three defenders, later with two front row players and two backcourt players.

Variation:
(1) In order to give the one, or at most two defender/s, typical beach volleyball defensive functions, this game may be played with three players at the net and one backcourt defender.

Photo 71: "Gator"
beach-dig

7.7 SPECIAL DRILLS

For the improvement of the blocker's and defender's co-ordinative abilities, the organization and execution of these drills should be done according to chapter 6.5.1 .

Beach volleyball player with blocking function:

- Block→set→block.
- Block→self-coverage→block.
- Fake block→backcourt defense→attack.
- Fake block→backcourt defense→set.
- Serve→block→attack.
- Serve→fake block→backcourt defense.
- Serve→abatement of the running movement to block→backcourt defense →attack.
- Block→defensive save→block.
- Serve→block→set.
- Block→self-coverage→set.
- Set→block→running down a tactical shot.
- Running down a setter's trick attack→attack→block.
- Block→fake block→block.
- Fake block→block.
- Block→deep court set→block.

Beach volleyball with backcourt defending function:

- Serve→defending a spike→attack.
- Serve→running down a tactical shot→attack.
- Backcourt defense→attack→backcourt defense.
- Deep court set→block→self-coverage.
- Running down a setter's trick attack→attack→block.
- Defensive save→attack→defensive save.
- Backcourt defense→deep court set→defensive save.
- Attack→backcourt defense→attack.
- Attack→running down a tactical shot→attack.
- Serve→defensive save→attack.
- First pass played as a set→defensive save→set.
- Deep court coverage→attack→block.
- Running down a trick attack→attack→block.
- Running down a setter's trick attack→attack→defensive save.
- Backcourt defense against 5 spikes in a row with a return to the starting position each time.

- 3 consecutive ball saves with a return to the starting position each time.
- Running down 3 consecutive tactical shots with return to the starting position each time.
- 5 defenses of hard-driven balls hit at the body with beach techniques.
- defending/ setting of 3 consecutive balls that have been touched by the block.
- 3 consecutive ball saves, as the team's third ball contact.
- 3 receptions of a down-ball with subsequent attack.

Photo 72

8 DEFENSIVE AND OFFENSIVE STRATEGIES

In the following pages, strategies and counter-strategies, and their practical application, will be presented and explained. The strategies are always based on systematic player- and game-observation (scouting, see chapter 9). The player's and trainer's talent lies in choosing the most effective training step from numerous possible training steps based on one observation feature. Moreover, he must choose the one technique that will be most likely to give that player(s) a certain edge.

8.1 SERVICE STRATEGIES

Considering the explanation of the problems of specialization (see chapter 3.3) and of the server's individual tactics (see chapter 5.4), the following observations are important for the development of a service strategy:

According to the fact that every beach volleyball player must be an outstanding receiver, his passing strengths and weaknesses must be registered in detail. The following key points should receive special attention (see chapter 9, game observation):

a) Observation of the reception-performance of his good/ weak side (see chapter 5.4), also with respect to weather conditions.
b) The player's reception-quality after movement.
c) The player's reception-quality with respect to his offensive action, especially regarding his speed and coordinative abilities.
d) Observation of his mental strengths and weaknesses during reception.
e) Observation of the possibility of a corresponding connection between reception and offensive performance. It should be noted if follow-up mistakes in the reception occur after an attacking fault has been committed by the same player. The comparison of the pass and the attack performance and vice versa should be done through data preparation of the action *sequences*.
f) Observation of the players' cooperation during the reception, especially when receiving serves in the 'husband and wife area' between the players.

The choice of the service position and technique from all of its variations, as well as the target is of great significance. The execution of serves and especially the flight of the ball are profoundly influenced by external conditions. Basically it can be said, that the following factors influence the individual and team tactical decisions of the serving team:

- The external conditions, especially wind direction and force, the sun light conditions and the character of the ground along with the player's own service strengths and weaknesses.
- The external conditions along with the opponents' strength and weaknesses, not only regarding their pass, but also their set and attack.
- The team's and the opponent's physical load. In beach volleyball, this is of enormous importance. When one takes into consideration, that the players possibly must play more than four matches during the first of two tournament days and up to six more matches until they reach the final.
- The team's and opponent's mental state.
- The score and, for the American pro-level, the remaining time on the rally clock.

For individual tactical decision, different goals for different types of serves depend on the weather conditions and should be considered:

1. The choice of the service location depends on the one hand on the external conditions and on the other on the intention to make the ball's trajectory as short as possible.

Therefore the serve from pos. I to the opponent's pos. I is less useful, since, due to the ball's longer flight time, the receiving player can anticipate the serve easier and assume a better position to run down, save or pass the ball. Here, it makes more sense to choose the service location pos. V in order to serve deep to pos. I with a short ball flight. However, the beach volleyball player should be able to serve from any service-position to any area of the opponent's court.

2. For the choice of the service technique, the serve's direction and the service location, the player's skills are the decisive factor. Principally, the player tries to use his 'best' serve. Only as a second priority the server can include the opponent, the wind conditions and all already mentioned factors into his considerations. He will then vary *his* technique accordingly or change his position and the serve direction.

The opponent, and his strengths and weaknesses, represent an important factor in determining the individual and team tactical decisions of the serving team. In most cases, the service strategy will be that one player will receive the majority of serves and that he, therefore, will be under a higher psycho-physical stress. Here, the following considerations affect the decisions:

- One shall attempt to recognize and to take advantage of an opponent's momentarily passing weakness, therefore the serve will always be aimed into this area!

- One shall attempt to recognize and to take advantage of an opponent's momentarily attacking weakness by serving directly at him! Here, it must be considered that the evaluation of the opponents' offensive performance also depends on the preferences of the defending team, which means, against whomever they more like to block or dig.
- One shall attempt to try to wear out the player who already is executing more jump actions due to his own service and defensive tactics. This is done by serving the main share of serves toward him. This can be done:

    a)   if it is known how many matches the opponent has played,
    b)   if the defensive tactics of this team are known.

- One shall attempt to try to hit a 'surprise'-serve to the one player, who has not received a serve for a longer period of time.
- One shall attempt to try to recognize and take advantage of an opponent's momentary setting weakness by serving at him!

Moreover, the player takes the current wind conditions into consideration for his individual tactical decision on the serve technique, direction and location. Here, a **good** and **bad** court-side can be distinguished. The team facing the wind and therefore serving into the wind is playing on the so-called good side, since more risky service techniques are available. For the receivers, the balls' trajectories in **headwind** are usually difficult to anticipate, since the serves can suddenly drop. Consequently, they are more dangerous than serves with tailwind. In this context, wind directions 'between' headwind and crosswind may also be regarded as advantageous for the serving team. Therefore, the basic recommendation is:

> At the coin toss, prior to a match, always choose the **good** side, meaning the headwind-side! The option to serve should only be chosen in calm wind conditions!

Given are the following recommendations concerning service locations, techniques and directions for serves in **headwind**:

- When facing a headwind, a riskier serve should be played.
- The "best" serve is usually a hard and deep serve toward the court center, between the two receiving players (Fig. 41 a). This is done to create misunderstandings. This *is* a potent serve, and the risk of a service-mistake is kept relatively low.
- Vary short and deep float and jump-serves! The opponent should thereby be tempted to take an inappropriate receiving position.
- A receiving player (A) positioned too close to the net should be passed by a deep jump serve over and beyond him (Fig. 41 b).

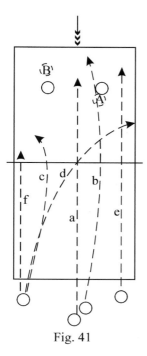

Fig. 41

- A receiver (B) placed too far from the net should be surprised with an extremely short jump serve (with a lot of top spin; Fig. 41 c)!
- Jump serves with a intense top spin should be hit cross-court (Fig. 41 d)!
- Deep float serves, should force the opponent to move before or during the reception (Fig. 41 e)!
- Jump and float serves should be deeply hit in order to force a long attack approach for the opponent (Fig. 41 b-e)!
- Short (tactical) floaters should be hit in cases where an opponent is showing obvious signs of exhaustion (Fig. 41 f)! A deep posture during the reception of short serves, along with a quick alternation of the excentric and the concentric muscle contractions, should tire out the passer and force him to make mistakes during his subsequent attacking action.
- The wind direction must always be taken into consideration when making the choice as to the one's position behind the baseline,
- In light, normal or medium wind headwinds, deep serves should be played more often or at least *as* often as short serves!
- Shorter and harder serves should be increasingly hit only in strong or very strong headwind!

In a crosswind or a slanting headwind the following recommendations are given:

- The service location (A) should usually be chosen in such a manner that the serve can be hit into the wind (Fig. 42 a, b)!
- The 'best' serve is the jump serve with side spin toward the 'short cross-court' (Fig. 42 a)!
- Jump serves should preferably be hit with side spin. Therefore, the ball should severely change its flight direction. The fact, that the ball will first travel at one player and then change its direction towards the sideline (Fig. 42c), the court's center or the other player, should force misunderstandings between the receivers (Fig. 42b).

- If the jump serve with side spin has not been mastered (middle or lower performance level), the spin serve from a standstill with top and side spin is a good alternative!
- Float serves should only be hit in light crosswinds!

The serving team finds itself on the so-called bad side, if it must serve with a tailwind or with a slanting tailwind. For the receiving team, the ball trajectory is more easily judged. This applies specifically to float serves. Moreover, serves with side or top spin do not drop as abruptly as in headwind conditions. Additionally, the flight direction does not change as severely as in crosswinds. The considerations made prior to serves with tailwind therefore focus more on the opponent's weaknesses than on the wind conditions.

- The 'best' serve is the serve hit between the opposing players, such that it leads to misunderstandings! Moreover, tailwind only allows for few risky variations.
- Jump serves should be hit, as long as wind conditions allow it!
- For a physical rest or in case of obvious fatigue, float serves should be used!
- As soon as the wind gets too strong or if it is deemed useful due to other factors, deep float serves should be hit between the opposing players. (Fig. 43a)!
- All serves should be hit deep! The opponent's attack approach should be as long as possible. This should take him out of his usual rhythm/ timing (Fig. 43a-c)!
- Deep float serves should be hit at the receiving players' body to surprise them with a ball that does not drop! In this case the receiving player will not be able to move to the side or backwards to get out of the ball's way (Fig. 43c)!

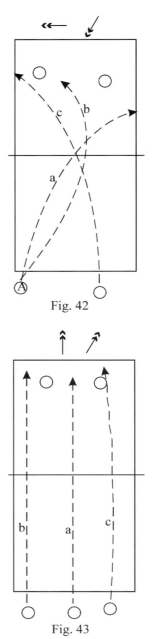

Fig. 42

Fig. 43

- One should serve down the line in order to shorten the opponent's reaction time (Fig. 43b)!
- Especially in light tailwinds, **skyballs** and all risky serves with a high and deep trajectory should be used! The wind and light conditions, the ball's instable flight path and the increasing speed of the sinking ball make the reception more difficult and may lead to follow-up mistakes in the attack.
- Skyballs should always be hit deep, so that the receiving player will be forced to move backwards (and not forwards)

It is easy to consider the players' passing strengths and weaknesses, because each player will receive and accordingly executes many receiving actions.

Since, with the exception of the attack *on two*, the receiver executes the attack at all times, the service strategies must always be seen in connection with the player's offensive performance. A player's offensive performance, not his reception performance, might often even be the decisive factor for deciding the service strategy. For example it might be very useful to serve to the better passer and weaker attacker, in order to improve the chances of the team's own block and court defense (see above).

Basically, each service strategy should take the team's own good/ bad side, depending on the wind conditions, into consideration (see above). However, this fact has less influence on the principle, that every player should always try to use *his* most effective type of serve.

Moreover, **jump serves** are recommended as the most effective offensive action in the service situation, especially,

a) because time for communication between partners, will be reduced, particularly with serves hit in between the players,
b) because, due to a hard-driven ball's nature and shorter traveling time, the pass is made more difficult,
c) because the receiving player can be urged to back far off of the net to the backcourt. This leads to a longer approach to the intended attacking location,
d) because a jump serve toward the front of the court, produces a surprising effect. In particular, if the receivers starting position is far from the net,
e) when hit as a risky jump-serve toward the front of the court and mainly toward the short cross-court.

The **tactical serve**, almost as effective as the jump serve, can be recommended in order to,

a) take advantage of a player's reception weakness. For example in the case of movements prior to the pass, weaker reception sides, etc.,

b) force the passer into the backcourt. This makes the transition from pass to attack more difficult,
c) put the technically or mentally weaker player under pressure through series of serves. Additionally, deliberately extended eye contact will help to weaken the passer's mental stability,
d) put a physically weaker player under pressure through series of serves and attacks. This will tire him out even further. Short serves, which result in long distances to be covered prior to the pass that forces a new attack approach, are suitable in this context,
e) physically wear out a team's blocker to completely exhaust him. This is done by hitting a series of serves (and therefore forcing series of attacks) at him. This is effective when the team is using a specialized blocker and backcourt defender. Here, accurately recorded observations made of the opponents jumping actions during earlier games of a tournament are of enormous importance.
f) "choose" the attack location and the attackers,
g) determine the weaker setter,
h) force misunderstandings among the players by serving into the "husband and wife area",
i) surprise the player/ players using short/deep serves, to force longer running distances. This will make them tend to choose an incorrect starting position for the reception,
j) surprise a player who has not passed the ball for a longer period of time and who has therefore lost his rhythm for the pass-attack sequence.

The **skyball** as a tactical variation is highly effective, especially because it

a) **is a forceful serve with tailwind,**
b) causes problems for the passer through the increasing speed of the sinking ball,
c) requires a different receiving tactic,
d) puts mental pressure on the opponent and makes him look "ridiculous" during a passing mistake,
e) takes the opponents out of their usual rhythm during their transition from reception to attack,
f) forces the receiver player to look up into the sky/sun for a long time instead of having a view of the whole court and the play action.

In beach volleyball, float serves are hit from a distance of up to 4m behind the baseline. They are useful, if an opponent has weaknesses in receiving these serves and if tactical serves do not appear to be highly effective. Float serves have an increased floating effect at the cost of accuracy. Overall, they increase the receiver's difficulties.

By utilizing the US-professional rules, the following advice can be given:

1. The team's more effective server deliberately takes advantage and serves consecutive times in a row during his right to sideout, until the opponent/ referee recognizes and eventually corrects it.
2. The execution of a skyball in order to give the opponent less playing time and put him under time pressure. Here, a few seconds can be the decisive edge. This step is recommended in the case of a clear point advantage and immediately before the remaining effective playing time ends.
3. On the contrary, the team under time pressure should execute risky serves in order to at least force a tie during the remaining time. In this situation, especially if there are less than three seconds left to play, the server should toss the ball *very* low and serve it aggressively. For example, with high risk in order to reach a tie through an ace serve.

Serve strategies in the tie-break

During a **tie-break,** the following advice may be given for the service strategy:

1. Basically, the service-strategy should not differ from the strategy in the previous set, especially if only a few direct service mistakes were committed.
2. On the contrary, if many serves were hit out of bounds or into the net and if the number of aces was very low, the service strategy should have to be changed. The willingness to use risky serves in order to avoid direct service mistakes should be reduced. This might lead to a situation where possibly each player, independent of the serve strategy, uses his favorite serve. In this case, his willingness to use risky serves is kept.
3. Safety-serves should be rejected, since they build up the opponent mentally.
4. In case of a score of 14 : 12 or higher, the server should serve with total risk. The goal is to serve an ace.

USA: In tie-situations in the professional game or in "sudden death", where the next point will decide the game's final result:

Here, neither the serve-strategy nor the willingness to use risky serves, should be changed.

8.1.1 GENERAL STEPS FOR THE SERVICE STRATEGY

Here, generally valid measures, which also refer to aspects of individual tactics, shall be explained along with the previous illustrations:

- The set and match score and, if applicable, the remaining time, the opponent and the team's own mental condition, previous incorrect calls by the referee and similar situations can lead to a change in the service strategy. For example, a momentarily stressed out player may be served to.
- If a team has weaknesses in blocking and backcourt-defense, it **must serve with a higher risk!**
- If a team is clearly superior in terms of reception, attack build-up and attack situation, but again inferior in blocking and backcourt-defense, **it must serve with a higher risk!**
- In contrast, the serve's risk should be **minimized** after the following situations:

  a. the time-out,
  b. sideout win through a long fight,
  c. the partner's service fault,
  d. preceding one's own service faults,
  e. one's own spectacular attack or block action,
  f. several points won by one's own team in a row.

Service strategies based on a systematic opponent observation, which do not immediately show the desired effectivness should not hastily be abandoned. The service strategy not only starts at the beginning of the match. Rather, serves before, during and at the end of the warming-up-time are already included in it. These serves help the player acclimate to the wind, ground and light conditions.

- Every time, during warm-up, when the partner does not receive the serve, the players should serve more intensely, than during the competition. This will intimidate the opponent, without adding to one's own insecurity by committing too many service faults.
- When serving to the partner, one should first execute easy and later competition-like serves. This will give the partner the opportunity gain "feeling".
- Moreover, one's own physical condition must always be considered. For example, if fatigue already occurs, jump serves should not be hit during the warm-up.

Finally, it must be emphasized, that it is only in a few games, that a service strategy, independent of individual abilities, may be used by each player. Consequently, the strategy must consider the server's individual abilities as well as actual reception situation. The strategy must be developed for every player separately.

To sum everything up, in a beach volleyball team, **at least one player must have mastered the jump-serve** as his main serve. Furthermore, it shall also be pointed out that the service location depends on a certain goal. This means that the server should choose the shortest distance to the target, almost every time. **Excluded** from this are serves which utilize the wind-conditions.

8.2   RECEPTION STRATEGIES

As the service strategies may be assigned to offensive strategies, the reception strategies may be associated with defensive strategies. The reception strategies can also be called counter-strategies, since they represent counter-measures against the service strategies that they must react to.

For the preparation of a reception counter-strategy, the following observation aspects are essential:

1. Type of serves:
   It should observed, which player uses jump-serves and which player uses tactical serves. This must be noted in connection with the weather-conditions.

2. Service location:
   Here, it should be observed whether or not the player/ players prefer/s one or more service locations. This should be noted depending on the weather conditions, with respect to the good/ bad side for the serve.

3. Opposing service strategy:
   Are the players using the same serves independent of whoever is the receiver, or can it be observed that they serve differently to different receivers?
   Is the opponent serving with risk? With or without tactical intention?
   Is each player using the same service strategy?
   Does the opponent generally change his service strategy during the match or only in critical situations?
   Is it noticeable whether or not that the server executes better or even worse serves following interruptions, for example after sand-time-outs or time-outs?

Any promising service strategy is based on detailed observation and analysis of the one's own reception performance! This fact should be paid particular attention to, for choosing the receiving court-side (right or left). This on the one hand, emphasizes the players' passing strength and on the other it hides his weaknesses.

The players' systematic analysis of the reception situation will seek to optimize the reception training and to eliminate weaknesses (see also chapters 5.3, 8.1 and 9). The recognition and exposure of the team's own players' passing weaknesses and peculiarities by the opponents will have an adverse effect on that team. For example, it can often be noticed that one player has more difficulties passing jump-serves than the other or that he has transition problems from pass to attack.

The following examples shall explain the counter strategies for the reception. It must clearly be emphasized, that the offensive strategy should always be subordinated to the reception strategy:

1. In strong tailwind, the players should usually shift their starting position, 7 m from the net, slightly forward (see Fig. 13a+b in chapter 5.2). A more drastic forward relocation must be rejected, since the receivers could easily be outplayed by a serve over and beyond them. Vice versa, the starting position should be shifted to 8m from the net in strong headwind. This is tactically useful, since a short serve with a low trajectory and high speed is difficult for the opponent to execute.

2. Even in light headwind, the players shift their start position about 1 m backwards. This allows them to avoid using a backward motion *prior to*, or *for* the pass (see Fig. 13c+d in chapter 5.2). Short serves will only come at low speeds and can therefore be easily run down.

3. If the serves are executed in a strong crosswind, the passers shift their starting position, with respect to their distance from the sidelines, slightly to the side of the wind (see Fig. 13e+f in chapter 5.2).

4. In light winds, independent of the wind direction, the basic starting position should not be changed.

5. For the reception of skyballs the tactic may be changed (Fig. 44):

   – If there is a better "skyball-passer" (A), the one-man reception formation may immediately be used following the serve (1). Thus, this better passer is covering the whole court on his own (2).
   – When the players are equally skilled in receiving skyballs, the more effective attacker should mainly pass the ball.
   – Exception: If the skyball comes down close to the net and on the side where the player, who already left the reception formation, is located, the player should pass the ball himself in order to simplify the attack build-up. This is with respect to the maintenance of the preferred, stronger or weaker attack side.

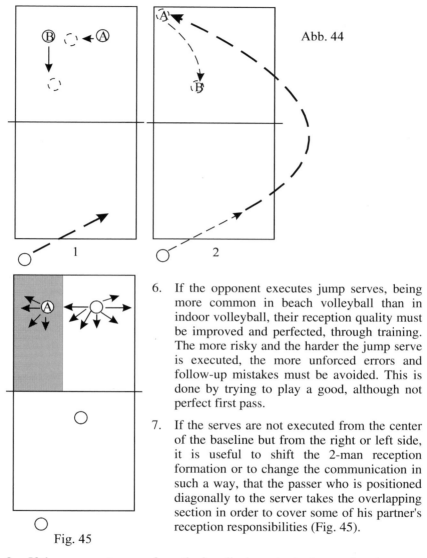

Abb. 44

Fig. 45

6. If the opponent executes jump serves, being more common in beach volleyball than in indoor volleyball, their reception quality must be improved and perfected, through training. The more risky and the harder the jump serve is executed, the more unforced errors and follow-up mistakes must be avoided. This is done by trying to play a good, although not perfect first pass.

7. If the serves are not executed from the center of the baseline but from the right or left side, it is useful to shift the 2-man reception formation or to change the communication in such a way, that the passer who is positioned diagonally to the server takes the overlapping section in order to cover some of his partner's reception responsibilities (Fig. 45).

8. If the opponent serves from the baseline's center to the overlapping zone to induce misunderstandings and therefore make the attack build-up more difficult, the momentarily stronger passer or the receiver with the stronger passing side towards the overlapping zone should receive the ball (see Fig. 45).

9. When an opponent uses tactical serves in order to take advantage of a passer's weak reception side, the reception formation should be changed. It should be done in a way, that this player covers more space on his stronger side. Additionally, he might consciously take a starting position which only allows movements toward the stronger reception side (see Fig. 45).

10. If the opponent uses tactical or jump serves to make the transition to the player's attack more difficult, the court distribution of serves could be accomplished in such a way, that the receiver, currently taking a series of serves, must cover less court space for example $^2/_5$ or $^1/_3$. Through this measure, the server would be forced to either hit into the player's smaller receiving zone or to change his service strategy (Fig. 45).

11. If the service strategy aims to put one of the players under mental pressure, the measure mentioned in point 9 must be used. In any case, the players must particularly prepare themselves mentally for this service strategy.

12. If the opponent always serves deep into the backcourt, the players' position should be shifted slightly backwards to avoid being outplayed by serves that travel over and beyond the receivers.

13. If the opponents are serving in a highly effective manner or if they are weaker in block and backcourt defense, the players should prefer a reception of medium quality to avoid direct receiving mistakes or follow-up mistakes.

14. If the players are very successful following deep-court sets, the first pass must be played with less risk. In the case of potent serves, a reception of medium quality should be preferred.

USA: In competitions played according to the AVP-rules, the receiving players must pay attention to the following facts, especially toward the end of the effective playing time:

1. The clearer their point advantage is, the earlier they should attempt to extend the duration of rallies using a high pass and set. However, this should not be done at the cost of reduced effectiveness.
2. In contrast, if they are trailing, they should shorten the rallies through preferably fast passes and lower sets. Again, this strategy should not lead to a reduction of their playing effectiveness.
3. Especially if only a few seconds of playing time remain on the rally clock, the player should try to induce the sideout by an attack *on two*. Additionally, this should be done even by playing the first pass directly into the opponent's court.

These delay- or speed-up tactics should only be used no earlier than with a remaining effective playing time of less than one minute.

In the tie-break as well as in the final phase of matches with a rally-clock, the reception strategies should not be changed if previously during the course of the match, direct reception mistakes were hardly made.

If, on the contrary, many direct mistakes have been committed, the reception strategy should be changed with an increase in the tendency to make a good first pass, rather than always pursuing the perfect beach volleyball pass.

Safety-receptions may be played if the receiving player is attacking effectively.

8.2.1 GENERAL STEPS FOR THE RECEPTION STRATEGY

The following explanations represent basic measurements, complete the already explained steps and partially discuss individual-tactical aspects:

1. With respect to the receiving player's individual tactics, the team's own psycho-physical condition as well as the set and match score or the time remaining shall be considered.

2. The willingness to take risks during reception could be consciously decreased,
    –   following unforced errors,
    –   following mistakes made by one's partner,
    –   after time-outs/ "sand" interruptions,
    –   for the reception of effective/ potent serves,
    –   in case of follow-up-mistakes during the attack,

3. Individual-tactical behavior with respect only to the server and the passer, can be very effective:
    –   Through his position, visual contact or signals, a player who currently feels mentally strong, will offer a gap or area to the server in order to make him unsure. This could also make him change his original strategy as well as to force him to commit faults.
    –   After and before reception and especially following good receptions, the receiver should show the opponent his strength. Following mistakes, he should act "unphased".

4. In every situation, the receiver must take into account fakes by the server. For example a change of the serve's depth and/or direction, executed by a not observable wrist-motion.

5. Particularly, in the case where there were only a few preceding passing actions, a very good receiver must be attentive. This will allow the player to avoid being surprised by a change in the opponent's service strategy or by a surprise-serve at him.

6. The reception strategy does not start with the first serve, but before warm-up. The players should get used to the external conditions of their designated match-court early.

To sum everything up, it must be emphasized, that there are not many reception strategies and that they mostly have an individual-tactical character. Apart from that, there is a strong connection between the reception and the attack strategy: All the above mentioned explanations are to be seen in the context of the service strategy and with the explanations in chapter 5, reception and serve situation.

8.3   SET AND ATTACK STRATEGIES

The setting strategies are affiliated with the attack strategies and together they are represented as one unit. This is one of the decisive factors the beach volleyball player must take into consideration. The setting player does not only execute the set, but also influences or, sometimes, **determines** the attacker's actions through the use of calls. In the end, a setting strategy does not exist since the setter has the **obligation to play the perfect set** according to his partner's attacking abilities in every situation. Consequently, the explanations in chapter 6 are largely authoritative for this unit. However, further considerations are given here, since the set is the most important prerequisite for the execution of the attack strategies. The analysis of one's own team includes the following observation aspects with respect to the attack strategy:

1. The individual-tactical abilities of the setter, especially seen under the aspect of technical abilities,
2. individual-tactical abilities of the attacker,
3. team-tactical abilities in all options of the attack build-up.

The analysis of the opponent must specifically include (see also the explanations on player observation, chapter 9):

1. The players' individual tactics as blocker and backcourt defender,
2. the possible specialization in the block and backcourt defense-situation,
3. the analysis of the defending team's actions before and during the set and the attack,

4. a detailed analysis of the opponent's blocker, with respect to:

    (1) The strategy-concept:
- if the block is always up in cases of good and medium quality sets,
- if the fake block is used even in the case of a good set,
- if the blocking strategy, with respect to the zone block, is often or rarely changed,

    (2) The execution of the technique:
- if the player blocks over and penetrates the plane of the net immediately or if he blocks rather unaggressively,
- if the blocker blocks the *ball* more than actually covering an *area* from the attacker,
- if the blocking player often uses the spread, resp. split block,
- if the blocking player jumps very late,
- if the opponents show technical mistakes and if so, which mistakes. Specifically, the arm and hand-position should be observed.

    (3) The athletic abilities, especially with respect to the transition ability, for example.:
- from the block to self-coverage action,
- from block to set,
- from touched balls to attack,
- the anthropometric preconditions.
- The detection of early fatigue should be emphasized.

    (4) Performance actions rooted in mental stress, especially after successful actions, failure, or follow-up actions:
- Will the blocker change his performance or behavior if the attacker is frequently hitting past him?

For the **setter's individual tactics**, more factors and features are important:

1. The knowledge of one's partner's strengths, weaknesses, and peculiarities with respect to his offensive performance.
2. The knowledge of one's own technical abilities in order to provide the optimum set for one's partner according to a certain situation.
3. The setter's ability to observe the opponents' backcourt defender's moves and performance directly following the set. This allows the setter to anticipate the optimum attack action sequence and to inform the attacker about best attacking direction, right before the spike.

4. The ability to analyze and interpret the set and attack action, thereby figuring out to what extent, for example, an effective attack may be traced either to his call or to technical/ tactical mistakes by the opponent.
5. The ability to assign successful set actions to different game situations in order to be able to repeat them during similar situations.
6. The knowledge of one's partner's abilities with respect to his speed and coordinative abilities, especially during the transition from pass to attack and from backcourt defense to attack.
7. The ability to perceive the position of the defenders using peripheral vision, during the first pass and just prior to the set. One can take advantage of this skill, by using a setter's trick attack or an attack *on two*.

The setter's "art" or skill is to select the one feature from many observations and influencing features that promises to be the most success in an actual situation.

Apart from all that has been mentioned above, it is important for the **attacker's individual tactics** to know about the technical, tactical and athletic abilities of the blocker and the backcourt defender.

1. If the blocker is not as athletic, a close set should be played and subsequently hit past him or simply over and across him.
2. If the blocking player has technical/ tactical deficiencies, such as for example, a late penetration, sweeping hand/arm movements during the jump, or a landing location that is far away from the takeoff location ("flying blocker"), the attacker should spike either very early or very late.
3. An attacker should always be analyzing the backcourt defender's characteristic moves *before* and *after* his attack action. This is done in order to be able to consider these observations in similar set and attack situations.

The following examples illustrate set and attack strategies:

1. The blocking player acts using an aggressive zone block, the attacker should try to hit hard past him or he should use tactical shots, especially trick attacks and poke shots (Fig. 46a).
2. If the blocker uses the fake block, the attacker should spike a hard-driven ball right in front of the backwards moving blocker, a hard-driven ball between the two defending players or a shot across and beyond blocker (Fig. 46b).
3. If the court defender has a weaker defensive side hard-driven balls should preferably be hit into this area.
4. If the net player uses a passive block, the ball should be hit off the blocker's outside hand (Fig. 46c).

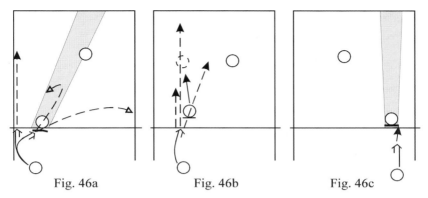

| Fig. 46a | Fig. 46b | Fig. 46c |

In general, the following hints for the attacker's individual tactical actions can be given:

1. A successful attacking tactic or a successful hit should only be changed if the blocking player and the backcourt defender adjust and therefore improve their play from one situation to the next situation and thereby increase their chances to defend an attack.
2. At the beginning of the game, very hard-driven spikes may be played in order to demonstrate strength and superiority.
3. In critical situations, to use a very well-mastered but deliberately rarely used spiking variation is highly recommended.

Recently it has been observed that the attacking team uses observers or, "spies" behind the opponent's court. These spies will show and try to betray the blocker's hand signals to the attacker. Ultimately, this is not fair yet very efficient, each team should be attentive and look out for such spies. Additionally, the signals should be changed from match to match or even better, the strategy should be discussed shortly before each serve. This is always done within the rules' limits.

All the explanations regarding the set and attack strategy are directly connected to the subsequent block and backcourt defensive strategies

8.4 DEFENSIVE STRATEGIES

The defensive strategies concern the block and backcourt defensive actions and must be regarded and trained as a team tactical action in order to be successful. The knowledge of the setter's and attacker's tendencies and performances is critically important for successful court defense. The communication between blocker and backcourt defender is an absolute prerequisite for successful defense. Every block and backcourt defensive strategy is primarily based on one's own strengths, and secondarily based on special consideration of the opponent's set and attack strengths and weaknesses.

In beach volleyball, the service strategy eventually implies the block and defensive tactics, since the attacker can almost always be determined by the person the serve goes to.

Therefore, individual player observations with respect to reception, set and attack, are essential for the development of one's own block and backcourt defensive strategy. Concerning one's own team's analysis the following observation points must be focused on and paid attention to:

- The technical-tactical and physical-mental characteristics of both players. Differing blocking and backcourt defensive qualities, may lead to a specialization in defense.
- A detailed analysis of the players in block and defense.

The opponent analysis refers to the following main observation aspects (see also chapter 9, player observation and chapter 8.1, serve strategies):

1. Strengths and weaknesses of the receivers also with respect to their transition qualities from the block to the attack (see chapter 9.2).
2. Analysis of the setter's tendencies and performance (see chapter 8.3).
3. Detailed observation of the players' qualities and effectivness as attackers, including attacking direction (see chapter 9.2).
4. The co-operation of both players in the reception and attack situation.

In general, teams and players may be classified into three different categories, according to their preferred types of attack:

1. Players/ teams who primarily prefer to use tactical shots. Here, the backcourt defender should act from a medium-low to high posture from the court's center (Fig. 47a).

2. Players/ teams who mainly prefer to hit hard-driven spikes. Against these players/ teams, the blocker must take

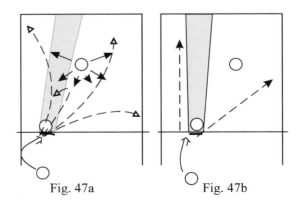

Fig. 47a   Fig. 47b

212

blocker must take away the main hitting direction and the backcourt defender should cover the larger, unscreened area from a medium-low to very low posture (Fig. 47b).

3. Players/ teams use of both types of attacks almost equally. As a counter-strategy, an alternation or an occasional change between the above mentioned strategic measures is recommended.

For the backcourt defender, the following factors with respect to his individual tactical decisions apply:

1. The currently determined **blocking strategy,**
2. **knowledge** of the preferred attacking directions and tendencies of the receiving attacker,
3. the quality of the **setting action** with respect to spacial relation between the ball and attacker as well as that between the ball and the net as well,
4. his anticipatory ability, especially regarding the attacker's arm swing,
5. his ability to **suspect** changes in the opponent's attack tactics,
6. his reaction time and speed of motion, along with the situation and rules regarding the use of any defensive techniques.

By giving selected examples which are similar to real-life situations, the following steps specifically take, yet simplified, the frequency of attack locations along with the attack directions into account. Here, it shall be emphasized once more, that communication between the blocker and backcourt defender takes place prior to each serve and each defensive action:

1. Player A often attacks deep over and beyond the block into the area screened by the block (Fig. 48a):
   - The blocker should jump as late as possible.
   - The blocker should use the fake block and back off from the net toward backcourt defense.
   - The backcourt defender fakes a defense in the unscreened area, but actually defends the screened area, in motion.

2. Player B spikes hard in prolongation of his approaching direction (Fig. 48b):
   - Directly before the ball is hit by the attacker, the blocker covers the main hitting direction and the court defender covers the larger uncovered area.

3. Player A mainly attacks hard and diagonally (Fig. 48c):
   - The blocker takes away the cross-court at the last moment.
   - The court defender takes over the longline-area.

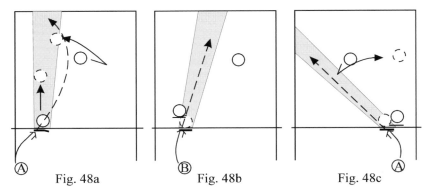

Fig. 48a   Fig. 48b   Fig. 48c

4. Player B mainly spikes down the line (Fig. 49a):
   - The blocker will show the attacker, that he is either taking cross-court - he will change his blocking direction to a longline-block shortly before the attacker contacts the ball (1) - or
   - the block player uses the fake block (2).
   - The backcourt defender covers the unscreened area.

5. Player A mainly uses tactical shots to the opposite of his approach direction (Fig. 49b):
   - The blocker jumps very late and the backcourt defender acts, at the moment of the opposing setter's call, toward the defensive area which is opposite of the attacker's approaching direction.

6. If the balls are set close and therefore cause more attacks with wrist action and rotation, toward the extreme cross-court, both players will defend the cross-court (Fig. 49c).

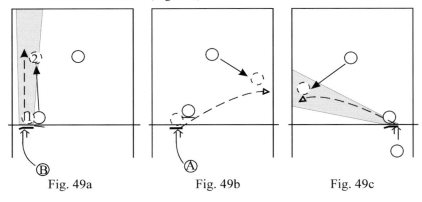

Fig. 49a   Fig. 49b   Fig. 49c

7. From difficult reception situations, under time pressure, player A attacks exclusively very hard in prolongation of his approaching direction (Fig. 50a):
   - The court defender acts in the cross-court and
   - the blocker, fakes the block, as well defending the backcourt.

8. In case of good sets, player B attacks with tactical shots (Fig. 50b) and in case of bad sets he attacks with hard-driven spikes (Fig. 50c):
   - In the first case, the blocker should initiate his block very late and the backcourt defender should take the rear of the covered area or the extreme cross-court following a fake move (Fig. 50b).
   - In the second case, the blocker should take the main hitting direction. Accordingly, the court defender should cover the edges of the blocking screen (Fig. 50c).

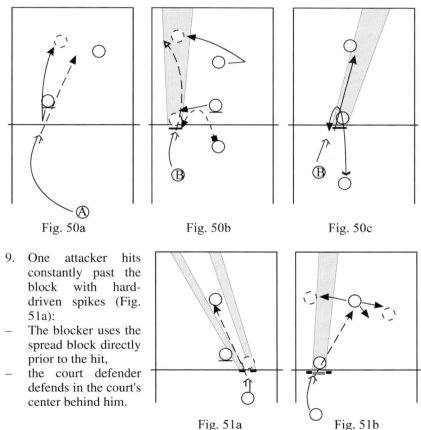

Fig. 50a   Fig. 50b   Fig. 50c

9. One attacker hits constantly past the block with hard-driven spikes (Fig. 51a):
   - The blocker uses the spread block directly prior to the hit,
   - the court defender defends in the court's center behind him.

Fig. 51a   Fig. 51b

10. The attacker acts very variably, but mostly past the block (Fig. 51b):
   - The blocker should fake the spread block and change the split arm position into an aggressive zone block directly before the ball is hit.
   - The court defender makes his own decision as to the size of the zone not covered by the block.

11. One player uses trick attacks or poke shots in critical game situations:
   - The blocker should jump earlier to have an increased chance to save the ball through a self-coverage, or
   - very late in order to be able to hit back a not perfectly executed poke during his blocking action.

In the following, generally valid aspects, specifically characterized by individual tactical considerations, are discussed in keywords:

- During the game, the blocker, as well as the backcourt defender, must especially recognize and analyze the attackers characteristics in order to develop new and different strategies.
- The same applies to the observation of the opponents' mental and physical condition.
- A block jump initiated either too early or too late, can possibly make the attacker feel unsure. The same applies for the fake block.
- During the landing, the ball should be observed. The landing itself should enable the player to take a ready posture from which he may take his next action.
- During the execution of the fake block, the net player should **always** keep visual contact with the **attacker and the ball**.
- Prior to an attack, the backcourt defender never acts very far to the back, but rather more closely to the net, ready to dig hard-driven balls over shoulder level.
- Holding on to a defensive strategy makes the attack strategy for the opponent easy. Therefore, strategy variations are necessary and tactically useful.
- After long rallies and during critical game situations, it can be observed that the attackers will usually execute their normally most successful spike.
- After a successful block, a different attacking direction or attacking variation must be expected.
- In case of inaccurate sets, the predetermined blocking strategy should be changed:
   - if the ball is set close to the net, the blocker must block *the ball*,
   - if the ball is set farther off from the net, the blocker should back off to play backcourt defense.

- If an attacker is not hitting very hard, but often hitting off of the block, it is recommended that one pulls the arms back almost at the moment of his hit or to take the cross-court and to have the longline-area be covered by the backcourt defender.
- A one-arm-block will only be useful if the blocker is late. This would happen, for example, because of a misread *close* set while he was already backing off for a fake block.
- If an attacker hits down the line and "out of bounds", the blocker should cover the cross-court on the next attack.
- When executing the fake block, the cross-court should preferably be defended and the line-area be neglected. This court defensive formation applies even more to balls set further than 2 m from the net (not similar to a down-ball-situation).
- After an opponent's time-out, a new offensive strategy must be expected.
- In case of a bad reception or a down-ball-situation, the court defender moves toward his receiving and attacking half of the court.
- In the case of frequent and effective setter's trick attacks, the backcourt defender may reorientate himself slightly closer to the endangered defensive area during the first pass. Following the set, he must quickly take his starting position at the court's center.
- The higher the opposing attacker's action height, the more forward the court defender should take his position.
- If the attacking spot is located outside of the antenna, the court defender must move to the extreme cross-court while the blocker tries to deflect the ball toward the base line, while not penetrating the plane of the net.
- After a long rally, especially one that has been lost, one should try to create or even fake some kind of game interruption. This could be done by pushing the game rule's limits. For example, one could call "sand", although a sand-break might not really be necessary at that moment.
- If the defending team realizes, that the opposing team is receiving substantial information with respect to that team's own blocking strategy through the use of spies, and if the spy can not be removed, then there are three counter-strategies which can be employed. These, of course, will have to be practiced and tested:

1. The communication takes place after the serve or shortly before the blocking action.
2. The signs will receive a different meaning. A finger pointing downwards does no longer mean zone-block longline, instead it would then be designated as a cross-court block etc.
3. The third step is easier to execute: The players discuss the block strategy shortly before each serve, so that they will use signals only during the course of complex 2.

The explanations in chapter 7 with respect to individual tactics of the blocker and backcourt defender, must be seen in a conjunction with the theories regarding block and backcourt defensive strategies - specifically the motion and action sequences of the blocker and the backcourt player, as well as the action sequences leading to the block and backcourt defense. The transition situation, 'attack from defense', should be observed in more detail.

Photo 73

9 BEACH VOLLEYBALL PLAYER OBSERVATION

Interviews show, that so far, only casual and unsystematic observation has exclusively been used. Especially, at the US-professional level, this is incomprehensible, when taken into consideration, that the prize money has already reached denominations of up to 300.000 $.

It may clearly be recognized, that the professionalisation so far only applies to well planned training. With respect to preparation for a match against a certain opponent, the professionalisation has remained at an **amateur level**. When considering the development of beach volleyball as an Olympic sport and the fact, that teams are surely trained/ coached in the near future, and given the importance of player observation in indoor volleyball, it can be concluded, that player observation methods for beach volleyball will be developed and soon be integrated into training and competition.

To be able to control the training, game or competition successfully, one must combine an analysis and discussion of player observation, every time. Eventually, the optimization of training and competition performance can only take place with a planned and systematic observation of the individual and team tactics. Every player and game observation from one's own as well as the opposing team aims at the detecting and filtering a team's strengths and weaknesses.

An unsystematic or casual observation, most of the time will lead to unprovable and accidental results. This is presently common in beach volleyball and must be **rejected** for the upper national and international performance levels.

At middle and lower performance levels, the observation of one's own team should have priority in order to specifically reduce one's own weaknesses through training. The game of beach volleyball is even more suited for player and game observation than indoor volleyball, since it consists almost exclusively of standardized situations and only two players must be analyzed. Several reasons promise success concerning the use of player observation:

a)   the execution of player observation does not take much time,
b)   the 'to be expected' professionalisation, of a beach volleyball-team's entourage, with the addition of a **coach, scout**, physical therapist etc.

The detection and notation of the performance determining factors of that respective performance level is a necessity for the successful use and application of each observation. Furthermore, a critical prerequisite for observing an opponent is, that a team may dispose of alternative strategies in attack and defense and that the players have learnt to apply these counter-strategies effectively during training as well as in test-competitions. Here, the following principles apply:

- The appropriate observation method has to be chosen and used.
- A critical precondition is the correct choice of performance-determining factors.
- The number and type of observation criteria or categories depends on the respective level of performance and on the rating/ evaluation of the certain observed features.
- Counter-strategies must be developed, practiced and used during training and during the match.
- Every strategy will attempt to emphasize one's own strengths by taking advantage of the opponent's weaknesses or rather, by suppressing his strengths by hiding or neutralizing one's own weaknesses.
- A precondition for the successful execution of each strategy is the correct evaluation of the team's own individual- and team-tactical abilities, especially at the mental and technical-tactical level. If it is easier to be applied, the second best measure should be used prior to the best.
- Each team at the international level, and later at the national top-level, should have a scout/ game-analyst, who is accepted by both players and by the trainer/ coach. If such a scout/ game-analyst is not available, the co-trainer or the coach must take over this function themselves, as much as possible.
- The players must be trained systematically on a long-term basis and thereby be enabled to convert action-hints/ instructions, coaching measures and counter-strategies into effective play.
- Both players' must contribute their share to the observation analysis and the development of counter-strategies. This must be demanded and supported in order to favor a success-promising execution of the counter strategies. Players are more likely to be able to identify themselves with decisions made by them.
- The players must be trained systematically to read observation results, to interpret them and, if given, to analyze video footage on their own.
- Counter-strategies may only be successful if they are theoretically understood, accepted and intensively worked on in practice.
- The players' training must always be seen as a continuos process. Measures successfully tested against very weak opponents should therefore basically apply to the next stronger opponent.
- With an increased level of performance, the game observation is gaining significance.
- The player or game observation is an essential for the coach in order to

1. organize his team's training more efficiently,
2. be able to optimize the match and therefore competition control,
3. be able to control and compare training performance with competition performance,
4. have the possibility to confront a player without prejudice and more objectively,
5. control his own strategies with regard to their effectivness.

– The validity of the single observation depends on the following factors:

1. The more of the opponent's games are analyzed, the more reliable the results will be;
2. the more important, harder fought and longer an observed game is, the more valid the registered data will be;
3. the more of the opponent's games have been analyzed, the larger the probability to detect his strategies in all situations and therefore know and expect an opponent's counter-strategy. Accordingly, one's own counter-strategy can be determined more precisely.

Other than the systematic game and player observation, the collection of more information about the opponents, such as for example the players' relation to each other, aversions, competition related behavior etc., is of enormous significance in beach volleyball.
This information can lead to simple, but effective counter-strategies, especially if the information is confirmed through the video analysis. Information can be collected through the media, rumors and by talks among trainers and players. Accordingly, information about one's own team should not be given to other players/ coaches.

In the following, knowledge and methods of the indoor volleyball player observation will be modified and transferred to the beach volleyball game. This chapter shall represent the first step in this direction, which has already been proven effective indoors and successfully been employed in a few beach volleyball tournaments as well. If more than one scout/ observer is available, the observation tasks shall be further divided and the results shall be registered depending even more on the preceding and the subsequent action.
The player observation during competition shall be done in written and in graphic form as well as by videotaping the match.

> The goal of a professional beach volleyball team shall be **to set up a cardfile** for each beach volleyball player and for teams which often play together. The data should be with respect his/ her/ their strengths and weaknesses in all situations of play and it should be compiled through video observations.

For the single player, this step is important, as well since many players do not have a constant partner. Instead, they shift partners from tournament to tournament. At the professional level, this tendency will not change in the long run. At the national top-level and in international tournaments (World Series) the prohibition of a partner change during a single season can be expected in the near future.

With respect to video footage, it is important to first note the daytime and the weather conditions in order to be able to interpret the player's/ team's actions depending on the weather.
If a team has not done any player observation, the players should analyze an opponent using written player observation during the game. If the team has a scout/ game-observer, he should observe the next opponent, especially if the players are playing, recovering or being treated by a physical therapist.

Photo 74

PLAYER: *Bruk*

SERVE:

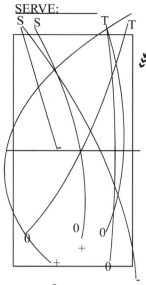

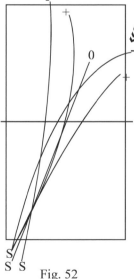

Fig. 52

9.1 OBSERVATION AND NOTATION OF THE SERVER'S TENDENCIES

Here, the observation must specifically take the external conditions into consideration by clearly distinguishing the player's actions on the "good" side of the court from the actions on the "bad" side. The following information about the server should be noted in written form.

- His preferred serve,
- if he prefers longline or cross-court serves,
- if the skyball is used,
- if he varies deep and short serves,
- if it can be noticed that he is using a strategy where the majority of serves are hit to a certain player,
- if a special serve is preferred in critical situations,
- if he changes his serve after one or two service-faults.

The service location behind the baseline and the touchdown-spot of the ball shall be graphically connected by a continuous line (Fig. 52). At the touchdown-spot, the effectivness of the serve will be rated using a "+", "0" or "-". In order to graphically note the type of the serve, jump serves will be denoted with a "J", the float serve with an "F", the spin serve with an "S" and the skyball with an arched line. It is necessary to prepare two drawings for each player for each side of the court, each drawing is marked with an arrow for the showing of the current wind direction (see Fig. 52). For the notation of the game's actions of a score of above ten points, the graphic representations shall be highlighted with a red pen.

9.2 OBSERVATION AND NOTATION OF THE RECEIVING ATTACKERS

> The observation of the players in the passing and attacking situation must have absolute priority above any other game observation.

Therefore, in cases where there are too many overburdening demands on a single scout/ observer, he should concentrate exclusively on this situation. The game observation should be done graphically with additional written remarks on the player's tendencies. For the observation sheet, the following principles apply:

1. The following areas with respect to the single player's reception will be noted: To the sides, in front, to the side and backwards, to the side and forwards of the body and at the players body. These reception areas are illustrated in Fig. 53. The dividing lines are usually not featured on the observation sheet, they are only shown in order to illustrate the areas more clearly. Zone A is in front of the player, B is on the lateral front right, C is on the lateral backward right, D is behind/at the player, E is on the lateral backwards left, and F is on the lateral front left. Here, reception in the various zones shall again be rated using a 3-category quality scale consisting of "+", "0" and "-". The assignment of a grade to one of the zones is done at the moment of reception. This means that if a player moves forward to receive the ball 3 m in front of his original position, it will be noted as a reception in front of him.

   The player's tendencies should also be noted in written form. For example, if a receiving player is more or less effective passing a certain jump serve or if he shows deficiencies during the attack or after a reception in the rear part of the backcourt, resulting in a long approach.

   Fig. 53 shows that the player, "Tim" has a strong receiving side on the right and that he has the most difficulties with balls on his left side, and behind him. However, he shows no distinct weaknesses on his "good" side.

   Furthermore, the attacking directions are registered along with the effectivness of the attacking action. The effectivness is noted at the touchdown spot or the location where the spike is defended. Straight lines indicate a hard-driven spike, arched lines the indicate trick attacks or tactical shots (see Fig. 53).

   Fig. 53 clearly shows, that player "Tim" rarely plays poke shots and hard-driven balls toward the extreme cross-court. He mostly plays tactical shots. From these results one could infer that the court defender must be ready to run down far reaching tactical hits.

RECEPTION - ATTACK

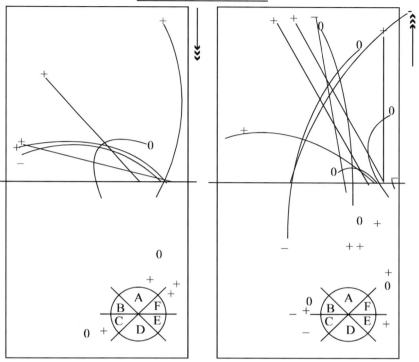

Fig. 53

2. The passer's attacking actions are noted on the same sheet, but without recording the approach. The action sequence of reception-attack, whose analysis can lead to very decisive interpretations in beach volleyball, must be recorded in written form by the observer. The action's effectiveness is also noted (Fig. 54).

In the left column, the reception-quality is registered, in the center column the setting-quality and in the right column the quality of attacking actions. In the right column, the attack is classified by applying the letters "T" for a tactical hit, "S" for a smash and "F" for a fake resp. trick attack. A dot (.) beside a letter means that the attack takes place without a block.

Pass Quality	Set Quality	Attack Effectivity	Type
+	+	+	S
0	0	0	F
0	+	+	T
+	+	+	T.
+	+	+	T
+	+	+	T

Pass Quality	Set Quality	Attack Effectivity	Type
+ 0	+	+	S
+ +	+	+	S.
0	+	+	T
-	+	0	T
-	0	0	T
-	0	0	F
0	0	0	F
+	+	-	F
+	+	+	S.
+	0	-	S
-			

Fig. 54

The **action sequence** (Fig. 54) might show,

1. whether a player executes tactical shots only following poor receptions and poor sets,
2. whether the attacker mostly attacks hard after a good set,
3. whether the attacker executes hard spikes only when the block is not up,
4. whether the attacker hits hard into the cross-court, only in critical or stressful situations ,
5. if the trick attack (poke shot) is only used after a good set etc.

9.3 OBSERVATION AND NOTATION OF THE BLOCK- AND BACKCOURT-DEFENSE

Here, a written observation will primarily concern itself with the following aspects:

1. The team's possible specialization in this situation of play.
2. Strengths and weaknesses of the blocking player,
    -   if he always blocks aggressively (penetrates),
    -   or mostly passively,
    -   if he usually does not change his blocking direction,
    -   if he usually takes another direction at the moment of the hit,
    -   if he covers the extreme cross-court using a slanting jump,
    -   if he uses the fake block often,
    -   if he uses the spread (split) block often,
    -   if he delays his takeoff severely,

- if he is successful in his self-coverage,
- if he holds on to, or changes his blocking direction in either one of the main blocking locations,
- the quality of the setting action following the defense.

3. Strengths, weaknesses and tendencies of the backcourt defender,
   - if his starting position already reveals his intended subsequent actions,
   - if he mostly fakes moves to the right in order to subsequently reorientate himself to the left,
   - which is his stronger defensive side,
   - if he often defends the ball directly toward the opponents court,
   - if he acts less successfully with certain techniques,
   - if he acts better while defending either hard-driven balls or shots,
   - if he is quickly and effectively able to execute his approach following a save in the deep backcourt ,
   - if he mostly acts outside of the block screen, rather preparing himself for hard-driven balls etc. (see Fig. 55).

For an analyst registering of all the above mentioned observations the following procedure is recommended. The analyst observes the player's service actions as well as blocking and backcourt defensive actions on one sheet. This is done by **keeping** the serve-observations **in mind** and not recording until the conclusion of the rally, **after** he has registered his observations of the blocker's and backcourt defender's tendencies

Photo 75

On the next sheet, the notation of the reception and attack situation proceeds in a similar way. He keeps track of the reception location, the quality of the reception and the quality of the set in mind. First, he marks down only the direction of the attack and its effectiveness. Subsequently, he records the reception location and the qualities in the action sequence. This requires a systematic education of the observer, over the course of several matches employing videotape as well as notation of a live match. (Following pages: Fig. 56, sample sheet A+B).

BLOCK: *Spezialized*

aggressive angle 0
aggressive angle 0
Fake 0
Fake +
Fake -
aggressive angle -
aggressive angle +
Spread 0, self-coverage +
aggressive angle 0, set -
passive, extreme angle, late 0
aggressive angle -
aggressive angle -
Fake -
Fake 0
Fake +
Fake 0, set -

BACKCOURT DEFENSE:

- after Fake
- after Fake
+ down-ball, subsequent attack +
+ after Fake

Photo 76   Fig. 55

PLAYER: *Bruk*

Serve:

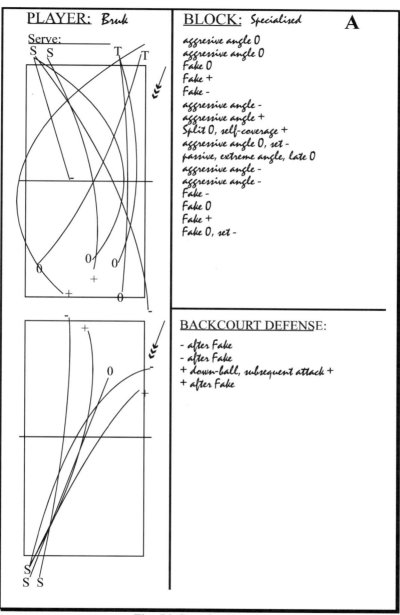

BLOCK: *Specialised*   **A**

aggressive angle 0
aggressive angle 0
Fake 0
Fake +
Fake -
aggressive angle -
aggressive angle +
Split 0, self-coverage +
aggressive angle 0, set -
passive, extreme angle, late 0
aggressive angle -
aggressive angle -
Fake -
Fake 0
Fake +
Fake 0, set -

BACKCOURT DEFENSE:

- after Fake
- after Fake
+ down-ball, subsequent attack +
+ after Fake

Fig. 56: Sample sheet A

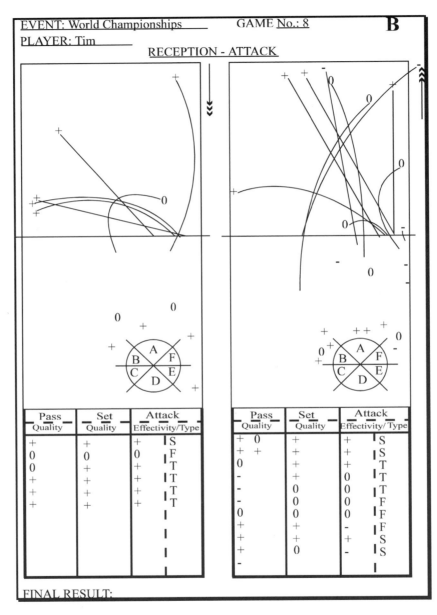

Fig. 56: Sample Sheet B

PART 3: SPECIAL ASPECTS OF PLANNING AND ORGANIZATION OF TRAINING

10   THE PROFESSIONALS´ OPINION ON TRAINING

Nine US top players and one coach were interviewed. The interviews were compiled in 1991. All showed, that they **systematically planned their training** and that they did so ranging from the whole year to certain periods of a season as well as for single weeks. LINDA CARILLO, PAT ZARTMAN and PATTY DODD underline the fact, that there were only a few full-time female professionals and that therefore, the training volume was reduced, when compared to male pros.

In the second part of the interview, the players were questioned about the **contents and methods of training during the transition, preparation and competition period**. With respect to contents and intensity, the answers are

so different, that they could not have been classified into a few categories. Therefore, the basic statements of each player have been summarized:

KATHY GREGORY has been a beach volleyball player for more than 20 years. In 1974 she won her first tournament. As of 1990 she has not been playing in professional tournaments. Since then, she has been a television tournament announcer. She is also the coach of the women's volleyball team of the University of California at Santa Barbara.

Photo 77:
Kathy Gregory

Kathy Gregory states, that most players based in California, keep up their training during the *transition period* at a full level. There is no real training break for these players. Players not based in California, are forced to reduce ball training. She explained that players try to build up an athletic basis during winter. An important aspect of training in the *transition and preparation period* would be strength training. Players, moreover, train their endurance base. The training methods of choice were the stairmaster, the jumprope and running.

Concerning the competition period, she explained that most players, as far as she knew, were executing ball-training which would combine drills and training matches. She further explained that players were also working with trainers to help in conditioning during the season.

MIKE DODD has been a beach volleyball professional since 1983. He has mainly played together with partner Tim Hovland. Apart from Smith/ Stoklos, they were the most successful team in the 80´s with more than 60 wins to date. He won the beach volleyball world championship four times and was also a member of the American indoor national team.

Mike Dodd explained, that he would begin intensive strength training directly *after the conclusion of the season*. He first employed the method of repeated submaximum contractions This refers to methods whose main

Photo 78: Mike Dodd

effect is to develop muscle cross-section. He underlined, that he would not play any volleyball from the end of September until January and that he would stay in shape by playing basketball and golf. Starting in January, he would begin strength training methods which would aim at mainly intramuscular-coordinative effects. Additionally, he would try to play beach-volleyball for 4-5 hours a day. Dodd explained, that during the season, he would replace the strength training using weights with "leaner" methods using only his body weight, for example push-ups. For the jump training he would use a machine in which he would jump against the resistance of a bicycle tube or other rubber bands. Until April, his ball training consisted of 4-5 training matches daily, similar to the preparation phase. Starting in April, he would play no more than three times a week, and from July on, he would reduce the ball training to 1-2 weekly units.

The former Colombian national player **PATTY DODD** played for the University of California at Los Angeles and as a professional in Italy, before she became a beach volleyball professional in the US. Since 1988 she has

Photo 79: Patty Dodd

Photo 80: Jon Stevenson

belonged to the most successful players. In 1989 she and partner Jackie Silva made up the best female beach volleyball team.

Patty Dodd, has also explained, that she would begin with strength and endurance training in September, in order to build up an athletic basis. She would undergo strength training 90 minutes a day from October to December, using strength-endurance methods (methods which increase the anaerobic local and overall muscle endurance). She would set a high value on endurance training using the stairmaster. She explained that she would finish the strength training by February and then start with ball-training. During the season, she would employ strength training with light weights, and, additionally, would regularly receive physical therapy treatment. Her ball training would consist exclusively of training matches.

JON STEVENSON has been the AVP's president since 1986. He is the author of the beach volleyball book "Hot Sand" and with 25 tournament wins, he is one of the most successful players of the last ten years.

Jon Stevenson explained, that he emphasized strength training *during the transition and preparation period*. He would undergo strength training two times a week, at which he would use the repeated submaximum contraction method in the first unit and methods of maximum contractions in the second unit. He underlined that although he would occasionally run short distances in the sand, he is of the opinion that special training for basic endurance is wrong. Concerning the *competition period*, Stevenson explained that he preferred drills in ball-training. He emphasized, that he practiced match elements in exercises, and that he would then include these elements in his play. During the season he would also maintain, his already mentioned strength training.

LINDA CARILLO was a member of the American national team at the Olympic games in 1984. She became a beach volleyball professional three years later. She was the WPVA'S president until April 1993. In 1987 and 1988, she was the most successful player. In 1990 she won the American national and the World Championships.

Linda Carillo explained, that she used the first six weeks *after the season* as a break. During that time, she would just run and do some weight control. After that *transition period*, she would begin with ball-training over the weekend. Additionally, the building-up of an endurance basis was one of her training goals. Three times a week she would use a weight belt as her preferred training tool. She underlined that she tried to keep up her endurance by short-distance running. She would not tend to emphasize too much towards strength training. She

Photo 81: Linda Carillo

thinks that the sand's soft surface would support her jumping ability to a satisfactory level. She would maintain the level of training for an athletic basis until the *beginning of the season*. In March, she would intensify the ball training. It would consist of exercise forms and training matches. *During the season* she would practice three times a week. The volume and duration of the week's first training would depend on the tournament results of the preceding weekend. If she would have come off badly, a large training-volume on Monday would be the consequence. During her training matches, she would concentrate on the improvement of some elements of her play, besides, she would also use drills.

PAT ZARTMAN is a personal coach for many female beach-volleyball players. With his help, many players have for the first time systematically prepared themselves for tournaments. He has worked, with Linda Carillo, Janice Opalinski-Harrer and Jackie Silva, among others.
Pat Zartman explained the training he uses with for training group during the *transition and preparation* period:
After a two-month break following the end of the season, wherein he would have no influence on the players´ training, he would start with a preparation

period consisting of three stages. During the first two-month stage, sprints with a weight-vest represent the majority of training. He described his so-called "on and off" training methods, as follows. Directly following a sprint wearing a weight vest, the players repeat the same sprint without the vest. The running patterns resemble the patterns found during a match. This sprint training would begin with a series at the beginning of the preparation period and be increased to six series during the following weeks. The players would practice over two hours, three times a week. In the second and third stages, ball-training would become more and more focused upon. During the third stage, the amount of the described endurance training, would be reduced by 50%. The ball-training would then mainly consist of drills.

Zartman explained that the players of his training group would then only try to maintain their endurance level *during the season*. Special strength, endurance or speed training would therefore only be undertaken in a reduced form. The players would train three times a week for four hours. The first half of the training would be exclusively used for special endurance training as well as for ball training with drills. Subsequently, the women would play games for two hours.

Photo 82: Kent Steffes

KENT STEFFES has been a beach volleyball professional since 1989. Since 1993 he is ranked as the No. 1 AVP player. Since 1992 he won the vast majority of tournaments, with his partner Karch Kiraly.

Steffes explained, that his *season preparation* would begin five weeks after the season's conclusion and that he would stay fit during the *transition period* through participation in other sports.

Steffes reported that he would start a four month *preparation period*, in November, which is split into four stages. The strength training would represent a major part of the training during all the phases. He would undergo strength training three times a week, choosing exercises in such a manner that he would never have to do the same exercise during two subsequent units. During the first four-week stage, he would start with lower loads and lower volumes. The second four-week period would be characterized by an increase in the training volume. The number of series would be increased to 8-10. Apart from that, the number of repetitions during a single series would be increased using the pyramid method (strength training intermediate method, with affecting intramuscular coordination, as well as increasing of the muscle cross section). During the next two stages he would use the maximum contractions method. Steffes explained that he would change either training method, as soon as no further increase of the maximum strength could be achieved. The weights used in strength training at the end of the preparation period would be the appropriate loads for his season-strength training.

Steffes explained that he would undergo additional intensive combination training of endurance and speed during the preparation period. From week to week he would increase the running distances and the running speed. He would run or sprint 16 times per training over distances of 100 to 400 meters. At the end of the preparation period, he would combine the jogged and sprinted distances to an interval training or a combination of slow and faster running as well as sprints. The ball training during the preparation period would mainly consist of drills.

Steffes said that *during the season*, he would perform an intensive training of strength, speed and endurance as well. The ball training would then consist of training matches. When asked why he would not use exercise forms during the season, he answered that it would probably be impossible to find training partners who would want to drill with him instead of playing games.

STEVE TIMMONS: The volleyball professional has also been playing professionally indoors in Italy. He was a regular player on the US national team's roster until the 1992 Olympic games. He won two Olympic titles with this team and is playing in the AVP tournament series since 1990. Steve Timmons explained that he did not do any special *preparation* for the beach volleyball season, since he plays indoor volleyball in the winter. Furthermore he stated that due to his obligations to

Photo 83: Steve Timmons

the national team, he would not have time for a transition period or recovering period. Consequently, his preparation consists of playing indoors. Following the beach volleyball season, he would have to complete the preparation period with his indoor team. During the competition period, he would try to keep his athletic level through weight training. The ball training during the season would mainly consist of training matches.

BRUK VANDEWEGHE was elected the AVP tournament series "most improved player" of 1993. His best results to date include a second place at the prestigious Manhattan Beach Open Tournament (1993) and a win in San Antonio, in 1993 as well.

He said that his transition period lasts for four weeks. He would just play a little basketball or football during that time, from time to time he would be mountainbiking. It would be important to approach each of these activities with a competitive disposition.

Starting in November, he would systematically prepare for the season, paying special attention to the four tournaments with the highest prize money as season climaxes. In November and December he would start his first adjustment to strength training, employing short runs (< 3 km) in the deep sand, co-ordination drills and other kinds of sports as well as 1-2 beach volleyball matches per week.

Photo 84: Bruk Vandeweghe

From January on, the special preparatory period would begin with 3-7 ball training units, five strength training units and further units of coordination and speed training per week. In January and February, Vandeweghe would work on the upper body two days a week and jumping power three days a week with an extensive exercise program, usually with repetitive submaximum contractions and various other methods (see above). Starting in March, he would concentrate on developing jumping power, mainly through the use of repetitive maximum contraction. An exclusive program for the development of the abdominal and back muscles as well as a final 20-minute stretch, would be also part of each unit.

Vandeweghe explained that he would undergo ball training daily, starting in February. The load and volume of his strength training would not be changed. In March, shortly before the first tournament, loads and training volume would reach their peak.

During the competition period, his strength training days would be Tuesdays and Thursdays. However, each series would then be performed with decreased loads as well as decreased numbers of repetitions.

Monday would be his day "off" and Wednesday his high volume day and Thursday would be his ball training. Friday, as a traveling day, would hardly be used for training at all.

To sum everything up, it can be said that Bruk Vandeweghe focuses his training on ball training as well as strength training. He emphasized that he did not consider endurance training to be of high importance. However, important factors include good nutrition, sufficient consumption of liquids before and during the competition as well as to have fun playing all matches and practicing exercises. However, to also play competitively at the same time.

Photo 85

11 RECOMMENDATIONS FOR THE PLANNING OF TRAINING AND FOR THE TRAINING OF ATHLETIC ABILITIES

The following will attempt to convey findings from the training sciences for the preparation of a beach volleyball player. The game's further development will definitely require an annual time table for the planning of training. This applies as well to all athletic abilities, since it has clearly been shown in the previous chapters, that players proceed in training following a more emotional path more so than scientific facts. Here, recommendations regarding all aspects of the training of athletic abilities will be given. However, basic knowledge is a prerequisite for the optimum use and application of these recommendations.

11.1 ANNUAL PLANNING

Because of the current situation and the further development of beach volleyball, three very realistic annual training plans will be explained and discussed here.

1. For the US-professional player either, male or female.
2. For the European player who focuses exclusively on beach volleyball.
3. For the indoor volleyball player, who plays beach volleyball during the summer as a secondary sport.

Annual planning, training periods and their respective goals, contents and methods will be discussed with respect to these three groups of players in the following.

11.1.1 U.S.-PROFESSIONAL

The AVP-**competition period (CP)** stretches from the middle of March to the end of September, covering almost 6 months of weekend tournaments. The very first tournament, the first weekend of February, however, is purposely shown in the **preparation period (PP)**, which lasts from the beginning of November until the middle of March. The **transition period (TP)** includes 4-5 Weeks, starting at the end of September until middle/ end of October (Fig. 57).

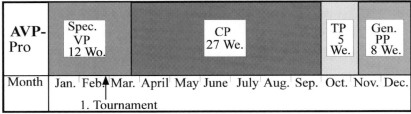

AVP-Pro	Spec. VP 12 Wo.	CP 27 We.	TP 5 We.	Gen. PP 8 We.
Month	Jan. Feb. Mar. April May June July Aug. Sep. Oct. Nov. Dec.			

1. Tournament

Fig. 57

As in professional tennis, the annual periodization in beach volleyball is profoundly influenced by various factors, for example the rankings and the different amounts of prize money. This means, that with the exception of a few of the best players in the world, none of the athletes can determine where his season peak will lie prior to the season. Therefore, the competition period can be regarded as a season of "**permanent peaks**", which means that with the exception of the priority granted by the best endowed tournaments, each match and each tournament is regarded as a season peak.

Over the course of this 6-month **competition period**, the 16 best US-professional teams can complete up to 25 weekend tournaments, each consisting of 10 possible games. Consequently, the season's best beach team plays more than 180 matches during the competition period. The teams ranking between positions 17 through 32 may participate in 20 tournaments. In cases of high success they may play a maximum of 150 matches. If one of these teams has greater success at the beginning of a season, it will get the chance to qualify for three out of five invitational tournaments. Thereby allowing the team to be able to play even more competitions.

Teams, ranked lower than the 32nd spot, must play qualification tournaments with at least three matches, in order to join the seeded teams in the main tournament. That means, that even the qualifiers, in the case they qualify for a tournament, play more than 120 matches during the competition period. The above mentioned reasons clearly show, that a microcycle (weekly training plan/ schedule) is identical for each of the top 32 players. Here, the main competition days are considered to be Saturday and Sunday.

The qualifiers' weekly training schedule differs greatly from the pros' schedule, since their first days of competition are probably Wednesday or Thursday. The given time frame mainly determines the weekly training schedule. The **time frame of a microcycle** of one of the best players could resemble the following:

–   Sunday afternoon: Final in Hermosa Beach, return trip home on the same evening (up to 2 hours).

- Monday, Tuesday, Wednesday and if given Thursday may be used for training at the usual site (near the player's residence).
- Thursday or Friday are traveling days, spent getting to the next tournament in Cincinnati.
- After Sunday's competition: return flight to Los Angeles.

The **qualifier's** time frame resembles the following:

- Elimination in the qualifying tournament on Wednesday/ Thursday. Return trip home, up to two hours.
- Friday, Saturday and Monday are practicing days at the residence site.
- Tuesday or Wednesday are the traveling days, spent getting to the qualifying tournament.
- Wednesday or Thursday: 1-4 matches.
- Friday: No competition.
- Saturday/ Sunday in case of a successful qualification: Tournament.

TRANSITION PERIOD

The transition period, which can stretch to a duration of four to five weeks, plays a decisive role for the annual planning:

- The player should strive to put some distance between himself and beach volleyball. In the end, this will have a mentally and physically positive recharging effect on him.
- The player should take part in other pleasant and joyful sports during this period. This includes sports, ranging from golf to basketball or baseball to even track and field. It is very important, that the player works out athletically **at least 2 hours on every other day**.
- The practice times shall be adjusted to the individual's daily rhythm.
- If the player chooses to perform individual sports, he should deliberately keep the intensity at a medium level.
- Once a week, a game sport is recommended.
- This period should preferably be used for the treatment of injuries, even if it will have negative effects on athletic abilities.
- Principally, this period should mainly focus on recovery and physical and mental regeneration.

PREPARATION PERIOD

The preparation period can be worked out in a similar way for all professionals as well as qualifiers. Here, the months of November and December can be regarded as **general preparation period** (gen. PP) and the period from January until the middle of March as a **special preparation period** (spec. PP). All the explanations with respect to the number of tournaments and competitions determine the goals as well as the contents and methods of the PP.

The game's structure and the fact, that 'walking in the sand' can be regarded as a physical load, instead of recovery, show that special **endurance training** is necessary (see chapter 11.4, endurance training).

During the gen. PP, basic endurance shall be trained 3 times a week.

During the spec. PP, endurance training can be reduced to 2 weekly units and it can be performed in a rather beach volleyball-specific manner.

Jumping and running actions on a sandy surface require a good speed strength based on a high maximum and explosive strength level. The same applies to the development of the hitting-strength, since the ball is heavier than the indoor ball and moreover, it must frequently be spiked into the wind (see chapter 11.5, strength training).

Except for the TP, **strength training,** like endurance training, should be performed all year round.

In the gen. PP, strength training shall aim at the enlargement of muscle cross section.

In the spec. PP, training shall almost exclusively be performed with the goal of improving of **intramuscular coordination (IC).**

The latest studies show, that particularly well-trained top-level beach volleyball players who have been pursuing a strength training for several years, do not perform hypertrophy-training for more than four weeks. This time span is sufficient enough to reestablish the original muscle-cross section level.

In the gen. PP, strength training shall be executed 4 times a week, in the spec. PP, 3 times a week.

The necessity of speed training and its consequences for the beach volleyball-specific speed is not doubted. It becomes clear through the structural analysis (chapter 3).

The basic speed qualities shall be developed in the gen. PP, the reaction time in the spec. PP and noncyclic speed in connection with technique training, while practicing certain motion and action sequences. The training goals and contents should shift from basic speed to the specific speed demands of the game. At first, these will be practiced in the spec. PP, gradually and then after 4 weeks, exclusively (see chapter 11.3, speed training).

In the gen. PP, speed training will be done 2 times a week, in the spec. PP up to 3 times a week.

In contrast to all other sports players, the beach volleyball player needs even better developed coordinative abilities, since he must play on an uneven and soft surface under constantly changing exterior conditions.

Like speed training, the **training of coordinative abilities** is undertaken 2 times a week in the gen. PP and 3 times a week in the spec. PP. In the spec. PP, the beach-specific abilities in conjunction with a ball shall receive more attention and shall basically be trained along with speed.

Technique training shall be done 2 times a week in the gen. PP, in order to work on deficiencies. The detection of deficits should be a result of the observation and analysis of one's own playing performance. If, for example, someone has difficulties with the set or if he is not satisfied with the effectivness of his jump serve, he will have to improve his technique under the instruction of his coach/ partner.

– No more than 2 weekly training games shall be played in the gen. PP. This would create a physical load that would be too competition-like, and have a negative effect on the gen. PP.
– In the spec. PP, individual and team tactics must be combined with the training of technique.
– In the spec. PP, ball training should at least be done once a day. Here, first the Saturday should be loaded with 3-5 test games. Four weeks before the season opener, additional test games should be added Sundays as the next 'tournament day' four weeks before the season.

> The below outlined microcycles are based on the assumption that the whole **professional's daily rhythm will be subordinated to his training**, meaning that he will practice up to 3 times a day and at very various times of the day.

– This so far only applies to very few professionals. Looking ahead, it can be said that the professionalization, which refers to interpretation of the findings of training sciences, will prevail in the next years, even in the **field of planning of training, training execution and analysis**.

Without changing the content sequences, the microcycles must deliberately be adjusted in such a manner, that they will be carried out at different times of the day under the most random external conditions (see chapter 12, principles of training). The examples assume the weekend rhythm of tournaments. Monday has been assigned as the regeneration day or 'day off'. Sunday will be the regeneration day for players who were already eliminated from the tournament on Saturday. They shall then go for a 30-min. regeneration-run on a **more solid sand surface** (close to the water). The intensity of the regeneration-run, which should be very low, can be judged appropriate if a conversation is possible during the run.

The sample microcycles of the PP are principally based on at least 12 **training units (TU)** a week. Each TU lasts 1.5 - 2 hours. It has been scientifically proven, that 2 or 3 well-dosed TU's a day make much more sense then 1 or 2 very extensive practices. Due to organizational reasons, the following training plans must be regarded as more suitable for **one** player and less for a team. During a **gen. PP microcycle**, (table 12), speed-training, training of coordinative abilities, of technique and the practice-game are all carried out with a submaximum to maximum intensity. Muscle-hypertrophy training follows the standard method I (see chapter 11.5, strength training). Endurance training is undertaken following the steady method (see chapter 11. 4, endurance training). A 10-minute regeneration-run with a subsequent stretching may not be missed at the end of each TU .

Monday	Regeneration		
Tuesday	9-11 a.m. Basic speed	5-7 p.m. Strength (Hypertrophy)	
Wednesday	8-10 a.m. Technique/ Individual tactics	1-3 p.m. Strength (Hypertrophy)	6-8 p.m. Gen. endurance
Thursday	9-11 a.m. Basic speed. gen. coordination	Off	
Friday	8-10 a.m. Technique/ Individual tactics	1-3 p.m. Strength	6-8 p.m. Endurance
Saturday	8-10 a.m. Coordination/ Speed	12-2 p.m. 2 Games	
Sunday		12-2 p.m. Strength	6-8 p.m. Endurance

Table 12: Microcycle gen. PP

Monday	Regeneration		
Tuesday	9-11 a.m. Noncyclic speed without and with ball		5-7 p.m. Strength IC
Wednesday	8-10 a.m. Technique/Individual tactics		4-6 p.m. Spec. endurance with/ without ball.
Thursday	10-12 a.m. Speed/ Coord. with/without ball	12 -1 p.m. Strength IC: legs	
Friday	8-10 a.m. Technique Individual tactics Team training	1-3 p.m. Speed/ Coord. with/ without ball	7-9 p.m. Endurance
Saturday		11 a.m.-2 p.m. 3 Games	
Sunday	8-10 a.m. Strength IC	2-4 p.m. 3 Games	7-8 p.m. Reg.-run

Table 13: Microcycle spec. PP

COMPETITION PERIOD

Endurance and strength training are executed twice a week during the CP, in order to maintain the achieved athletic level. The endurance training should possibly be included in ball training. Speed training as well as the training of coordinative abilities shall also be performed 2 times a week with ball in order to stabilize the achieved level. Technique training as well as training of individual and team tactics shall be done, with the exception of Monday as a 'day off', 3 to 6 times a week. The number of ball training sessions also depends on the distance between the tournament site and the player's residence, therefore on the traveling constraints (Table 14).

Monday	Off-day, regeneration-run	
Tuesday	9-11 a.m. Speed/ Coordination with ball	5-7 p.m. Strength IC
Wednesday	8-10 a.m. Technique individ. & team tactics	6-7 p.m. Speed/ coord. with ball, 7-91h endurance with ball
Thursday	10-12 a.m. strength IC	1-5 p.m. Individual-and team tactics, also as games/ playing endurance
Friday	Traveling	6-7 p.m. easy ball training, preferably on the tournament courts
Saturday	Tournament	Tournament, in the evening, after the last match: Regeneration-run, app. 25 min.
Sunday	Tournament	Tournament

Table 14: Microcycle CP

The **female professionals** have a 1-2 month shorter CP. Accordingly, as clearly shown in Fig. 58, the TP lasts app. 7 weeks and the PP about 6 months. With a duration of 3 months, the gen. PP can be extended as long as the spec. PP.

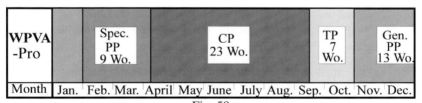

Fig. 58

Observations have shown, that women, in contrast to men, must incorporate a larger share of technique training and more training units with a ball into the gen. PP. Consequently, they also play more practice-games. Since the women's game is almost identical with men's beach volleyball with regard to the physical load and since the playing format is not any different, all other previous explanations on the men's game, with respect to aspects of annual planning and therefore of the microcycle, apply here as well.

11.1.2 EUROPEAN PROFESSIONAL

The following explanations refer to the European professional as well as to professionals originating from other continents:
Based on the current performance level of the "to be expected" European professionals, it can be unconditionally recommended, that these players take part in competitions in the USA at a preferably high level, in order to improve their caliber of play. It should be the goal of the European professional, to reach the US-professional level of play by qualifying for the subordinated AA- and AAA-tournaments. If the players succeeded and actually take part in the professional series, as well as in World-Series-tournaments, then the following descriptions must be combined with the explanations for the US-professional. It shall be clearly emphasized, that a distinct PP will no longer be possible and can not exist under the current temporal circumstances. Fig. 59 shows the possible annual time table for a European professional considering World-Series-competitions, the US-season and the important national tournament series.

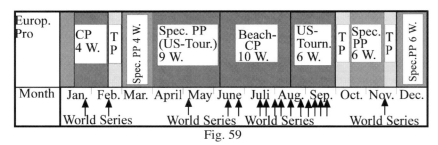

Fig. 59

The expected development implies, that **all pro-beach volleyball players** should adapt and come to use the knowledge and the **findings** of the **professional tennis players**.

This means, that each player must plan his year's training following preferably monthly and weekly cycles as well as depending on specific tournaments and on success in the previous tournament.

11.1.3 INDOOR PLAYER IN BEACH VOLLEYBALL

Indoor players, who play beach volleyball as their secondary sport, must consider the annual periodization of their respective indoor top-league (Fig. 60).

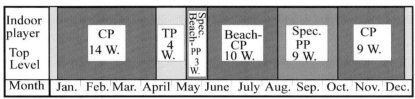

Indoor player Top Level	CP 14 W.	TP 4 W.	Spec. Beach-PP 3 W.	Beach-CP 10 W.	Spec. PP 9 W.	CP 9 W.
Month	Jan. Feb. Mar.	April	May June	July Aug.	Sep. Oct.	Nov. Dec.

Fig. 60

In contrast to the displayed seasonal divisions of a top-league player, a national team player will usually not even be able to get a TP of several weeks. Based on the exaggerated statement, that the game of beach volleyball is as different from indoor volleyball as table tennis is from tennis, it is not recommended for national team players, to play beach volleyball-competitions regularly. A systematic and regular beach-training, combined with competitions on sand-surfaces, will definitely have a negative effect on that respective national team's competitiveness. In case the national teams' schedule does not include important games such as the World League or World Championships/ Continental Championships or the Olympics or qualification tournaments, the national team players can take over the annual periodization of top league players with slight modifications.

Top indoor players without any national team obligations, who want to take part in beach volleyball competitions, can start their beach volleyball training during Christmas time, in their TP. The consequence for Europeans would be, that the players will have to spend their Christmas competition break in a country which allows outdoor volleyball training on sand. The only restriction that applies here, is that players must return to indoor training for the last week of the TP, if their first indoor competition is of significant importance. Depending on their athletic condition, the players should practice once or twice a day. The training contents shall be limited to only exercises with a ball and to games. This means that attention will primarily be paid to technique and individual tactics in all situations of play as well as team-tactical aspects.

It is believed that **beach volleyball has a very positive effect on indoor volleyball in almost all aspects of the game,** as in for example technique. Particularly defensive techniques, individual tactical performance, anticipation, reaction and coordination and especially the all-around and universal education are positively affected. The **soft character** of the sand surface, especially easy going on knees, ankles, hips, lower back etc. joints, allows high training volumes. Here, the danger of injuries or further sports related damage is considerably lower. This especially applies to ankle injuries, which are very frequent in the indoor game.

The sand has a **negative** effect on reactive strength and on the player's timing. Therefore, the player should counteract this negative development of muscle stiffness/ reactive strength by performing skip-series on hard surfaces. This should always be done in a fully rested condition prior to a TU.

In the TP, directly following the indoor season, ball-training can be undertaken. Depending on athletic condition as well as possible injuries, it may be done once instead of twice a day, in order to first make the adjustment/ transition from indoors to the beach. This should be accomplished before attempting to achieve a considerable increase of performance. The indoor player as a beach volleyball player should regard the CP in beach volleyball as his **gen. PP** for the indoor season, consequently he will start his preparation for the indoor season directly with a **spec. PP**.

The beach volleyball-endurance should always be trained with a ball. The weekly schedule (see table 15) should include 2 TU's for the maintenance of the strength level. With respect to the weekly schedule, it is important to adjust the practicing times to the competition times. Otherwise, all other fundamentals of the professional beach player as well as all the beach-specific training principles apply. It becomes clear, that many practice games must be played in order to achieve the transition to beach volleyball faster.

Monday	Regeneration day: 30-minute regeneration-run on more solid sand	
Tuesday	10-12 a.m. Technique, indiv. tactics	5-7 p.m. 2 Games
Wednesday	9- 11 a.m. Team-tactics	7-9 p.m. Strength training
Thursday	8-10 a.m. Technique, individual tactics	5-8 p.m. 2-3 Games (spec. endurance)
Friday	9-11a.m. Strength training	Off
Saturday	after 2 p.m., more than 4 games	
Sunday	8-11a.m. 3 Games	12-15 p.m. 2 Games

Table 15: Microcycle spec. PP

During the CP, strength training shall be reduced to once a week. Gradually the number of practice-games will be reduced in favor of training of individual and team tactics as well. Special attention must be paid to the service/ reception situation as well as to the blocking and defensive situation with focusing primarily on the players' communication. For further hints regarding the indoor-players' speed-training and coordinative training, the reader can refer to the training sequences and the chapters on special forms of training (11.2, 11.3 as well as 6.5.1 and 7.7). This should then be taken into consideration within the TU's for technique and individual tactics. However, this is only done once the techniques have already been mastered. The indoor player should plan a regeneration period of at least 2 weeks after the beach-CP.

11.2   COORDINATION TRAINING

The coordinative abilities must be specifically and systematically trained on sand. The second half of the spec. PP and the CP is suggested for this. The exercises can be looked up in chapter 6.5.1, "Special forms of training" (for the coordinative abilities of the setting player and for the passing and attacking player) as well as in chapter 7.7, "Special forms of training" (for the coordinative abilities of the blocker and the backcourt defender).

The arrangement of the below listed principles for training follows the temporal succession, in which they become relevant during the training process:

– An intense warm-up is an absolute must in order to establish an optimum mental-physical state.
– The training may never be executed in a fatigued mental or physical state. In case fatigue occurs or can be felt, the training has to be broken off immediately.
– With regard to technique, the player must be able to execute the exercises perfectly.
– Only use the **repetition method**, making the duration of physical load be up to 8 sec. Here, the exercises must be performed with maximum intensity. The breaks in between the exercises shall last longer than 2 min. and shall be filled with some activity. The break after each series, after app. 5 repetitions of the exercise, shall last about 6 min.
– The training lasts about 45 minutes.
– The maximum-load intensity requires and demands very high motivation.
– Because of the necessity of regeneration time, a maximum of 2-3 highly intensive and demanding TU's, shall be planned within one microcycle.

- The general coordinative abilities will be trained and restored in the gen. PP. Here, special attention must be paid to **balance**.
- In the spec. PP, beach-specific coordinative abilities shall be trained.
- They shall be stabilized in the CP.
- The coordination training will be reduced in the TP and generally maintained through participation in other sports.

11.3 SPEED TRAINING

All the principles for the training of coordinative abilities must be observed unconditionally. In the following, 3 selected examples with different goals will be presented:

Forms of exercises:
1. Speed training for the improvement of basic speed in the gen. PP:

- 5 sprints over 15 m from varying starting positions.
- 3 - 5 sprints over 25 m with flying start.
- 5 sprints with increasing speed over 35, 25, 35, 25 and 35 m.
- 10 sprints from a lying position over 12 m.

2. Speed training for the improvement of non-cyclic speed in the final phase of the gen. PP and the beginning of the spec. PP:

- Block-jump, body turn, sprint over 10 m
- Diagonal retreat (running backwards) from the middle of the net toward the court's center with a subsequent explosive sprint over 3 - 4 m.
- Dive and subsequent sprint over 5 m.
- 2 - 3 m running backward with subsequent sprint over 6 m.
- Start in the court's center, dash to the right over 2 m, followed by a dash to the left over 6 m.
- Imitation of a jump serve with subsequent sprint toward the starting position of the blocker.

3. **Speed training with a ball**, starting halfway through the spec. PP and in the CP for the improvement of the beach volleyball-specific speed:

- Since speed training with a ball is to a large extent similar to coordination training with a ball, the simpler exercises of the special forms of training (chapter 6.5.1 and 7.7) should be used here.

11.4 ENDURANCE TRAINING

The **steady method** and the **extensive and intensive interval methods** are explained as methods for endurance training. The steady method may be used for working on a basal level. Here, this method is recommended in three variations with a ball and one without a ball:

1. Continuous method.
2. Changing method.
3. Fartlek (Cross Country running with alternating speed).
4. Steady method with a ball.

To 1.: This method shall be used at the beginning of the gen. PP. The beach volleyball player shall maintain a constant speed over a duration of 30 min. with a heart rate of about 150 beats per minute.

To 2.: Here, the player shall increase his speed systematically in predetermined sections of his run. During the constant physical load, for example, the speed shall be increased slightly, after another 5 min. it should be decreased again etc.

To 3.: Here, the beach player shall choose his desired speed independently. The topography and the surface should be varied in order to provocate changes of the running speed. In the following, two examples for the beach volleyball - fartlek will be given:

a)   with a speed-orientated phase,
b)   with a strength-orientated phase.

a)   Speed-orientated fartlek:
⇒   10-minute relaxed warm-up jog with relaxation exercises on a solid sand surface,
⇒   10 min. stretching,
⇒   10 min. steady run in deep sand, the intensity should be below the aerobic-anaerobic threshold and a conversation should be possible,
⇒   Initiation of the speed-orientated phase by hop-runs, bounding runs and acceleration runs in hilly terrain,
⇒   Exercises on the court: Start and sprint over 5 m from the various starting positions/ runs with changing directions up to 10 m. For example, sprint s from the court's center to the sideline and back, from the net's middle to the court's center and back could be used. More examples can be looked up in the program for non-cyclic speed,
⇒   relaxed jog with relaxation exercises on solid sand (10 min.), 10 min. steady run with low intensity in deep sand,

⇒ 3 sprints over 20 m in deep sand and relaxed jogging in shallow water in between,

⇒ 10 min. regeneration run and stretching on solid sand.

b) Strength orientated fartlek:

With the exception of the speed orientated phase, the process is similar to the above described example. The strength orientated phase may be filled with the following exercises:

⇒ 10 jumps with full body extension form a low ready posture or 5 functionally executed knee-bends with the partner sitting on one's shoulders,

⇒ 25 functionally executed repetitions of a dynamic exercise for the abdominal muscles,

⇒ the same for the back muscles,

⇒ 10 one-legged jumps for each leg on solid sand or 15 block jumps or 15 reps. of jump-combinations,

⇒ two-legged long-/ high-jumps from a standstill,

⇒ 3 x 20 push-ups of varying different types.

The exercises shall be combined in such a manner, that different muscle groups will be trained from one exercise to the next.

The fartleks may be used up until halfway through the spec. PP.

To 4.: Endurance training with a ball is recommended for the spec. PP and for the CP. Players at the medium performance level shall prefer endurance training with a ball over all other methods, since it profoundly contributes to technical improvement and stabilization. However, training should be limited to already well-mastered exercises. Endurance training with a ball can be undertaken with a partner as well as by the single player.

EXERCISE-EXAMPLES FOR SINGLE-PLAYER TRAINING

– Serve/ jump serve and, then slowly running to shag the ball, execute jump serve etc.

– Execution of an attacking technique, for example the extreme cut shot after tossing to one's self, shagging the ball, etc.

EXERCISE-EXAMPLES FOR THE TRAINING WITH SEVERAL PLAYERS

Here, small-court games *with each other* and, in the case of many players, *against each other*, combined with alternating positions/ functions each time the ball crosses the net, are recommended. The power-games with numerous balls play a special role. Here, the ball toss, initiating play, shall be performed in such a manner, that the physical load will not transcend the match-specific load. Power-games shall first be played *without* jumping actions. This means playing from a standstill without spikes. Later *with* jumps in the game *with each other* and lastly *against each other*. Concrete examples can be looked up in the training sequences.

When using **interval** methods, a systematically planned alternation between load and recovery shall be undertaken. The subsequent load shall not start after a full recovery but at a heart rate of about 120-130 bpm. During the daily practice of a beach volleyball player, the control of the physical load through other parameters can hardly be converted.
Interval methods can on one hand be classified with respect to the duration of load and on the other hand with respect to the intensity. With respect to load-duration, the load will last between 15 s and 2 min. in the short-term interval method, between 2 and 8 min. in the medium-term interval method and between 8 and 15 min. in the long-term interval method. With respect to intensity, the extensive interval method with low to medium intensity can be distinguished from the intensive interval method with relatively high intensities. For the beach volleyball player, it makes sense to work on basic and specific endurance with the steady method with or without a ball during the gen. PP.

The interval methods with or without a ball should particularly be used, if the player's mental attributes, specifically his mental resistance, needs training.

For this purpose, power-games above a competitive level with the respective incomplete recovery breaks may strongly be recommended. These games fit particularly well into the weekly schedule if the following day, at least that morning will be a day-off.

11.5 STRENGTH TRAINING

According to the explanations on annual planning (chapter 11.1), recommendations on strength training, especially on the development of weekly and monthly schedules for the respective training period, will be given in this chapter. One difference between the indoor and the beach player, with respect to the choice of methods and therefore to the goals of their strength training, must be clearly highlighted:
Besides the improvement of all other speed-strength related components, the strength training of the indoor player aims especially at the development

reactive strength qualities. Such as the ability to utilize the elastic attributes of muscles and the neuronal reflexes during muscle contractions which are preceded by a lengthening/stretch of the particular muscle, the so-called muscle-stretch-shortening-cycle during jumps.

In contrast, the pro-beach volleyball player restricts his strength training to methods which increase the speed strength exclusively by the development of maximum and explosive strength, never working on his reactive strength. This significant distinction for strength training can be traced back to the fact, that all takeoff, start and sprint actions take place on soft ground/ sand. Therefore, the very short ground contact times of under 200 ms, necessary for the activation of reactive strength abilities, can not be reached. This extreme difference results in the fact, that the indoor player who does not play much beach volleyball in the summer, must perform exercises during the beach-CP, which contribute to the preservation of his reactive strength. He should therefore perform ankle-initiated hops, hop-steps, bounding runs, and/ or depth-jump training three times a week. This must always be done on a hard surface and in fully recovered condition.

The **prophylactic functional strength training** is important for the indoor player, however, for the following reasons, it is an absolute must for the beach volleyball player:

a) He needs very well-built, balanced, and strong muscle groups, since he must move very quickly on soft, instable ground.

b) Moreover, this high level of strength will help him to maintain his balance during resting periods as well as during periods of movement. Balance is one of the most important coordinative abilities for the beach volleyball player .

c) The functional strengthening of abdominal and back muscles represents the main basis for the beach volleyball player's strength training.

The following principles must always be observed in strength training:
–   Execution of a general and a discipline specific warm-up at all times!
–   During the gen. PP, the intensity (loads) should be increased gradually.
–   A proper technique in each strength training exercise is the most important prerequisite for training with heavier weights.
–   The strength level of the spine-stabilizing muscles (abdominals/ back) is the **performance-limiting factor** in each exercise. This is **independent** of the performance level of a muscle group that is specifically trained in its respective exercise. As a result, each player must strengthen his trunk muscles daily with functional exercises.
–   With respect to the muscle groups which must be trained, the beach volleyball player can, in contrast to the indoor player, neglect his calves in favor of his thigh muscles, particularly his quadriceps.

- Antagonists must always be included in strength training in order to avoid muscular dysbalance and therefore harmful body positions.
- At the end of each training, stretching exercises for those muscle groups that have just been worked on, is necessary. This is to avoid a shortening of muscles, so-called contraction-holdovers.
- The exercises should possibly be game- and competition-like.
- Typical beach volleyball moves should be carried out after training with weights.
- One-sided loads, especially on the weak wrists, ankles and elbows, should be avoided if possible.
- Balancing moves, especially involving the spine, (f. e. lordosis, sideward movements), must be precisely observed and avoided. If they occur, the exercise must be broken off immediately.
- In situations of intensities under 80% of the maximum strength, 'pressed' breathing is to be deliberately avoided.
- Training with a partner, in order to be able to help each other in technically difficult exercises.
- Each new exercise must be thoroughly learned and initially executed with low intensities.
- The training principle of progressively increasing loads must be respected. Consequently, a valid and suitable performance-diagnosis method must be used every two weeks in order to determine the strength performance level.
- The individual training control is the most important precondition for an optimum strength training.
- If a chosen strength training method no longer leads to an increase of maximum strength, a change of methods becomes necessary.
- In cases where three or more strength training units are undertaken a week, especially when using hypertrophy methods, a slightly increased need for protein must be considered.
- Free weights are preferred over machines, since more muscle groups and larger parts of one muscle group will be trained.

Based on the publications of BÜHRLE (1985) and SCHMIDTBLEICHER (1987), **useful strength training methods for the beach volleyball player** are presented in the following. Additionally, methods promoted by MARTIN and others (1991) will be considered. These methods use the so-called muscle performance threshold for an athlete to determine of the training load. In contrast to the other mentioned methods, the effectiveness of these methods has yet to be proven.

	Standard-method I (constant loads)	Standard-method II (progressive increasing loads)	Bodybuilding-method I (extensive)	Bodybuilding-method II (intensive)
Speed	rapid	rapid	slow	rapid
Load (intensity)	80%	70-80-85-90%	60-70%	85-95%
Repetitions	8-10	12-10-7-5	15-20	8-5
Series	3-5	1-2-3-4	3-5	3-5
Duration of break	≥ 3 min.	≥ 3 min.	≥ 2 min.	≥ 3 min.

Table 16: Methods of repeated submaximum contractions for the enlargement of the muscle cross section
(Source: BÜHRLE 1985, p. 96; SCHMIDTBLEICHER 1987, p. 368; MARTIN and others, 1991, p. 128)

Methods of repetitive submaximum contractions (Tab. 16) primarily aim at an enlargement of the muscle cross section. An improvement of the intramuscular coordination will barely be reached. In contrast to methods using maximum loads, the training with methods of submaximum loads can be performed in an already fatigued condition, following another TU.

- 3-5 series with 8-10 reps. and loads of 80% of the diagnosed concentric maximum strength are executed when the **standard method I** is used. The breaks in between series should last at least 3 min.
- The **standard method II** already represents a mixed method in the shape of a pyramid. The first series with 12 reps. at 70% intensity, the second series with 10 reps. at 80% intensity, the third with 7 reps. and 85% load and the last series includes 5 reps. at a 90%-intensity. The breaks last at least 3 min. Especially with respect to this as well as other methods, the necessity of a spotter using supporting/security posture by the partner must be emphasized again.
- The **bodybuilding method I** with 3-5 series, loads of 60-70% and reps. of 15-20 leads to the total exhaustion of the person being trained. This can be traced to the shorter breaks and the therefore induces "excessive" exploitation of the muscles.
- Working out with the **bodybuilding method II** also leads to total exhaustion. The reason for this can been seen in the high number of reps. (8-5) at a very high intensity of 85-95%. 3-5 series with breaks of at least 3 min. will be completed.

	Quasi-maximum contractions	Maximum-concentric contractions	Concentric-excentric Contractions	Method following the principle of the muscleperformance threshold
Speed	maximum fast			
Impact	explosive			
Load	90-95-97-100%	100%	70-90%	55-60%
Repetitions	3 - 1 - 1 1+1	1	6-8	6-8
Series	1 - 2 - 3 4+5	5	3-5	3-5
Break betw. reps.	10 s	-	10 s	10 s
Series breaks	≥ 4 min.	≥ 4 min.	≥ 4 min.	≥ 4 min.

Table 17:   Methods of maximum contractions for the improvement of the intramuscular coordination
(Sources: BÜHRLE 1985, p. 98; SCHMIDTBLEICHER 1987, p. 367; MARTIN and others, 1991, p. 130)

If **components depending on speed-strength (starting force, explosive and maximum strength), which are most important for the beach volleyball player**, are to be improved using methods of maximum contractions, a maximum explosive starting force exertion will be an absolute precondition.
It must be emphasized that the improvement of speed strength can be accomplished much more effectively using methods of maximum (explosive) contractions than by the traditionally used "speed strength methods" such as repetitions with light weights. The moreover necessary development of speed strength through an improvement of the discipline-specific intermuscular coordination will be accomplished in the spec. PP and the CP through:

a)   other training contents (speed/coordination-training; see chapter 11.2),
b)   a possibly discipline-specific choice of exercises in strength training.

The **methods of maximum contractions** (table 17) must be executed after an extensive warm-up, since they primarily aim at improving explosive strength and a more effective utilization of the available muscle mass. (Improvement of intentional activation) These training effects are results of neuronal adaptations. The player must train in a fully recovered condition. Moreover, each repetition must be executed with maximum will-power and explosive starting force impact exertion.

–   Strength training in general, but especially training with high loads (90-100% of the maximum strength) and free weights, requires well built up trunk muscles. Therefore, it is only recommended for the professional athlete who has strength training experience along with well-trained abdominal and back-muscles (s.a., "principles").

Training using high loads, more than 90% of the maximum (concentric) strength, only leads to a modest enlargement of the muscle cross section. Instead, the increase in strength is accomplished in an, for the beach player, ideal way, namely without **gain of body weight.**

–   The **method of quasi-maximum contractions** again follows the principle of pyramid-training. Here, the first series is executed with 90%-intensity and 3 reps. The second, third and fourth with 95, 97 and 100% intensity and one rep. In the fifth series, 1 kilo will be added to the 100%-load.
–   The **method of maximum concentric contractions** (5 series with always one rep. and a 100%-load) will only lead to an optimum training effect, if the maximum strength is determined prior to each TU.
–   With regard to motion sequences, the **method of concentric-excentric maximum contractions** may be performed resembling beach volleyball moves. A free falling weight (barbell) smoothly "caught" and immediately accelerated with maximum explosive force. The load is 70-90% with 3-5 series and a 6-8 reps each.
–   For the determination of the load-intensity, the **method following the principle of the muscle performance threshold** is orientated at the maximum possible force impulse, which is supposedly around a load of about 60-70% of the concentric maximum strength. This method represents a mixture between methods of maximum and submaximum contractions. It is, therefore, a compromise which aims to improve intentional activation ability, while at the same time improving intermuscular coordination and increasing muscle cross section. This is done through higher motion speeds than in "normal" IC-training.

At least 4 TU's shall be undertaken in the gen. PP and 3 TU's in the spec. PP. The following methods are recommended.

–   In the first four weeks, extensive use of bodybuilding method I,
–   In the next four weeks, standard methods I+II.

The volume shall be kept very high, at about 4-5 series. The standard method II (pyramid-format) should especially be used at the end of the gen. PP, in order to simplify the transition to heavier loads and the transition to the training of intramuscular coordination in the spec. PP.

The pyramid method or the method of quasi-maximum contractions will be used during the first four weeks of the spec. PP. In the next four weeks, the intensity will be increased to 90%-100% by using the method of maximum concentric or maximum concentric-excentric contractions.

The number of TU's can be decreased to two a week during the transition from the spec. PP to the CP. The number of series should also be reduced, however, even though the intensity will still be increased. This is done following the method of maximum contractions. Later it will be kept at a maximum level.

During the whole CP, the player should basically use methods that aim at the improvement of intramuscular coordination. A change of methods towards submaximum contractions for the improvement of the muscle cross section is recommended only if the CP includes longer periods without competitions, for reasons of scheduling or injuries.

A description of certain strength training exercises is deliberately neglected by this handbook, on one the hand for reasons of limited volume, but on the other because the specific literature on strength training offers numerous exercise collections and the reader may find these in general and technical sports literature.

12   SPECIFIC PRINCIPLES OF BEACH VOLLEYBALL TRAINING

These principles should help the player/ trainer arrange all aspects of training in an appropriate and suitable manner for the beach volleyball game. The principles refer to training itself and are closely linked to the exercise and training sequences found in chapters 5, 6 and 7. In general, training must be arranged and organized according to the specific structure and requirements of each sports-discipline:

The structural analysis of beach volleyball (see chapter 3) reveals, that the repetition-method (ib) *is the appropriate method* for technique training, with respect to individual and team tactics. Here, the repetition method is not meant to be an appropriate method for *learning* a technique, rather it should resemble the *situation and competition application* of a technical/ tactical action under competition conditions.

12.1   GENERAL PRINCIPLES

1. **During the transition period as well as during the general preparation period, every indoor volleyball player should utilize the advantages of beach volleyball for the indoor game.**

2. Training should take weather conditions into consideration, for example a practice should not be canceled due to moderate rain.

3. The same applies to training on different sand surfaces.

4. Players at the low and medium performance levels should more or less neglect the training of the athletic abilities, favoring instead a technical, individual and team tactical improvement.

5. It must be observed, during training, that each player always has a larger share of practicing time on "his" side of the court.

6. A beach volleyball player who does not act as a blocker in competition, must, however, practice the block intensively. This will minimize his only weakness as a beach volleyball player.

7. Professionals: Always practice with players of the highest caliber or the best possible players currently available at your beach training-site.

8. Medium and lower level: Always practice with players of a slightly higher caliber of play.

9. A beach volleyball player, who never or rarely acts as backcourt defender, must however practice backcourt defense intensively, in order to minimize his only weakness as a beach volleyball player.

12.2 PRINCIPLES FOR THE WARM-UP WITH A BALL

The warming up with the ball should preferably consist of exercise forms that prepare the players for the focal point of the respective training. The shorter the practicing time or the training-volume, the more the warm-up without a ball should take place outside of the court's boundaries *prior* to the beginning of the practice. This will allow for the possibility to actually start the practice directly from the warm-up with a ball.

Two person warm-up play

1. The players play opposed or diagonally positioned to the net since all receiving and defensive actions are played toward the net's direction.

2. The positions should be changed often in order to let both players get accustomed to sunlight and wind conditions.

3. First, the players spike accurately and mildly so that different defensive techniques can be used and practiced. The defending player should dig the ball within his reach in such a way that he is able to catch it. Afterwards he himself spikes the ball. This warm-up practice helps the players to get accustomed to the necessary level of ball control.

4. Afterwards the players will spike accurately and harder toward the defensive reach of the partner. This will help to get accustomed to the proper choice and execution of defensive techniques for specific situations.

5. Subsequently, the warm-up without catching the ball follows. Here, the net player should frequently jump. This of course makes regularly alternating between the net player with the backcourt player necessary.

6. As a transition form, small-court games *with each other* are recommended. They are suitable for warming up because the players can work on the motions and actions with respect to the net in a more match-like situation.

Warm-up attacks at the net

1. The attacks should always be executed indirectly. This means, that a receiving action must be played prior to the attacking action. This corresponds exactly to the beach volleyball attacking situation.

2. The attacks should take match-like running patterns into consideration. Thus, the attacking player plays the reception about 7 m from the net before he attacks. Starting positions for warm-up attacks that are located close to the net (3 m-line), as practiced in the indoor game, are useless in beach volleyball!

3. Also during practice, each beach volleyball player should hit more than 80% of all warm-up attacks on *his* original attacking side.

4. The warm-up attacks should be played, when more than two players are available, against a block if possible.

5. Even in warm-up attacks, attention should be paid to net violations.

Warm-up before the competition

The following points should be taken into consideration for warming up before a competition:

1. The service and the reception should definitely be components of the warm-up. At first, serves should be hit accurately in order to allow the partner to quickly become accustomed to the receiving situation. Afterwards, competition serves should be practiced. In general, each player should include the serving/ receiving situation into the warm-up. This should be done on each side of the court and as often as possible.

2. During the course of a tournament, a warm-up without and with a ball should be executed prior to each game. If there are obvious signs of

fatigue or if the breaks between games are very short, the volume (duration) of the warm-up should be reduced. In this case, the basic warm-up can be reduced in favor of warming up with a ball.

3. The team/ coach must follow the course of events in the tournament in order to be able to assess the team's own match time, even prior to an official announcement. This is the only way to warm up sufficiently, at least 15 minutes before the tournament director's announcement.

4. Internationally, the match announcement must be made 10-15 minutes before the match's first whistle. Subsequently, three minutes will remain for the warm-up at the net in case another court was previously available. Otherwise, five minutes will remain for the warm-up. The AVP-rules grant 15 minutes for the net-warm-up.

5. For the FIVB and other non-US national circuits, this means that the warming up without a ball should take place 10-15 minutes before the match announcement. The warm-up with a ball should start simultaneously with the match announcement and should preferably be done on the actual designated court or any other available court.

USA: The professionals should act similarly, however they will, in any case have access to their designated competition court for their warm-up.

6. The warm-up should be executed as follows:
    ⇒ Warm-up without a ball (running, stretching, easy work on main muscle groups, sprints, jumps etc.).
    ⇒ Warm-up with the ball diagonally to the net, frequent change of positions.
    ⇒ Easy spin spikes, the defending player digs the ball close to his reach so that he is able to catch it. Afterwards he spikes.
    ⇒ Like the prior exercise, now with harder spikes.
    ⇒ Like the prior exercise, now the ball is hit toward the whole defense range, high, short, to the side etc.
    ⇒ Warming up without catching the ball. Here again, the main focus is the proper execution of defensive techniques in certain situation.
    ⇒ Indirect attacks, meaning that a receiving action is played prior to the attack action. Here, attention must be paid to whether match-like running patterns and distances are being executed. The players will only attack their specialized sides.
    ⇒ Execution of at least 10 serves and receptions; with respect to all service locations and techniques.

12.3 PRINCIPLES FOR THE ORGANIZATION AND EXECUTION OF FORMS OF TRAINING

1. Only a few forms of training should be practiced per training session. All match situations should be considered but only with one or at the most two main focuses.

2. All forms must be played until a final decision!

3. In all forms, the 'out' balls may not be received or defended against.

4. In practice, no rule violations may be consciously or unconsciously ignored. That also includes practice using net antennas.

5. The more beach volleyball-balls that are available, the more the prior and the subsequent actions in the action sequence must be involved or executed in a game-like fashion. If less balls (or if only one ball) are available, the players shall concentrate on the execution of the basic motion or the action they are actually attempting to perfect. The prior and subsequent actions can be executed by tossing and catching balls.

6. In practice, it must be considered that, with regard to physical demands and load, all small-court games, especially the games played with each other, are *above* match level.

7. Playing without a ball should always be considered and observed in all forms of training.

Number of players in training

1. With five or more players, the training of the individual and team tactics should always be performed against an opponent. This means that for example service or attack training are only appropriate with a simultaneous training of the reception and defense.

2. Four players can be regarded as a good amount of people for training because fewer balls are necessary.

3. Training with three players also allows good execution and application of most game situations.

4. Training with two people is recommended for the improvement of technique. However, it requires the availability of several balls.

5. Single-player training is only suitable for practicing certain techniques. Here, the availability of several balls is essential for an effective training execution.

6. Traditional practices, such as spiking at a target, are only useful in single-player training.

Training of technique and individual tactics

1. During the special preparation period and in the competition period, the serves during training, with respect to the service-type, should be risky. They should always be hit as if in actual competition. Here, mentally stressful training forms are recommended.

2. During the special preparation period and the competition period, the training of the backcourt defender should always be undertaken in connection with the blocker's training. Here, if given, the attack build-up from the defense shall be included by throwing a second ball into play.

3. In order to pay attention to the individual tactical training of the receiver and the defender at all times, a ball which has been directly defended at the opponent, may be penalized as a fault.

4. In games with each other, which aim at technique training, game-interruptions should be deliberately lengthened.

5. In professional beach volleyball, corrections concerning technique should only be given during the preparation period. For players at lower and medium performance levels, who are not pursuing any kind of periodization, corrections may be given during any stage of the training process.

6. For training individual and team tactics, first the player's strengths should be developed. Then, later his weaknesses should slowly be reduced.

7. In technique training, different situations should be paid attention to. Therefore, motion and action speed and accuracy must be practiced together.

The training of team tactics

1. In any form of training, communication between the setter and the attacker through calls and between the blocker and the court-defender using signals may not be neglected or disregarded.

2. During the development and application of strategies and counter-strategies, other players take over supportive functions by simulating the previously observed actions of certain opponents.

12.4 PRINCIPLES FOR TRAINING UNDER MENTAL STRESS

The planning, execution and application of training can be very positive but nevertheless ineffective because training forms do not address competition-like levels of mental stress. The factors shown in chapter 3 on structural analysis, are playing a decisive role in beach volleyball. Consequently, the measures listed below must **always** be considered during training:

1. Complex or game forms which always include the demand that one choose appropriate actions. The serving player should for example force the receiving player to move about. Here, the result represents the control of the action.

2. Passing serves to special zones.

3. Repetition of a training form or an action as long as it is executed correctly and/or effectively.

4. Notation of the quality of a player's action during a training unit.

5. Creating a more intensive level of mental stress than in competition.

6. Repetition of a training form until one, three or five faults occur or until a given number of successful actions is reached.

Changing of forms of play

1. The beach team with partners accustomed to each other plays against a beach team whose partners are not used to playing together. This team will have a point-advantage (0:5/0:10; **handicap-games**).

2. Matches of a shorter duration attempting to reach a tied score. A team starts the match for example with a three-point advantage, thus 13:10.

3. Matches of shorter duration attempting to reach a tie in a certain time span. One team for example starts with the an three-point advantage with a remaining effective playing time of one minute.

4. Training matches with short sets, until one team reaches a 3-4-point advantage. A set then ends for example at a score of 3:0, 5:0 etc.

5. Training matches in tournament format, where the teams have certain point advantages corresponding to their strength. This should always be considered during training practice, since it often happens that several teams of the same caliber of play train at a single location (for example the strongest team starts with 0 points, the second strongest with 3 points, the third strongest with 5 points etc.).

6. Training matches with main focus on certain tournament formats.

7. Training matches in tournament format following the principle of progressively awarding of points. This means, that the serving team will get one point for the first successful action, two for the next, etc.

8. Challenge games with short sets at which the winner holds the court.

9. If there are more than two courts available, the winner on court A stays on the court. The winner of court B advances to A and challenges there. The loser from court A must challenge on the next lower court etc.

10. Competition of three or more teams in a tournament format with sets of a short duration. The winner of the set always stays on the court. Winner is the beach team that first wins five or three sets in a row.

11. Training matches in tournament format where only two, then three points in a row lead to a set point (Big point).

12. Tie-break-matches.

13. Sudden death-matches.

14. Matches in tournament format with rally scoring.

15. Creating critical match situations:
    –   giving one team a point advantage,
    –   match score 13:13,
    –   match score 14:12 with a remaining time of 50, 30 and 10 sec .

16. One point for every successful attack from the defense, two points in case the defending team had sideout.

17. Deduction of two points after a failure, for example a service fault would yield a 2 point deduction.

18. Training matches in any kind of tournament format or as challenge matches. The winner or the stronger team always plays on the "bad" side.

19. Additional demands, such as changing of the net's height, of the court's size or of balls.

20. Creating unequal preconditions, for example the tactical serve/ jump serve from a 6-7 m net-distance.

21. A conscious provocation of players by unfair rule interpretation, strictness etc.

22. Matches in which the coach arbitrarily and without prior information
    – restarts a set,
    – determines a new set score,
    – designates the next point as the deciding one.

Reward and/ or punishment actions

Many of the above mentioned, as well as the following principles are appropriate for the achievement of a desired level of competition performance during the course of the training process by means of reward/ penalties:

1. The desired performance level of the player is achieved through positive reinforcement.

2. Execution of performance controls by clearly objectivizing demands which, if not fulfilled, will result in sanctions.

3. Promise of materialistic rewards, for example premiums etc.

4. Punishment of a single player in case of a fault/ failure by means of additional tasks, such as block jumps, runs, push-ups etc.

5. Creating an extremely technically-tactically stressful situation, for example the training is not going to end until ten perfect receptions or five successful jump serves in a row have been performed.

6. Punishment of the whole team in case of a single player's fault.

7. Punishment of a player/ team who is/ are not responsible for the fault.

8. In games with each other: Punishment of all players, if a player has committed a fault.

9. Matches in which the winner imposes a penalty on the loser, or the loser gets a predetermined punishment.

10. Cancellation of the promised reward, if the expected training performance has not been achieved.

Finally, it shall be pointed out that many of the above mentioned sanctions are applicable to players at all performance levels. However, some are to be exclusively used at the professional beach volleyball level and only very few are exclusively applicable at the international level. From the structure of beach volleyball, it can be inferred that the game requires a high degree of mental stability of all players. Therefore, the training should motivate, activate and mobilize the players, but it should especially create stressful situations and then consider them. Every professional should have a mental regulation (relaxation) technique in order to better overcome stressful situations and to prepare for an upcoming competition more efficiently. Here, it is important to reduce states of mind that might lead to a decreased performance, such as pre-start anxiety ("hypermotivated, nervous") or start-apathy ("too relaxed"), and increase the "optimum fighting spirit" (or better: willingness). The athlete must learn how to keep this motivational level stable over the course of a long tournament. The perfect utilization of breaks, for example the day following a tournament, is very important.

12.5   PRINCIPLES FOR THE COACH'S BEHAVIOR

As mentioned above, beach volleyball players mostly coach themselves. Presently, only very few players are coached, as in for example in professional tennis. The following explanations presume that in the near future beach volleyball national teams as well as professionally practicing teams and players, can no longer get by without coaching from a third party. With regard to the necessity of a coach, the experiences of any sports discipline have confirmed, that money will not be the most important factor for contracting a personal coach. The trainer/ coach in beach volleyball should not only have the essential technical knowledge and qualities but should also be able to take over supporting functions for the successful execution of a training form. As in tennis, training with no more than four players will be undertaken. This does not mean that the coach's self realization must be the most important prerequisite for a coach's work. Much more important are the following tasks:

- creating training plans and schedules,
- the match-like control balancing between load and relaxation,
- the analysis of mistakes and the application of appropriate corrections.

He must be able to register performances not only during competition but also during training. He must analyze these observations in order to employ adequate methods to control the training process. If possible, he must also be able to observe an opponent during the match with an objective eye, in order to further optimize his coaching (see chapter 9, player observation in beach volleyball). He must also know the strengths and weaknesses of as many players as possible at that respective performance level and to update this knowledge at all times. This requires an prior analysis of possible opponents' matches against each other in advance, in order to use this data for upcoming matches. The opponent-observation will become one of the coaches' main responsibilities because 'beach-teams' with partners who will play together on a regular or constant basis, are already common and are expected to be even more common on the international circuit in the near future. The following principles must always be observed by a beach volleyball team's coach:

Behavior towards players during training

1. The mutual respect and confidence between coach and player are the most essential prerequisites for perfect cooperation.

2. The player(s) must be made aware of the essentials and the aim of each training form.

3. Long explanations should be avoided!

4. Concrete instructions - no subjunctive language!

5. The remarks made by players should be taken seriously and discussed shortly thereafter, depending on their degree of importance. This applies especially, if the remarks were negative or if they aimed at the interpersonal relation with a partner!

6. The organizational procedure and planning of the training year, of training weeks and days as well as of competitions should be agreed upon early. The same applies to agreements on probable season-goals at the beginning of the training year.

7. The coach must be able to distinguish between the player's performance on the one hand and his human personality on the other hand.

8. The coach must bear in mind that beach volleyball is a *game of errors*. Therefore, he must distinguish very accurately between "acceptable" and "unacceptable" mistakes during practice.

Planning and execution of training

1. The coach analyzes the training load, especially regarding the microcycle, by assigning each exercise to the following intensity levels in a simplified form:

   – above match level = higher intensity than in a match,
   – on match level = match intensity,
   – below match level = lower intensity than in a match.

2. Technical-tactical as well as mental-physical, training must be worked out and performed in competition-like fashion.

3. In any case, a training must be prepared and, subsequently, analyzed thoroughly. This should be done in written form in order to be able to control the planning of training afterwards. From time to time, performance controls of players are essential.

4. Talks with players can give clues as to their mental-physical levels of stress and therefore allow appropriate modification of the planning of training.

5. The coach should assign special value to the development of communication between the blocker and the backcourt defender through the use of signals or calls between the attacker and the setter. If applicable, he should change the signals/ calls during training and also during a competition.

6. In case the coach takes over supporting functions, he must consciously warm himself up!

The explanations in chapter 8, with respect to the defensive and attack strategies, must be observed for competition-coaching. So far, competition-coaching at the professional level is, as in tennis, not permitted; national associations will, however, in all likelihood admit competition-coaching. However, the FIVB-rules, which also apply to most national circuits, so far lack any comment on coaching. Therefore, it is recommended to every beach volleyball player outside the AVP-sphere, to regard coaching as permitted. Consequently, the following principles shall be understood to be clues to successful coaching.

Coaching

1. The coach must systematically prepare himself for coaching prior to each competition match or tournament. This not only includes the preparation with respect to the first-round-opponent, but also on any other potential opponent during a tournament.

2. The coach must be able to anticipate the opponent's strategy and to make his own strategic changes.

3. The strategy created, based on opponent analysis, must be made clear to the players so that they are able to apply the measures effectively.

4. Coaching must be organized individually. The knowledge of the strengths and weaknesses of a single player, is the only way to demand adequate performances from each individual. The same applies to the factors influencing the mental condition of the players which almost always requires treatment with special attention to the *individual*.

5. When preparing a team for the next opponent, first the defensive strategy and *then* the attack strategy should be developed.

6. It is one of main responsibilities of a coach to plan the course of a tournament day as accurately as possible (see chapter 13).

7. The strategies to be used against the next opponent should be explained shortly prior to the tournament's start and prior to each match. Information on weather conditions, officials, spectator behavior etc. should also be added in every case.

8. The coach should make full use of all factors within his power to influence, however only acting within the rule's limits.

9. Information, for example, with respect to the team's own blocking actions, *can* be given loudly, thus audible to the opponent, since it is often likely to irritate the opponents.

10. The coach should take time-outs early; no later than after three consecutively lost points. He has twice as many times-out available, compared to indoors, but with no possibility of a player substitution. He should exercise the time-outs as follows:

    – Positive influence on players. Listing their mistakes is always forbidden, because the players are already cognitively processing those faults on their own.
    – Transmit up to two messages to each player. They must be short, resemble instructions and they must be repeated at least once.
    – The same behavior should be shown during one's own time-outs as well as opponents' time-outs.
    – Activation and motivation of the players is an important part of any time-out, and should therefore not be neglected.

11. Since substitutions are not allowed in beach volleyball, time-outs are also fulfilling several substitution functions:

    – to give a mentally and physically overloaded player a possibility to relax,
    – to interrupt the opponent's momentum,
    – to disrupt the successful server,
    – to calm down an excited/ upset player.

12. The detailed analysis of competition matches after a tournament is one of the coach's main tasks. The instant analysis following a match as well as the tournament analysis, form the basis for the body of analysis discussions with the players.

13. The instant analysis of the competition after a match during a tournament should always be executed in a positive way and aimed at the next match.

14. Tie-break-coaching can not be practiced often enough during training:

    – Take time-outs early!
    – Make principal full use of all time-outs!
    – Give more responsibility to the mentally stronger player in defense/ attack!
    – Put pressure on the momentarily mentally weak opposing player!

15. The coach must be aware that he alone is responsible for the conceptualization of the match and his coaching measures.

Coaching-accompanying measures

1. Each practice, each test-match and each game in training is also a practice for the coach's behavior during competition.

2. Good coaching includes also self-observation in order to - if given -make changes with regard to the own behavior.

3. The coach should also learn relaxation techniques in order to better handle his mental stress.

4. The coach should always be prepared for co-operation with the media and carefully consider the effect of his statements, before he gives them.

5. Additionally, he must act positively towards spectators in order to bring the spectators on his team's side.

16. Prior to the beginning of match, the coach should have a positive talk with the referees.

Finally, it should be pointed out once more, that special coaching measures for example for service strategies, for block and backcourt defensive strategies as well as for coaching during the tie-break may be looked up in chapter 8.

12.6   PRINCIPLES FOR THE BEHAVIOR OF THE PLAYERS TOWARDS EACH OTHER

An essential precondition for the successful cooperation of two players in a beach-team is an intimate and friendly relationship. Therefore it is absolutely necessary to pay attention to the following recommendations:

- Refraining from negative comments towards the partner during a match. This applies especially to gestures!
- Each comment to the partner should have a positive character and should always refer to the next action/ match situation and never to the previous fault.
- During the tournament, criticism should only be given in a constructive way, thus it should already look for or offer solutions.
- Extensive conversations with a partner that do not refer to the next opponent may not be held during the tournament. The last two points also refer to conversations with the coach.

- Cheering the partner on will have negative results, meaning it will annoy the partner if it is done after one's own successful action or if it exposes him as the "weaker" player in front of the spectators.
- Demanding, helping hints or instructions pointing towards tactical realities, will always have a "negative" character.
- The player should divert opponent aggressiveness, aimed directly at his partner, toward himself.

During the warm-up prior to a match, the following suggestions regarding the positive co-operation and the mutual preparation/ cheering-up should be considered:

- Mutual control of the right "tension", thereby not being too relaxed, but also not too hectic. Firing each other up should not be done too intensely during the warm-up. This will only work if there is a total consensus between the players on the goals for the tournament and the season.
- During warm-up attacks, it must be observed that the partner spikes until he has completed an attack successfully, in order to exclude a silent overlook of faults and to only have successful experiences in every case.
- During the practice of the serve/ reception situation prior to a match it must be observed absolutely that the degree of the serve's difficulty is increased carefully and that no more than a competition-*like* risk shall be taken, in order to give the passer time to get used to these serves and to give him confidence.
- Service faults must be avoided absolutely!

Photo 86a: Have a good relation to your partner!

Photo 86b: Coaching will be a decisive part of beach volleyball in the future!

13 ACCOMPANYING MEASURES IN TRAINING

Apart from the already mentioned principles of training as well as the hints concerning the planning of training listed in chapter 8, the beach volleyball professional is asked to adjust his training and his training-accompanying measures to the specific competition-conditions of the sport of beach volleyball. This refers to the 15-25 weekend tournaments in mostly high temperatures and the influence of the sun rays as well as long traveling times along with time differences etc.

Each beach volleyball player must take different measures with respect to his competition-preparation and his behavior during the course of the tournament. These measures serve to optimize and maintain his mental-physical as well as playing performance.

The measures refer to:

a)   Nutrition.
b)   Fluid intake and balance.
c)   The prevention of sun or heat related problems/ diseases.
d)   The accurate planning of an undisturbed and stress-free arrival/ departure to/from the tournament site, which should include enough time for adjustment as well as relaxation.
e)   The mental-physical relaxation.

Referring to a) The high physical loads during training and competition, especially at the pro-level, are leading to an, in team sports, unusually high demand for energy. This becomes particularly obvious, taken into consideration that the players practice 4-6 hours a day and complete up to ten matches in hot climate during a tournament weekend. To optimally supply his energy needs, especially during tournament weekends, the following advice should be heeded:

–   With respect to the composition of his nutrition, a professional beach volleyball player with an intense daily training routine should follow these recommendations: 55-65% carbohydrates, 25-30% fat and 10-15% protein.
–   Complex carbohydrates with a high level of nutrients such as vitamins, minerals and trace elements must be chosen. For example, whole-grain products, muesli etc.; sweets and soft drinks containing too much sugar should be avoided.
–   Due to the large volume and high intensity that is to be expected during a tournament weekend, it must be seen to that the carbohydrate reservoirs

are filled up the day before. Here, pasta dishes represent the best possibility (no fatty sauces, preferably whole-grain pasta). A nutritional method following the principle of "carbohydrate loading" might be advantageous. The details or principles concerning this specific nutritional method may be looked up in the corresponding technical literature.

- On the competition day, a breakfast rich in carbohydrates, however easily digestible, should be taken 3-4 hours before the tournament
- During the competition day the player must satisfy, independent of his feeling of hunger, his high energetic demands with many small and very digestible meals, which should also be rich in carbohydrates.
- Here, less acidic fruits are a good choice, for example melons (additional high amount of water), **bananas or** muesli-bars as well as carbohydrate-drinks or fruit juices.
- The food intake should be controlled in such a way, that the player receives carbohydrates at the beginning of breaks of longer duration (> one hour) and not between two subsequent matches.
- Directly following each match, the player should drink 250 ml of a liquid enriched with a low glucose concentration (< 10%).
- On the evening of a competition day, the energy-reservoirs should again be filled up with food rich in carbohydrates (pastaparty!).
- Even 1-2 days following the competition, the player must compensate the existing lack of energy with pasta, vegetables, fruits etc.

Further proper explanations concerning the optimal supply of fat, proteins, minerals, vitamins, trace elements etc. would not suit this chapter's constraints, and therefore the study of further technical literature is advised.

Referring to b) Even among professionals, performance-breakdowns, muscle cramps and heat-related collapses, starting with dehydration and leading to unconsciousness and even heat stroke, occur during each beach volleyball season. With respect to fluid intake, the beach player should therefore consider the following:

- The beach volleyball player should perfectly regulate his fluid intake and balance daily, even on days without competitions. He must take in the lost amount of water, in order to rule out a reduction in his performance as well as any health-hazards. This can easily be accomplished by a measuring the body weight before and after training. The difference must be taken up again in form of fluids (**Advice**: Daily 1,8 liter of low carbonated sparkling water or water, enriched with apple juice + at least 150-250 ml every 20 min. during training).
- **Independent of his feeling of thirst**, the beach player must drink the following amounts of fluids **during matches**:

- Normal temperatures (< 20 C°): 0,5 - 0,7 liter per hour.
- Typical beach conditions, that means high temperatures, sun, etc.: at least 1 liter per hour!

- Basically, the choice of the beverage is a matter of taste, however, beverages with a high sugar content should be declined. Electrolytic beverages, water, mineral water/ juice mixtures (s.a. "Advice") are recommended.

Referring to c) In beach volleyball, the athlete is often exposed for long periods to intense **sun rays**. This requires appropriate prophylactic measures against possible health damage such as sunburn, heatstroke, eye damage or skin cancer:

- All the dangers mentioned above, especially today's high danger of skin cancer, make wearing a T-shirt and a hat/cap essential for the beach volleyball player! This applies to each day of training or competition!
- A sun screen (at least protection factor 15) should be used!
- The professional beach volleyball player should check himself regularly (monthly) for the first signs of skin cancer!
- Sun glasses with a large screening range (without bridge) and with a 100% UV-A/ UV-B protection not only protect the eyes, they also make playing with a deep sun or the reception of skyballs a lot easier. Consequently, the high-level player is obliged to wear them!
- In competition or training breaks, **the player must stay in the shade**!
- The beach volleyball player should protect himself against **burns** and foot-pain, caused by the **high sand-temperature**, by wearing socks.

Referring to d) Regarding long traveling distances to and from the tournament site, especially the professional player should follow the following suggestions (see chapter 11.1.1):

- Use the Friday morning for the trip. The type of transportation must be chosen in such a way, that the trip will not be too exhausting and that practice can still be executed during the afternoon/ late afternoon, in order to loosen up and get used to the local atmosphere. This means for example.:

  - for trips below 300 km: by car or better by train,
  - for trips above 300 km: by plane.

- For trips covering several time zones, the arrival should be advanced several days, in order to avoid the reduction of physical and mental strength, caused by the time difference. Here, the following applies for example:

- a time difference of ten hours: arrival five days in advance,
- a time difference of four hours: arrival two days in advance.

Referring to e) As with every top-level athlete, the beach volleyball player must pay attention to,

- a fast recovery after training and competition as well as in tournament breaks,
- the improvement and rehabilitation of possible injuries,
- the use of not only physical but also mental relaxation methods.

Here, functional gymnastics (in the sense of stretching methods), all physical therapy measures as well as techniques of mental regulation (see chapter 12.4), are of special importance. The following concrete measures are recommended, especially for the top-level beach volleyball player:

- Stay in the shade between tournament matches!
- Full body or partial massage after intensive training units and tournaments.
- Relaxing the muscles between tournament matches by functional stretching and/or massage (gentle rub massage).
- Prophylactic treatment (e.g. ice treatment) during match breaks.

Photo 87   Photo 88

14 GLOSSARY AND LEGEND

14.1 EXPLANATION OF TECHNICAL TERMS

The following beach volleyball-specific terms refer to technical terms that are internationally used. Terms which are exactly defined in the English/American volleyball terminology, and which are used in the book, are not explained in the glossary.

"Angle!": The setter's call to the attacker. Tells the attacker to hit cross-court.

ASSOCIATION VOLLEYBALL PROFESSIONALS (AVP): Operates the US-professional tournament series for men.

Beach-dig: Defensive action with open hands over or below head used against hard-driven balls.

CONFÉDÉRATION EUROPÉENNE DE VOLLEYBALL (CEV): European Volleyball Association.

"Cut!": The setter's call to the attacker. Tells the attacker the cross-court is the proper hitting-direction.

Cut shot: Cross-court spin spike or tactical spike.

Double-elimination-format: Tournament format, where one team, in contrast to the single-elimination-format, must loose twice to be eliminated from the event.

FEDERATION INTERNATIONALE DE VOLLEYBALL (FIVB): World volleyball association.

Hard-driven ball: Hard-driven spike, which travels with a straight trajectory. It may be momentarily held in the defensive action.

Husband and wife serve: Service between the receiving players, which should induce misunderstandings.

Knuckler: One-handed overhead defensive technique, where the ball is hit with the middle joints of the fingers.

"Line!": The setter's call to the attacker. Tells the attacker the line-area is the proper hitting-direction.

Novice: Player without any rating.

"Over!": call with two intentions:
1. Used when the ball set is traveling directly across the net.
2. Used when a player reaches over the plane of the net during an attack.

Rally-clock: Clock that measures the effective playing time.

Round-robin format: Group-system in a tournament, all teams play against each other (see also "Shot-Gun Format").

"Sand!": The player's call to the referee, when he needs an interruption in order to remove sand from his body.

Shoot: Playing the ball into the opponents' court with the tomahawk-technique (see below).

Shot: Tactical attacks, meaning all attacks that have an arched trajectory, for example all trick attacks and spin spikes.

Shot-gun format: Eight teams play in a format "each against each other". One set is played to ten points. The second and third placed teams play in the semi-final. The winner of this match then plays against the team which placed first after the group matches. In the final, one set to eleven points is played.

Sideout: Change of the right to serve.

Single-elimination format: Tournament format, where a team is eliminated after one lost match.

Skyball: High serve.

Split block: Block-attempt where the player jumps with wide spread arms.

Spread block: see split block.

Sudden death: In the case of a tied score after the expiration of playing time on the rally-clock, the so-called "Sudden Death" is played. Here, the team that wins the next point will be the match-winner.

Tomahawk: Two-handed overhead defensive technique used against tactical shots.

Unrated: Player who has not achieved a rating yet.

WOMEN'S PROFESSIONAL VOLLEYBALL ASSOCIATION (WPVA): Operates the tournament series of the female professionals.

14.2 SYMBOLS

───────►	Running path	════════⇒	Attacker's approach
─ ─ ─ ─ ►	Ball flight: set, serve, (hard-driven) attack	─ ─ ─ ─ ⇢	tactical shot
■─ ─ ─ ─ ►	Hand set	◄─ ─ ─ ─ ►	Bump set
◯	Player	◯▐	active block
◯●	Player with ball,	◯▕	passive block
◠	Setter ('3 vs. 3', '4 vs. 4')	◯▐	Spread block
◯▎	Blocker	⌒	Player after position change

Wind-direction/ -force		
──────► light	──────►►	medium
	──────►►►	strong

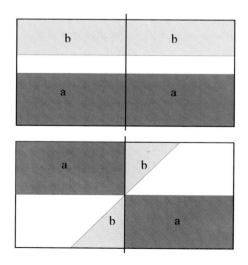

Fig. 61
a = 9 x 4,5m
b = 9 x 3m

Fig. 62
a = 9 x 4,5m with
diagonal arrangement
b = extremly diagonal

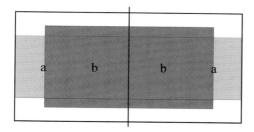

Fig. 63
a = 6 x 9m
b = 7,5 x 7,5m

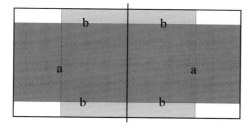

Fig. 64
a = 7,5 x 9m
b = 9 x 5m

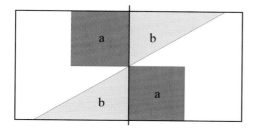

Fig. 65
a = 4,5 x 4,5m
b = Diagonal court

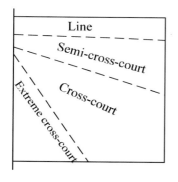

Line

Semi-cross-court

Cross-court

Extreme cross-court

Fig. 66

REFERENCES

ALLMER, H.: Psychologische Aspekte sportlicher Beanspruchung. In: NITSCH, J. R. (Hrsg.): Streß. Theorien, Untersuchungen, Maßnahmen. Bern 1981

ASSOCIATION VOLLEYBALL PROFESSIONALS (AVP): "Pro Beach Volleyball - Growth & Expansion. [unpublished]. Culver City 1990

AVP: 1991 Media Guide. Culver City 1991

AVP: 1993 Media Guide. Culver City 1993

AVP: The AVP NEWSLETTER 1 (1993)1

AVP (Hrsg.): Official Pro Beach Volleyball Rule Book, (Text by M. GAGE). Culver City 1993

AVP: Media Information [unpublished]. Culver City 1993

BEACH VOLLEYBALL MAGAZINE; 1, 2, 3, 4 (1982); 2 (1983); 1 (1984)

BRAMMERTZ, I.: Strukturanalyse des Sportspiels Beachvolleyball der Herren. Diplomarbeit, DSHS Köln. Köln 1993

BRANDEL, C.: Volleyball-Weltgeschichte. München 1988

BROWN, T.: Drinking it in. In: VOLLEYBALL MONTHLY 6 (1991), 34

BERKSHIRE, K.Q.: The Numbers Game. In: VOLLEYBALL 9 (1991), 28-32

BÜHRLE, M.: Dimensionen des Kraftverhaltens und ihre spezifischen Trainingsmethoden. In: BÜHRLE, M. (Hrsg.): Grundlagen des Maximal- und Schnellkrafttrainings. Schorndorf 1985

C. E. SPORTS: Budweiser 4-Man Volleyball Tour - 1993 Tour Guide. Van Nuys 1993

C. E. SPORTS: Bud Light 4-Woman Volleyball Tour - 1993 Tour Guide. Van Nuys 1993

C. E. SPORTS: American Beach Volleyball League/ Women's Beach Volleyball League (Bud Light Pro Beach Volleyball Tour) - Four-Person Beach Volleyball Rule Book. Van Nuys 1994

CHRISTMANN, E./ FAGO, K.: Volleyball-Handbuch. Reinbek 1987

CIARELLI, C.: Drilling for Gold. In: VOLLEYBALL MONTHLY 4 (1993), 42-44

DANNENMANN, F.: Gleichgewicht im Volleyball. In: DANNENMANN, F.(Red.): Volleyball erforschen. Ahrensburg 1989

DE MAREES, H.: Sportphysiologie. Köln 1992

EISINGER, M./ LEITZMANN, C.: Ernährung und Sport - eine Übersicht. In: DEUTSCHE ZEITSCHRIFT FÜR SPORTMEDIZIN, Sonderheft Ernährung, 43 (1992) Nr. 10, 472-494

FEDERATION INTERNATIONALE DE VOLLEYBALL (FIVB): Official Beach Volleyball Rules. Lausanne 1995

FIVB: Coaches Manual. Lausanne 1989

FISCHER, U./ GRANDE, U.: Das Spiel wird im Kopf entschieden. In: VOLLEYBALLTRAINING 2 (1991)

FLORSTEDT, C.: Mentale Tips für Zuspieler und Mannschaft. In: VOLLEYBALLTRAINING 3 (1990)

FONTANA, B.: Pumping You up. In: VOLLEYBALL MONTHLY 3 (1993), 32

FROST, D.: Sand Dollars. In: VOLLEYBALL MONTHLY 3 (1993), 52-59

FROST, D.: Make - or Break. In: VOLLEYBALL MONTHLY 4 (1993), 50-54

GREEN, T./ PATTERSON, D./ CASEY, M.: 10 Years after. In: VOLLEYBALL 3 (1993), 42-63

GROSSER, M. u.a.: Die sportliche Bewegung. Anatomische und biomechanische Grundlagen. blv-Sportwissen Bd. 415. München, Zürich 1987

HASTINGS, J.: 10 Events that changed Volleyball. In: VOLLEYBALL MONTHLY 8 (1992), 88-92

HERZOG, K./ VOIGT, H.-F./ WESTPHAL, G.: Volleyball-Training: Grundlagen und Arbeitshilfen für das Training und die Betreuung von Mannschaften. Schorndorf 1987

HÖMBERG, S.: On the Tactics and Technique of Beach Volleyball. In: INTERNATIONAL VOLLEYTECH 2 (1992), 15-19

HÖMBERG, S.: Technik und Taktik des Sportspiels Beach-Volleyball. Diplomarbeit, DSHS Köln, Köln 1993

HÖMBERG, S./ PAPAGEORGIOU, A.: Handbuch für Beach-Volleyball. Aachen 1994

HÖMBERG, S./ PAPAGEORGIOU, A.: Vom Hallen- zum Beach-
Volleyballer, Teil 1. In: VOLLEYBALLTRAINING 3 (1994), 33-46

HÖMBERG, S./ PAPAGEORGIOU, A.: Vom Hallen- zum Beach-
Volleyballer, Teil 2. In: VOLLEYBALLTRAINING 4 (1994) 55-61

HÖMBERG, S./ PAPAGEORGIOU, A.: Beachvolleyball - Auffassungen der
Profispieler. In: DANNENMANN, F. (Red.): Volleyball - Vielfalt,
Hamburg 1994, 193-209

HOLLMANN, W./ HETTINGER, Th.: Sportmedizin: Arbeits- und
Trainingsgrundlagen. Stuttgart, New York 1990, 3. Aufl.

JAGD, K.: Don´t Let the Sun Catch You Frying. In: VOLLEYBALL
MONTHLY 5 (1992), 114-117

JOHNSON, A.: Jump Serving Basics. In: VOLLEYBALL MONTHLY 3
(1992), 30-32

KESSEL, J.: Sand Volleyball Court Guidelines. In: INTERNATIONAL
VOLLEYTECH 2 (1992), 23-24

KIRALY, K.: Walls in the Sand. In: VOLLEYBALL MONTHLY 4 (1993),
38-40

KIRALY, K.: Make every Serve Count. In: VOLLEYBALL MONTHLY 8
(1993), 42-43

KIRALY, K.: Beach Defense. In: VOLLEYBALL MONTHLY 9 (1993),
36-37

KIRALY, K.: Hot Tips for the Cold Months. In: VOLLEYBALL
MONTHLY 2 (1994), 28

KIRALY, K./ KIRBY, K.: Strictly Beach. Videotape. Director: L.P. Mann.
VOLLEYBALL MONTHLY/ VIDEO ACTION SPORTS (Hrsg.)
1992, 60 min.

KIRBY, K.: Cut'em down. In: VOLLEYBALL MONTHLY 7 (1993), 55

KREMER, B.: Funktionsgymnastik im Volleyballtraining. In:
DANNENMANN, F. (Red.): Volleyball erforschen. Ahrensburg 1989,
133-146

KREMER, B.: Funktionalität von Gymnastikübungen zur Haltungs- und
Bewegungsschulung. Übungsbroschüre, IFSS Karlsruhe 1988

MARTIN, D. (Red.)/ CARL, K./ LEHNERTZ, K.: Handbuch Trainingslehre.
Schorndorf 1991

284

MOCULESCU, S.: Präzision, Perfektion und Flexibilität - die Markenzeichen der Spiele. In: VOLLEYBALLTRAINING 6 (1988), 82-86

NITSCH, J. R.: Zur Theorie der sportlichen Beanspruchung. In: J. R. NITSCH & UDRIS, I. (Hrsg.): Beanspruchung im Sport. Bad Homburg 1976

PALM, A.: The Wind Advantage. In: INTERNATIONAL VOLLEYTECH 3 (1992), 18-20

PAPAGEORGIOU, A./ HÖMBERG, S.: Beach-Volleyball, Ursprung, Entwicklung, Organisation und Spielstrategien der Profis in den USA. In: VOLLEYBALLTRAINING 4 (1991), 49-56

PAPAGEORGIOU, A./ HÖMBERG, S.: Das Sportspiel Beach-Volleyball. In: DANNENMANN, F. (Red.), Volleyball innovativ. Ahrensburg 1992, 24-46

PAPAGEORGIOU, A/ HUMMERNBRUM, B.: Sprunghandlungen im Volleyball. In: DANNENMAN, F. (Red.): Training und Methodik des Volleyballspiels. Ahrensburg 1988, 9-35

PAPAGEORGIOU, A./ EHREN, K./ KOSEL, B.: Gegnerbeobachtung im Volleyball. In: DANNENMANN, F. (Red.): Volleyball gesamtdeutsch. Ahrensburg 1991, 121-153

PAPAGEORGIOU, A/ KLEIN, B.: Die Rolle des Schnelligkeitstrainings im Volleyball. In: VOLLEYBALLTRAINING 6 (1993), 87-91

PAPAGEORGIOU, A./ SPITZLEY, W.: Handbuch für Volleyball, Grundlagenausbildung. Aachen 1992

PAPAGEORGIOU, A./ SPITZLEY, W.: Handbuch für Leistungsvolleyball, Ausbildung zum Spezialisten. Aachen 1994

ROQUE, E.: Beach Blocking Basics. In: VOLLEYBALL MONTHLY 5 (1992), 42-46

SATO, E.: Dig it! In: VOLLEYBALL 8 (1993), 62-66

SCHMIDTBLEICHER, D.: Motorische Beanspruchungsform Kraft. Struktur und Einflußgrößen, Adaptionen, Trainingsmethoden, Diagnose und Trainingssteuerung. In: DEUTSCHE ZEITSCHRIFT FÜR SPORTMEDIZIN, Schwerpunkt Krafttraining, 38 (1987) Nr. 9, 356-375

SMITH, S/ KIRBY, K.: Hitting the Cut Shot. In: VOLLEYBALL 9 (1991), 56-57, 73

SMITH, S.: Play, play, play... . In: VOLLEYBALL 7 (1993), 44-46

SMITH, S./ FEINEMAN, N.: Kings of the Beach: The Story of Beach Volleyball. Los Angeles/ Seattle 1988

STEFFES, K.: Soar before Spring. In: VOLLEYBALL MONTHLY 2 (1993), 30-33

STEFFES, K.: Pass perfect. In: VOLLEYBALL MONTHLY 6 (1993), 46-48

STEFFES, K.: Inside out. In: VOLLEYBALL MONTHLY 3 (1994), 32-34

STEVENSON, J.: Q&A with Jon Stevenson. In: VOLLEYBALL MONTHLY 6 (1990), 40-41

STEVENSON, J.: The Road to a Rating. In: VOLLEYBALL MONTHLY, 5 (1991), 33

STEVENSON, J./ OBSTFELD, R.: Hot Sand: The Beach Volleyball Handbook. Irvine 1989

STOKLOS, R.: Get to the Net. In: VOLLEYBALL 7 (1993)

TIMMONS, S.: The open-hand dig. In: VOLLEYBALL 6 (1993), 49-50

TIMMONS, S.: The Split Block. In: VOLLEYBALL 10 (1993), 85-86

WOMEN'S PROFESSIONAL VOLLEYBALL ASSOCIATION (WPVA): Tour Guide 1990. Culver City 1990

WPVA: Tour Guide 1991. Culver City 1991

PHOTO CREDITS

INDEX

Jump serve, 41; 76; **86**; 199
Jumping actions, 15; 38
Juvenile players, **45**

Kirby, Karolyn, 23
Kiraly, Karch, 21; 235
Knuckler, 278

Lee, Greg, 18
Line, 124; 278
Lollipop jump serve, 87
Lollipop serve, 84
Low performance level, 45

Manhattan Beach, 17
Masters tournaments, 27
Maximum strength, 36; 242
Medium performance level, 46
Menges, Jim, 18
Mental abilities, 15; 36; 75
Mental attention, 124
Mental relaxation technique, 68
Mental resistance, 39
Mental stability, 39; 267
Mental strength, 125
Mental stress, 39; 68
Mental-physical relaxation, 274
Method of concentric-excentric
maximum contractions, 258
Method of quasi-maximum
contractions, 258
Method of repeated submaximum
contractions, 232
Methods of maximum
contractions, 257
Microcycle, 240; 248; 269
Middle blocker, 57
Muscle cross section, 242
Muscle cross-section, 232

Muscle performance threshold,
258

Nina Matthies, 23
No one, 124
Non-cyclic speed, 250
Novice, 278
Nutrition, **274**

Observation, 76; 113
Olympic Games, 9; 26; 236
One-hand dig, 170
One-hand-screen, 150
One-man reception formation,
204
Opalinski-Harrer, Janice, 234
Open-handed digs, 129
Open-handed dink, 129
Outside hitter, 55
Over, 278
Overhead dig, 169

Pass
    frontal, **70**
    lateral, 61; **73**
    perfect, **65**; 75
    techniques, 70
Performance-determining factors,
45
Performance-limiting factor, 254
Periodization, **240**
Permanent peaks, 240
Physical demands, 35; 83
Physical load, 15; 35; 37; 243
Physical overload, 44; 145; 190
Physical resistance, 39
Player observation, 77; 212; **219**;
268
    receiver, 224
    server, 223

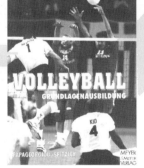

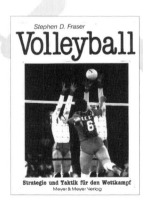

International Society on Comparative Physical Education and Sport (ISPEC), Volume 7

Sport for All into the 90s

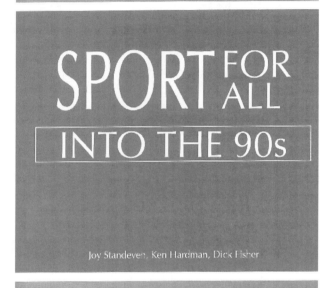

International Society for Comparative
Physical Education and Sport
Volume 7

SPORT FOR ALL

INTO THE 90s

Joy Standeven, Ken Hardman, Dick Fisher

Meyer & Meyer Verlag

Standeven/Hardman/Fisher
334 pages, paperback,
14,8 x 21 cm
ISBN 3-89124-150-X
DM 29,80/SFr 29,80/ÖS 233,-

MEYER & MEYER – Sportspublisher

Von-Coels-Straße 390, D-52080 Aachen
Telefon 0241/55 60 33, Fax 0241/55 82 81

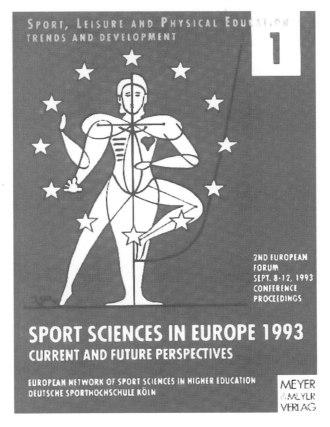